JAZZ COSMOPOLITANISM IN ACCRA

European and American modernist paintings and photographs have long evoked jazz and cosmopolitanism as night in the city, as dark shadowy buildings beaming the energy of bright lights into moody urban streets and skies. The vibe is not dissimilar in globally Afromodern Accra. Here, telecommunication towers now burst into night like the shimmering strings and swinging ostinatos of a *seprewa*, the Ghanaian harp. "Reach Out," "Stay Connected," "Pay As You Go," "Powerful Delivery," say the ubiquitous cellular ads, mixing consumer urgency and religious resonance. The words of the common obituary announcement, "Home Call," are simply flipped on the signboard of my local mobile phone kiosk: "Call Home." Jazz cosmopolitanism in Accra is a collusion of chronotopes, the time-space of the sky, of the road, and of the sea joining to sound an unending Black Atlantic musical motion, where older ancestral connections meet newer diasporic intimacies.

STEVEN FELD

Five Musical Years in Ghana

JAZZ
COSMOPOLITANISM
IN ACCRA

Duke University Press   Durham and London   2012

© 2012 Duke University Press
All rights reserved
Printed in the United States of America on
acid-free paper ∞
Designed by C. H. Westmoreland
Typeset in Arno with Din Schrift display
by Keystone Typesetting, Inc.

Library of Congress Cataloging-in-
Publication Data appear on the
last printed page of this book.

The 2009 Ernest Bloch Lectures in Music
University of California, Berkeley

Frontispiece: *Accra Calling*, photograph
© 2010 Steven Feld.

FOR ANITA AND BOB FELD

AND IN MEMORY OF MICHAEL BRECKER

*The artistic will to polyphony
is the will to the event.*

M. M. BAKHTIN

SET LIST

OPUS

Jazz Cosmopolitanism in Accra is the book and photographic companion to a multimedia project of DVDs and CDs produced from 2005 through 2010. These related films and recordings feature performances by and conversations with musicians Ghanaba (Guy Warren), Nii Noi Nortey, Nii Otoo Annan, and the La Drivers Union Por Por Group, as well as photographs and interviews by associate producer Nii Yemo Nunu. All are published by VoxLox (www.voxlox.net), with the exception of *Por Por: Honk Horn Music of Ghana*, published by Smithsonian Folkways (www.folkways.si.edu).

Jazz Cosmopolitanism in Accra (Steven Feld, DVD trilogy 2009)
    Disc 1, *Hallelujah!: Ghanaba and the Winneba Youth Choir*
        perform G. F. Handel's Hallelujah Chorus
    Disc 2, *Accra Trane Station: The Music and Art of Nii Noi Nortey*
    Disc 3, *A Por Por Funeral for Ashirifie*

Various Artists, *The Time of Bells, 3: Musical Bells of Accra, Ghana* (CD, 2005)

Accra Trane Station, *Tribute to A Love Supreme* (CD, 2005)

Accra Trane Station, *Meditations for John Coltrane* (CD, 2006)

Accra Trane Station, *Another Blue Train* (CD, 2007)

Virginia Ryan and Steven Feld, *The Castaways Project* (CD + DVD, 2007)

The La Drivers Union Por Por Group, *Por Por: Honk Horn Music of Ghana* (CD, 2007)

Accra Trane Station with Alex Coke and Jefferson Voorhees, *Topographies of the Dark*; sculptural paintings by Virginia Ryan (CD, 2008)

Nii Otoo Annan and Steven Feld, *Bufo Variations* (CD, 2008)

The La Drivers Union Por Por Group, *Klebo! Honk Horn Music from Ghana* (CD, 2009)

Steven Feld, *Waking in Nima* (CD, 2010)

Nii Otoo Annan, *Ghana Sea Blues* (CD, 2011)

FOUR-BAR INTRO

"The Shape of Jazz to Come"

I'm here to tell stories about encounters with jazz cosmopolitanism in Accra. While luminous and vexing to me, I don't expect them to be as memorable or unsettling to you. But I do hope they will be productive of surprise and critical reflection, certainly about the shape of jazz as diasporic dialogue in an African urban modernity, and even more about jazz cosmopolitanism as musical intimacy.

This was hardly what I had in mind when I first visited Accra in October 2004. Not at all. The idea was just a two-week look and listen. Ruti Talmor, then an anthropology graduate student at New York University, invited me to come as she was finishing her fieldwork about Accra's National Arts Centre and the local contemporary art world.[1] I'd help her out with some video work, and she'd introduce me to some musicians and artists.

I was at the time (and still am) at work on a project about how village, church, animal, and carnival bells have created senses of space and time over ten centuries of European pastoral history.[2] I liked the idea of finding out something about an even older yet very contemporary world of forged iron hand bells played as timekeepers in West African musical ensembles. But I wasn't thinking that Accra would become more than a short musical detour before heading back to Europe and bells, and then home to the last months of the generous Guggenheim support that had me on leave from teaching.

Ruti had been in Accra for more than a year and knew the city well. René Gerrets, another NYU anthropology graduate student, and on his way to begin fieldwork in Tanzania, was at the time visiting her too. We met diverse people connected with Ruti's research and cruised the city in her banana-colored sedan on days it cooperated. This brief scan made me aware of a kind of fieldwork unlike any other I had experienced, certainly distant from my work in a remote rainforest in Papua New Guinea, or from pastoral villages or towns in Europe. It was the possibility of art world fieldwork in a large and globally layered city, simultaneously engaged with multiple sites, locations, niches, scenes, and styles of production. And it was the challenge, within those multiplicities, to grasp something about the intertwined yet markedly race- and class-differentiated realities of artists, patrons, and institutions with their array of local to global connections.

Things happened quickly. On my first night we dined with Virginia Ryan, a visual artist working with the Italian Embassy in Accra and busy establishing the Foundation for Contemporary Art–Ghana.[3] A few nights later we dined again with Virginia and her FCA cofounder and codirector, Joe Nkrumah, a polymath art conservator, cultural historian, and "Uncle Joe" or "Prof" to everyone doing research in Accra. And just a few days later those two conversations led to meeting one of Joe's Accra art world friends, the sculptor, instrument inventor, and musician Nii Noi Nortey.

That crucial encounter streamed into others, an initial dialogue with Nii Noi about John Coltrane overflowing into what became five years of converging conversations, performances, collaborations, and recording and video projects about the feedback swirls situating Accra's jazz cosmopolitanism in the transnational diasporic currents Paul Gilroy calls the Black Atlantic and Caryl Phillips calls the Atlantic sound.[4]

Thinking back, those first two weeks in Accra were extraordinary. Never before in a life of much travel had I experienced such an immediate ease of attachment with place, people, scenes; which must have been why it was so easy to say yes when Nii Noi asked if I would consider coming back to Accra to work with him. He said it was "divined" by our first meeting, speaking of the moment I asked if he would like a recording of the rehearsal that Joe, Ruti, and I walked in on when we first arrived at his home.

If Nii Noi's word of choice was "divined," mine for that fateful encounter was "captivated." That was my instant feeling about the recorded material, so much so that on my return to the United States I immediately edited the tapes and sent the CD back to Nii Noi for review. He responded that we were hearing the music's contours the same way. "I'm telling you, man, it's the shape of jazz to come," he said on the phone, seductively quoting the title of a famous Ornette Coleman LP from 1959, one that really did herald a number of 1960s major jazz developments.[5] With that, I enlisted Ruti's help to arrange the rental of an acoustically bright loft designed and built by the architect Alero Olympio. And that's how I returned to Accra to set up a recording studio for a month in 2005 to record Nii Noi and Nii Otoo Annan's *Tribute to A Love Supreme*, in recognition of John Coltrane's classic LP.[6]

For many years before all this I had lived two simultaneous professional lives, one as a musician consumed by jazz, one as an anthropologist consumed by cultural poetics and politics. Of course music had long found its way into my anthropology, and anthropology into my music. But it wasn't until I went to Accra, met Nii Noi and Nii Otoo, and agreed to return that a new synthesis emerged, my lives as musican and scholar more deeply fusing in the possibility to explore how the performance of jazz in Africa, and Africa in jazz, could relate to the anthropology of globalism and cosmopolitanism.

What happened was that I began the *Love Supreme* tribute project working as a producer and as a recordist together with Nii Noi's regular sound engineer, Agazi. But the course of events changed wildly when I fell in love with one of Nii Noi and Nii Otoo's instruments, a bass *mbira* box, and took it away with me to continue and deepen the affair.

Things also changed wildly in that dense month when Nii Noi introduced me to other musicians in his immediate circle, the "divine drummer" Ghanaba (formerly Guy Warren), the country's leading experimentalist, and then the La Drivers Union Por Por Group, a union of minibus and truck drivers who invented a jazzy honking music for antique squeeze-bulb vehicle horns. Central to both introductions was meeting one of Nii Noi's close friends who had been working both with Ghanaba and the La Por Por Group for many years, the photographer Nii Yemo Nunu.

That month of work in 2005 led to spending up to six months in Accra during each of the following five years, exploring the African legacy of John Coltrane and playing in Nii Noi and Nii Otoo's Accra Trane Station band; following the intersections of African, European classical, and African American musical idioms in conversation with Ghanaba; tracing routes of music and transport, and of honk horn funerals with the La Drivers Union Por Por Group.

During those longer visits from 2006 through 2010, I lived in the neighborhood of Nima, remarkable for its blended overlays of village and cosmopolitan features. Each day I encountered a bustling mix of artists, politicians, business people, drivers, street sellers, tailors, carpenters, school children, local workers, and consummate hustlers. Down the road was the compound of the politically ever-present Akufo-Addo family ("as close to aristocracy as it gets here," in the words of someone who knows), as well as a longtime favorite restaurant haunt of international and local elites. All around was a class-mixed cross-section of Ghanaian neighbors, with a few Nigerian, Moroccan, Syrian, Lebanese, Ukranian, Thai, Serbian, Indian, Dutch, Swiss, and German in the mix. And in the blocks just beyond, a multilayered world of everything from "fitters" and "panel beaters" (mechanics and automobile body repairers) to computer dealers, dry goods sellers, and drug dealers, all their words, worlds, and works framed by the resonant soundmark surround of kids taking over the streets as *fufu* was pounded and local mosques (the area has a major Muslim history in Accra) and Pentecostal churches vigorously broadcast their faith. Among other things, life in Nima taught me a great deal about everyday listening to sonic stratigraphy.[7]

Over these years Nii Noi and Nii Otoo also visited me at home in New Mexico, and we've taught, toured, and performed together in Ghana, Europe, and the United States. Accra Trane Station CDs were issued year by year to document the work: *Meditations for John Coltrane* for 2006, *Another Blue Train* for 2007, and then, in 2008, Nii Otoo's *Bufo Variations* and *Topographies of the Dark,* a quintet collaboration with the American jazz artists Alex Coke and Jefferson Voorhees.[8]

Along with Accra Trane Station, the La Drivers Union Por Por Group was featured on *Musical Bells of Accra,* coproduced with Nii Noi in 2005–6, followed by their own debut CD, *Por Por: Honk Horn Music of Ghana* in 2007, and then *Klebo! Honk Horn Music from Ghana* in 2009.[9] Nii Yemo Nunu became my collaborating photographer, coresearcher, and Ga translator in these projects, also playing a critical production role in the three hour-long video documentaries that accompany this book, one each about Ghanaba's *Hallelujah!,* Nii Noi and Nii Otoo's *Accra Trane Station,* and *A Por Por Funeral for Ashirifie,* released as the *Jazz Cosmopolitanism in Accra* DVD trilogy.[10]

This body of work overtook my European bell project and much else over the last six years, but for most of that time, with the exception of copious diaries, I didn't write a word about the Accra jazz world. Why? Well, first, it felt more natural to let photographs, recordings, video, and performances express the sensuous substance and spirit of my inquiry as an artist among artists. Both as a matter of credibility and engagement, I wanted to make everything immediately accessible in Ghana, to make sound and image the centerpiece of our collective musical exchanges. Besides, I didn't set out to gather material to write another scholarly book. And as it all got going, I bluntly asked Nii Noi, and then the others, "What do you want out of working with me?" Their priorities were unanimous and pointed: first, to have their creative work well documented and to get paid for it, and second, through the prestige of that documentation, to get more gigs, income, and resources useful for the continuation of their work.

The time to write and the space for it arrived in a grand way, through a generous invitation to give the Bloch Lectures in Music at the University of California, Berkeley, in the winter–spring semester of 2009. Grand because January 2009 marked thirty years since my first setting foot in Berkeley, grand because once again I arrived with an intense writing project. The first time around I had returned from research in rainforest Papua New Guinea to sit down and write a dissertation. During that writing, Bonnie Wade invited me to her ethnomusicology seminar to give the first presentation of that sound-and-sentiment research. Thirty years later it was Bonnie, as chair of Berkeley's Music Department, who was facilitating a return to Berkeley to pour jazz cosmopolitanism onto the page, the pleasure enhanced by the opportunity to present six illustrated lectures and screenings of the three films.

The Bloch talks were academically hybrid, an attempt to present jazz cosmopolitanism through encounter stories and their global pre- and after-lives. My concern was first and foremost to convey some glimpse of the musical intimacy I gained in my Accra encounters, to voice the complexity of knowing African musicians with complicated lives, people whose unique practices and contributions were valorized neither in jazz, art, or experimental music discourses, nor in those of ethno/musicology. I wanted to tell stories about how my life as a musician and researcher became critically entangled in other searching musical lives, lives whose detail, nuance, and difficult positioning mattered to me far beyond academic intrigue. I wanted to focus on the poetics of irony in the making of musical cosmopolitanism.

But I also wanted to focus on the politics of con/disjunctions, and specifically to signpost an awareness of how telling stories and representing my encounters in the global city of Accra involved at least three overlapping genealogies of power: how jazz any-and-everywhere is about the place of race in musical history; how studying African music is always about spirituality and politics; how cosmopolitanism, mine, others', is embodied, lived, uneven, complicated, and not just some heady abstraction floating in the banalizing academic ink pool alongside "globalization" or "identity."

How then to write about musical cosmopolitanism? How to inquire into the substance of unanticipated global entanglements in contemporary musical life-worlds? How to render the entanglements of ethnographic precision and personal empathy? The kind of intervention I offer you means to clear space to talk about cosmopolitanism from below, to reimagine cosmopolitanism from the standpoint of the seriously uneven intersections, and the seriously off-the-radar lives of people who, whatever is to be said about their global connections, nonetheless live quite remotely to the theorists and settings that usually dominate cosmopolitanism conversations in academia.

My attention to subjectivity and voice thus comes out of work that disaggregates multiple and proliferating vernacular cosmopolitanisms from elite multiculturalisms, like the seminal work on "discrepant cosmopolitanism" by James Clifford in his *Routes*.[11] But it is equally a matter of ethnographic commitment to revealing how histories of global entanglement are shaping contemporary African musical life-worlds. Listening to histories of listening is my way to shift attention to acoustemology, to sound as a way of knowing such worlds, and particularly to the presence of intervocality, to intersubjective vocal copresence, to the everyday immediacy and power of stories. These are my means to represent the politics and poetics of cosmopolitan dialogues with my Accra interlocutors.

During the months of writing and lecturing in Berkeley, I was very much caught up in the complexities of finding this kind of storytelling voice for the work. And I understood that to be why I often encountered quizzical looks and comments from listeners when the talks were presented. Yes, I knew, many expected something more conventional: more conventional theory, more conventional analysis, more conventional critical distance, more of the familiar *locus classicus*—the music in its sociocultural context. A gentle edge was there in the reactions, a sort of "that was very interesting, but you didn't really analyze 'the music' or tell us what it means." While people indulged me in my storytelling, I could tell that some were anxiously waiting for me to get to the bottom of it all, to perform an analytic authority.

OK, stories are not analyses in the academic scheme of things. But this does not mean they are unanalytic. Stories, as shown many times and ways by Michael Jackson, as well as by Kathleen Stewart and Keith Basso, all brilliant among anthropologists for their equal talents as story writers, analyze by the ways they encode memorability.[12] They analyze by their narrative selection, juxtaposition, and sequence of lexical elements and vocalic performance. Stories create analytic gestures by their need to recall and thereby ponder, wonder, and search out layers of intersubjective significance in events, acts, and scenes. Stitching stories together is also a sense-making activity, one that signals a clear analytic awareness of the fluidity and gaps in public and private discourses. To listen carefully to stories is to take local subjectivity seriously; to repeat them shifts focus to remembering, to how musical experience becomes meaningful by being vocally emplaced, to how, as Alfred Shutz put it long ago, in *The Phenomenology of the Social World*, remembering "lifts experience" from "the irreversible stream of duration."[13] The work of "lifting" out from storied disjunctures, confluences, and contingencies makes the analytic gesture here of foregrounding irony in the poetics and politics of memory.

A vocal focus on encounters, memorability, and stories also turned out to be a form of mimicking that came naturally from the framing of local discourses in Accra. Locally, the indicative phrase "a story to tell" is a common way of marking the authority of having experienced something significant, particularly in relation to travel or newly gained expertise. In the Ga language, the framing phrases *mata nye adesa ko*, "I will tell you a story," or *miye adesa ko ni mata nye*, "I have a story to tell you," regularly set up and mark a narrative as one that comes from serious things, things well observed, seen clearly, heard profoundly, felt and taken in deeply. For my interlocutors, stories are rear-view mirror reflections; they are the mode of remembering things past, of resisting closure, of embracing life as reverberation. Ghanaba titled his autobiography *I Have a Story to Tell....*[14] And when told, stories produce heightened engagements, often eliciting many questioning frames, as well as confirmation of emphatic sorts I regularly heard rendered in diverse ways, but often enough in alternately melodic and staccato Ghanaian English with phrases like "By all means!" "You *see!*," "*Wond*erful!," *Eh hehh!*, or "It is *noo* small thing, not at *alll*."

Anyway, it was most often encounter stories and their poetics and politics of irony that I put on the table in the Bloch lectures. That was the centerpiece of the search for how to evoke and complicate jazz cosmopolitanism as musical intimacy, and throughout, to make the seeming contradictions palpably intervocal, to keep the whole a more-questions-than-answers sort of affair.

What went with it, in addition to audio and video clips, was an emphasis on how storied memoryscapes are narratively articulated with and through visual images. This was inspired by the everyday importance of image circulation alongside stories and sounds in Accra's public culture. It was also inspired by the interleaved image-text storytelling so poignant in the mixed genre works of W. G. Sebald, whose texts are broken up by photographic images, clippings, drawings, or engravings. Sebald's images foreground, pretell, retell, parallel, punctuate, dissociate, confuse, focus, or encapsulate textual storytelling elements in their immediate or not-so-immediate location. They make copresent text more resonant by pointing forward or back in ways that encourage rereading and re-viewing. They make memory at once soft, a shimmering flash to dream on, and hard, a precisely placed peg.[15]

Decisive moments came while discussing these text-image interplays with Virginia Ryan, both a visual artist and the author of an Accra memoir. Our conversation came naturally out of a collaborative book project, *Exposures: A White Woman in West Africa,*[16] sixty question-laden photographs of and by Virginia in African settings, accompanied by my essay on race and the photographic representation of whiteness. We talked about the textual and pictorial risks of othering in memoir voice, and the worries of making people (including ourselves) out to be strange curiosities. On the other side, we talked about the worries of embrace, of making everything a bit too wondrous or easy to naturalize. In both cases there was the gritty issue of getting close, but in that closeness, respecting the bounds of privacy and dignities of difference.

After leaving Berkeley, four returns to Accra in 2009 and 2010, plus U.S. performance tours each year with Nii Otoo Annan, provided opportunities to present, paraphrase, read, or reveal the shape and content of the lectures to key local interlocutors. What all of those dialogic editing conversations told me was that the only honest thing to do was to shape the book even more directly as a memoir of encounters. And that meant to do even more work that mimics the way many small moments add up to ever-repeating or recycling memories, and to keep the pieces short, ear-centered, and vocalic. Doing so also serves to better evoke what intrigues me most about the memoir genre, how the playback of my voice among other voices turns dialogism into intervocality. It also serves to evoke how stories, sounds, and images coalesce to blur the genre lines of memoir and ethnography.

So: am I aware that the memoir genre is risky when one lightly performs theoretical agendas in vocality, editing, and footnotes? Yes. All the same, I'm here to insist that stories clear substantial space for representing contemporary musical biographies at the cosmopolitan crossroads of modern jazz and modern Africa. I'm here to ask you to listen to how stories reveal Accra's jazz cosmopolitanism across the intimacy-making bridge of acoustemology.

VAMP IN, HEAD

Acoustemology in Accra

On Jazz Cosmopolitanism

1. Nii Noi and me. *Photograph © 2004 Ruti Talmor.*

"Where are you from?" asked the sculptor, instrument inventor, and musician Nii Noi Nortey when Joe Nkrumah introduced us on the porch of the Anyaa Arts Library, Nii Noi's home and studio about an hour's drive from central Accra.

"Philadelphia," I answered, "on the East Coast of the U.S.," not assuming what he might know of American geography.

"Philadelphia! Wow! The city of John Coltrane!"

"You know his music?"

He came back fast and with an uproar of laughter: "Know it? It saved my life!"

"Mine too! We've got to talk!" (More laughter.)

So Nii Noi took me into his house to see his sculptures and shrines to Coltrane. The walls were plastered with album cover collages that linked Coltrane to Archie Shepp and Pharoah Sanders, to Duke Ellington, Eric Dolphy, and Charles Mingus, to important Ghanaian musicians like Guy Warren, Kakraba Lobi, and the band Osibisa, to Nii Noi's lifelong study of Egyptology, and to a multitude of diasporic heroes like Bob Marley, Jimi Hendrix, and James Brown. His darkened hallways of posters and photographs, and his library of recordings, magazines, and books, wandered through African philosophy, Pan-African politics, and diasporan cultural history.

Books by Marcus Garvey, Malcolm X, and W. E. B. Du Bois were piled on the shelves, sitting next to Kwame Nkrumah, Frantz Fanon, Cheikh Anta Diop, Aimée Cesaire, Amilcar Cabral, and other Pan-African works. In the mix were numerous jazz magazines, cuttings, photos and posters, scrapbooks, documents and recordings from Nii Noi's long stays in London during the 1970s and 1980s, where his flute, saxophone, and percussion work was featured in the African groups Dade Krama and African Dawn, as well as in the celebrated black British reggae band Misty In Roots, central to the "rock against racism" movement.

2. Nii Noi's "Listen Closely" family shrine. *Photograph © 2005 Steven Feld.*

3. Nii Noi Nortey, left of tenor saxophonist Pharoah Sanders. *Photograph © 1992 Nii Yemo Nunu, Kotopon Afrikan Images.*

Similar materials were carefully displayed from the years since 1989, when Nii Noi returned to live full-time in Ghana: pictures, gig posters, and cassettes of his groups Mau Mau Muziki and African Sound Project. But the most touching moment arrived when Nii Noi pointed out a small shrine where he keeps an early picture of his two sons next to one of John Coltrane. "Listen Closely," it says. In the foreground is a world map, and in front of it, a smaller image of Nii Noi with Efua, his U.K.-based wife from Guyana.

Then we came to a photo on the wall of Nii Noi with the tenor saxophonist Pharoah Sanders, both a Coltrane alumnus and major avant-garde jazz presence for forty years. "Pharoah came in '92," he told me. "We were asked to open for him at his U.S. Embassy concerts. And Steve Coleman came a few years later and was supportive of our efforts," he continued, directing my eyes to a photo of the adventurous African American improviser and his alto sax posed next to Nii Noi and one of his sculptural arrays of instruments. And pointing to yet another photo of himself playing a two-string lute alongside another well-known presence on the contemporary jazz scene, he added: "I also got to play more recently with Antoine Roney. He's come a couple times, a deeply spiritual guy, and very positive about our music."

I was knocked out by this moment of contact with Nii Noi, by the sensation that as complete strangers we could so instantly know each other, by the sensation that we might equally embody closely overlapping genealogies of listening. I was equally knocked out by the question of whether my amazement was itself the historical product of an unwitting racism. I mean, why should I be surprised that an African musician has spent equally many years listening to what I've been listening to? Why should I be surprised by Nii Noi's similar passion for linking music, culture, and politics, by his distinct knowledge of Pan-Africanism, and by the central position he locates there for the legacy of John Coltrane? Why should I be surprised that in my first days in Accra I've met a man who dedicated himself to music because of the same musician who changed my life's path? Was it that hard to imagine that an African musician could be as deeply into the same sonic way of knowing and being that first inspired me? What could it mean that Nii Noi's was a cosmopolitanism that reached vastly beyond his modest and remote if not outright marginal location in the world of jazz?

In the moment of first encounter there wasn't much time to think about such heady questions. Within minutes Nii Noi excitedly showed me his instruments. He called them "afrifones," inventions he had worked on for several years, combining portions of African, Asian, and Western instruments with saxophone and clarinet mouthpieces. He showed and demonstrated soprano, alto, tenor, and bass varieties.

He told me that his first instruments were alto saxophone and flute, instruments he learned in the United Kingdom in the early seventies after dropping out of an economics degree program. He got some alto lessons from the remarkable Mike Osborne, an Ornette Coleman–inspired saxophonist who played in sixties and seventies U.K. avant-garde ensembles like Chris MacGregor's Brotherhood of Breath, collaborated with Louis Moholo and other distinguished South African musicians in London, and recorded memorably with John Surman and Alan Skidmore in the experimental sax trio SOS. Additionally Nii Noi told me that he stayed on in Zimbabwe after a 1982 Misty In Roots tour, spending several months there studying the Shona *mbira dza vadzimu*.

His instruments also included strings: a ten-string *seprewa* harp, two-

4. Nii Noi playing his mega-alto afrifone. *Photograph © 2007 Steven Feld.*

string *molo* plucked lute, and single-string *gonje* bowed lute. He told me that he played and practiced them all, but that his desire was to concentrate on the north African double-reed *alghaita*, and on his afrifones, to more deeply create what he called "pyrasonix" or acoustic pyramids, a sonic architecture fusing Pan-African timbres and sonorities in diasporic embrace with those deriving from the Coltrane legacy.

As Nii Noi played, I watched and heard his control of circular breathing, using the technique to shape undulating phrases with complex rhythmic and dynamic relations. I heard him take instruments with an ambit of little more than an octave and a half and double their range in both directions by fingering, over-blowing, and embouchure techniques I associated with jazz experimenters like John Coltrane, Albert Ayler, and Eric Dolphy. I heard him explore a range of open-hole and key fingerings combined with lipping techniques that gurgled and gargled their way into split tones and micro-tones. I heard him create a sound on his smallest afrifone that dialogued with the timbres Coltrane approached on the soprano saxophone, as inspired by Indian double-reeds as by the legacy of Sidney Bechet, the soprano's early jazz exponent.

When he switched to the bass instrument, I heard sounds that reached into those extraordinarily throaty places Eric Dolphy took the bass clarinet, crossing with the vibrant multiphonics he honked out of the bottom of his horn. The tenor instrument turned out an ever more powerful late-Coltrane sound, mixing an urgent edge perhaps even more in line with Albert Ayler, Archie Shepp, and Pharoah Sanders, a glidingly vocalic sound in the extreme altissimo register, with Dolphyesque swoops, swirls, and acrobatic register jumps, as swell as slap-tongue staccato accents that recalled the verve of Rahsaan Roland Kirk.

Playing what jazz ears might hear as Afro-Arabic-Asian vocal melody shapes in very postbop modal phrases of all lengths, Nii Noi liberally quoted the melody or well-known improvised phrases from recordings of Coltrane compositions like "India," "Africa Brass," or "Meditations," mixing in timbral arrays particularly resonant with Coltrane's late period of 1965–67, and with the overlapping artistry of numerous Coltrane disciples and inheritors.

When he played gonje, the one-stringed lute, he used a horsehair bow to saw into textures that immediately reminded me of saxophonist Ornette Coleman's approach to the violin. No wonder: out of the corner of my eye I spotted an Ornette Coleman Live at the Golden Circle trio LP[1] in one of the album collages that Nii Noi has created on his ceiling. When he switched to metal and wood gyil (pentatonic gourd-resonated xylophones), he laid into the instruments with a pounding physicality that nodded equally to the visceral bass comping might of McCoy Tyner's left hand, and the darting, right-hand, cluster-punch rhythmic runs of Cecil Taylor.

That afternoon I asked Nii Noi if he'd like a recording of his rehearsal with percussionists Nii Otoo Annan and Aminu Kalangu. "Yes, why not," he said, with an ease of trust, and after returning to the United States, I sent him an edited CD. Some weeks later, he called me in New Mexico to thank me for it and asked if I would consider coming back to work with him on a production. It was easy to agree. As soon as my teaching semester was over in late spring 2005, I returned to Accra to set up a studio with a local engineer, Nana Agazi, and worked with Nii Noi and

Nii Otoo for a month to record their tribute to Coltrane's LP classic *A Love Supreme*.

Coltrane's four-part suite comprises the pieces "Acknowledgement," "Resolution," "Pursuance," and "Psalm." Nii Noi and Nii Otoo's tribute is different, a three-part suite structure, a narrative idea linking three Coltrane titles, "Welcome" (from the LP *Kulu Sé Mama*), "Africa" (from his *Africa Brass*), and "Transition" (from the LP of that name).[2]

"Why not use the structure Coltrane used?" I asked.

"There's a difference between a tribute and a copy," Nii Noi replied. "Of course I find Coltrane's titles very meaningful. They're also challenges, like 'Acknowledgement' or 'Resolution,' which we can use. The 'Psalm' section I found very, very interesting, because it sounds like a hymn to the Christian ear, but for me, as an African, those vocalizations sound like a prayer from a traditional African priest. It's very meaningful music, the way it brings spirituality into our political struggles. But we can contribute more to the African recognition of Coltrane if we just show how we're inspired and moved by what Coltrane gave the world. Others can pay their homage by repeating his songs but our tribute should be different. It's about an African acknowledgment and resolution, and not just those words as Coltrane song titles or melodies."

Nii Noi's "Welcome" section is itself divided into three parts, again with Coltrane titles but different substance: "Acknowledgment" (also the opening title of Coltrane's *A Love Supreme*), "Spiritual" (from his *Live at the Village Vanguard* LP), and "Offering" (from his *Expression*).[3] Nii Noi took the melody vamp of Coltrane chanting the words "a love supreme" from the original recording's "Acknowledgment" section and substituted the vocal phrase *awo awo*. Colloquially "mother" in Ga, *awo awo* is a more formal honorific or deified invocation of Mother Earth as a source of bounty and sustenance, an African citation that creates a loving bridge from Ga spirituality to Coltrane's supreme being. Nii Noi added a more Afropentatonic harmony too, which transitions nicely to "Spiritual," a Mississippi Delta–meets–Afro-free-jazz exploration for plucked lute and bass box. And while resisting direct quotation of Coltrane's original melodic material, he brings the "a love supreme / *awo awo*" melody vamp back later on flute in "Offering," whistle-playing it in the style of a Fulani shepherd's call to the flock.

The "Africa" section is also divided into three parts: "After the Rain" (a title from Coltrane's *Impressions*), "Crescent" (from an LP of the same name), and "The Drum Thing" (also from Coltrane's *Crescent* LP).[4] The choice of "After the Rain" to open the "Africa" section came from the immediate situation; the sessions took place during the end of the rainy season, and on many afternoons we had to wait until after the rain stopped for enough quiet to record. Frequently it was the first recording take after the rain that was the most refreshing. "Crescent" is the CD's longest track and is itself a suite of Afro-Arabic-Asian textures, timbres, and moods. "The Drum Thing" is Nii Otoo's solo tribute to Coltrane's drummers Elvin Jones and Rashied Ali.

The final section, "Transition," opens with "Resolution" (the second title in Coltrane's *A Love Supreme* suite), and then closes with a personal tribute title, "For Trane." For this "Transition" section Nii Noi plays alto saxophone; the earlier pieces all feature him on afrifones, gyil xylophones, and plucked (molo) and bowed (gonje) lutes. "Resolution" is a slow melodic line reminiscent of Pharoah Sanders's extensions of Coltrane's spiritual melodies, accompanied by rolling free-time textures on bass and drums. On "For Trane," Nii Noi and Nii Otoo evoke the intensity of Coltrane and Rashied Ali's duos on the LP *Interstellar Space*.[5] Nii Noi takes the alto into sonic extensions of Coltrane's explorations, summoning saxophonic voices of Eric Dolphy, Albert Ayler, Marion Brown, Joseph Jarman, and Roscoe Mitchell along the way. Nii Otoo accompanies on his invention, the *gangofone*, a rack of *gangokui* double bells, plus hi-hat cymbal, all played with wooden curved sticks more typically used to play the underarm *odonno* pressure (talking) drum. "The bells bring a more ritual and spiritual sound, here and in the north," Nii Noi offered. "Otoo is ringing Trane's spiritual passage."

As we started the *Tribute to A Love Supreme* recording project, I asked Nii Noi if he would also like to do a series of video dialogues about Coltrane, his own musical history, his Coltrane-inspired sound sculptures, and his afrifones. He agreed, and we shot the first of what, three years later, amounted to some fifteen hours of conversations. Those conversations, along with footage of demonstrating the afrifones, making and discussing sound sculptures, of rehearsing and performing in Africa and the United States, and of Nii Noi's Anyaa Arts Library, shape the film *Accra Trane Station: The Music and Art of Nii Noi Nortey*.

The *Accra Trane Station* film begins with Nii Noi taking me on a guided conversational tour of some of his Accra Trane Station sound sculptures, each named by the title of a Coltrane composition, each a material distillation of the acoustic relationships and composite feelings of Coltrane's performances. He demonstrates his afrifones and makes links between the art and his instruments, showing how he uses PVC, plastics, metals, wood, shells, animal horns, bamboo, leathers, and recycled objects, and how he modifies bells, changes mouthpieces, and performs with each instrument in various stages of (dis)assembly to craft different timbral dialogues between African, Arabic, Asian, and diasporic jazz voices.

Also recorded in the film are scenes from different "Art in the Garden" exhibits organized by the Foundation for Contemporary Art–Ghana, showing Nii Noi's process of assembling sculptures. In other scenes, he takes me on tours of his library collections and discusses the relationship between musical and visual transmission of art and culture in Ghana, as well as his interests in critical pedagogy, particularly the use of music and

5. Nii Otoo and Nii Noi' s *Tribute to A Love Supreme. Photograph © 2006 Steven Feld, art © 2006 Nicholas Wayo.*

art to cultivate a higher national consciousness of Ghana as a nation within a Pan-African historical struggle for freedom and dignity. Woven into these segments are rehearsals in Ghana, concerts and recording studio sessions in the United States, and several critical conversations on Coltrane's African legacy, Ghana's freedom, and the significance of its fiftieth-anniversary celebrations.

In *Accra Trane Station* you also encounter the percussionist Nii Otoo Annan, Nii Noi's musical collaborator since 1990. Astonishingly, after I first heard Otoo play, Nii Noi quipped, "Did you check out my drummer? He even looks like Elvin Jones!" It's true. Nii Otoo's remarkable physical resemblance to Jones seems of a piece with his musical affinity for the famous polyrhythmic approach of Coltrane's longtime drummer. He expresses that affinity not on a traditional jazz trap drum kit, but on what Nii Noi calls the APK, or "African Percussion Kit," Nii Otoo's battery of *apentemma*, *kpanlogo*, *gome*, *brekete*, and *odonno* traditional

6. Nii Noi with "Africa Brass." *Photograph © 2006 Steven Feld.*

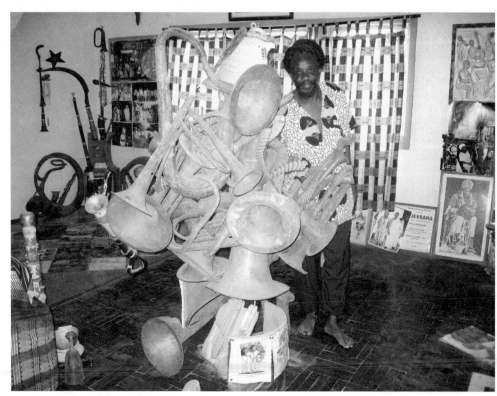

7. Nii Otoo at the "African Percussion Kit." *Photograph © 2006 Steven Feld.*

drums, joined by gyil xylophones, the "gangofone" rack of gangokui bells, and jazz-kit hi-hat and ride cymbals.

Nii Otoo's early musical background involved extensive participation in the world of Ga traditional ritual drumming. He later specialized in the jazz trap set in highlife and church bands, and is also on call as a bass and guitar player. Nii Noi introduced Nii Otoo to the work of the Coltrane drummers Elvin Jones and Rashied Ali, work that deeply influenced Nii Otto's fusion of African and jazz approaches to polyrhythmic improvisation. This is readily audible on all the Accra Trane Station CDs, where Nii Otoo not only creates that very-Elvin-ish sense of multiple drummers doing counterpoint-and-entity polymetrics, but continually explores tonal, textural, and timbral terrain on wood, skin, and iron, using Western jazz sticks, brushes, and mallets on his African drums as interchangeably as he applies palm and Ghanaian curved-stick techniques to his jazz hi-hat and ride cymbals.

The fusion of Ghanaian techniques and avant-garde jazz drumming also characterizes Nii Otoo's experimental *Bufo Variations* project.[6] With numerous instruments and instrument combinations, Nii Otoo recorded a series of overdubs to a six-minute recording I made of dense rhythmic sounds of night toads and crickets. Treating the toad and cricket interactions as a musical calculator, stimulus, and click-track, Nii Otoo improvised ten completely different variations on the metrical capacities of simultaneous play in three against two, four against three, and six against four. The project speaks to the generative polyrhythmic math of the so-called $\frac{12}{8}$ time line. It's a powerfully different imagination to the one you might have encountered in dozens of scholarly works on the topic, from the early theories and odd transcriptions of the Rev. A. M. Jones, to the recent recuperation of them by the musicologist Kofi Agawu, book-ending fifty years of ethnomusicological West Africanist scholarship and debate in between.[7]

After working together in Nii Noi's large ensembles, Mau Mau Muziki and African Sound Project, the name Accra Trane Station came to Nii Noi as he and Nii Otoo were recording their Coltrane tribute.

"Well, Accra Train Station–Coltrane Station is interesting because the music of Coltrane is universal and Accra has always served as the Pan-African capital. So Accra embracing Coltrane is part of the historical process. Accra becomes the new focus for John Coltrane. In other words, Coltrane has finally arrived in Africa. It's no longer just a dream on records and on titles, but now it's a real acceptance of the man's works in Africa. We can take our place in a Coltrane revival in Africa, which could be very, very important in the development of African music. So the Accra Trane Station is a projection into the future, and we are proud of it."

Nii Noi's choice of name combines the colloquial nickname for John Coltrane with the railroad metaphor so resonant in the historical movement of black people in North America. In full awareness that the word "station" meant "hiding place" in the coded lingo of the underground railroad network of nineteenth-century slave escape routes, Nii Noi created, in parallel to the music, an Accra Trane Station of sculptures in his studio annex, where he parked the material intersection of a diasporic train called jazz with the African presence of Trane's sound.

The *Tribute to A Love Supreme* project marked a culmination of musical conversations that Nii Noi and Nii Otoo had explored for years. But it also opened up a new horizon of jazz cosmopolitics. That came about because, during our month together, Nii Noi and Nii Otoo typically left all their larger instruments at the recording loft. One of them intrigued me, a bass lamellophone locally called *ashiwa* (the Ga name, in Twi, *premprensowa*, or pidgin, *sontin adeka*, "something box"). I recognized it as a larger version of the Caribbean "rhythm box" or "rumba box," an instrument of modest familiarity. Visiting Jamaica in 1963, my parents brought one home to me, a tourist model from Linstead Market, with garishly painted palm trees, but acoustically the real thing.

On many evenings alone in the loft I sat on my new fixation, the ashiwa box, and plucked away for hours, experimenting with tuning and fingering techniques. Perched in front of the hard drive digital recorder, I'd cue up some of the tracks we had recently recorded and play along, miming what Nii Otoo was doing with his left hand and lower-pitched drums to understand the time cycles, while exploring ways the ashiwa might overlay jazz or Afro-Latin bass figures to interlock, push, or pull. Some of this came quite naturally, as I had played low brass for many years, including ten years in TG3, Tom Guralnick's sax-brass-drums avant-garde trio, where I took the bass role on tuba, euphonium, or bass trombone, interlocking in just this way with Jefferson Voorhees, a drummer who had spent many years playing both West African traditional drums and Afro-Beat fusions in Bay Area ensembles.

One day at the beginning of our last recording week, I was upstairs practicing ashiwa with headphones on. Unbeknownst to me, Nii Noi, Nii Otoo, and Agazi had arrived. They walked up the stairs softly and all of a sudden appeared before me. Immediately I stopped playing and took the headphones off. But before I could greet them Nii Otoo was already seated at his drums and playing, and Nii Noi shouted out: "Keep playing, man! Get on our traaiin!" And before I knew it we were way into it, Nii Noi beginning with long-toned invocations reminiscent of Coltrane's "Dahomey Dance" as Nii Otoo's mallets rolled and tumbled jazzy *agbadza* variations on apentemma and kpanlogo skins, his cymbals echoing accents off of a pattern that I improvised following Jimmy Garrison's catchy bass vamp from the head of "All or Nothing at All," from the Coltrane quartet's recording of ballads.[8]

Well, the musical conversation that day got pretty animated, with Nii Noi and Nii Otoo clearly energized by additional layers of bass box Afro-jazz conversation triangulating their own rhythmic and melodic dialogues. Nii Otoo gave me some ashiwa technique lessons in the following days, Nii Noi ordered me an instrument from a local craftsman, and in the last sessions they had me join them for three of the last *Tribute* tracks.

This all happened quickly, and the absence of much about it in my diary reminds me of how speechless I felt in the face of Nii Noi and Nii Otoo's musical openness and inclusiveness in those last recording days. Yes, I had spoken to Nii Noi a bit about my musical history and had given him some CD recordings of different groups I had played in. But I had never suggested playing together, much less doing so as a complete novice on a local instrument. I was there strictly as recordist and producer. The only prior moment where my participation was requested had come when Nii Noi wanted to record a background figure and asked me to join him and Nii Nii Otoo on a third conch shell to thicken the texture and harmony.

By the time I returned to Accra six months later to spend the first half of 2006, I had devoted a great deal of time to practicing the ashiwa box at home in Santa Fe. After a first reunion session together, Nii Noi and Nii Otoo declared Accra Trane Station a trio. That meant not only the opportunity for a Coltrane conversation and musical exploration unlike any other in my musical history, but a location from which I could begin to acoustemologically apprehend something of how Nii Noi and Nii Otoo conducted their Ghanaian roots–infused diasporic dialogues with the late sixties black avant-garde.

What fascinated me here was exploring how playing a mix of Ghanaian bell and drum *and* jazz (including Afro-Latin jazz) bass parts on my "box" simultaneously extended the interactive relationships in Nii Noi and Nii Otoo's conversation of melodic and rhythmic layerings. While Ghanaian ashiwa players typically employed busy figures, filling space continually with rolling and tumbling triplets, eighth runs, and dotted eighths, I heard the instrument in a sparser and more accentual jazz bass framework, alternating vamp figures with more open space to create tension and anticipation in interplay with the drums.

In its Ghanaian usage, the ashiwa is always played as a seated rhythm box, the player utilizing only the three pitches of the upper sections of the three lamelles. In the spirit of invention and modification that flowed from Nii Noi and Nii Otoo's own homemade or hybrid instruments, I elevated the box onto a stand in order to extend its capacities to six rather than three tones, the upper portions of the lamelles with three fingers of the right hand, the lower ones with the left thumb. This way the four fin-

8. Me with my upright ashiwà bass box. *Photograph © 2006 Nana Agazi.*

gers could play the two ends of the lamelles in independent interlock, to
mix bass line ostinato with anticipation and counterfigures that grooved
with the inner drum parts played by Nii Otoo.

While I was gone, I also did some background research and learned
that the box was not Ghanaian in origin. From a Congo birthplace it
developed diasporically in Santo Domingo and Cuba, and then Jamaica,
where as the "rumba box" it was featured in mento, an early 1950s precur-
sor to ska and reggae. Numerous Black Atlantic variants of this instrument, often named *marimbula*, are found from Puerto Rico to Colombia,
with configurations of three to eleven keys. Repatriated Jamaicans intro-

duced the instrument to Nigeria and to Ghana, where it became part of diverse early twentieth-century acoustic popular musics on the coast and then the interior. In Ghana it was particularly important to the early Asante palm wine trio sound of guitar, beer bottle or bell, and the box, the three lamelles tuned in fourths to easily accompany guitar.[9]

With the regular presence and participation of Agazi at each session to record, Accra Trane Station's 2006 work was documented on *Meditations for John Coltrane,* a collection of textural pieces inspired by Coltrane's late-period *Meditations* suite. But this time, rather than give the pieces individual names, Nii Noi suggested that we just name them Meditations 1 through 9. "Meditations, 1" is the only track that directly references Coltrane's *Meditations* suite, with Nii Noi playing an Africanized alto sax transformation of the melody Coltrane titled "Love."[10]

The other tracks explore textures, instrumental combinations, moods, and emotions, from tranquil and serene to thunderous. The emphasis is on the percussive element of the instruments and ensemble dynamics. And this, Nii Noi told me, was because he was particularly impressed by something he read in the liner notes of *Meditations,* Coltrane's first re-cording with Elvin Jones and Rashied Ali drumming together. There Col-trane told the writer Nat Hentoff: "I feel the need for more time, more rhythm all around me. And with more than one drummer, the rhythm can be more multi-directional. Someday I may add a conga drummer or even a company of drummers." Reading those lines out loud Nii Noi said, "You see, that's where he recognized the African base of it all."

After the *Meditations* sessions I wrote to an old friend, Jean Schwarz, about how the Accra Trane Station project joined Coltrane, Africa, and experimental jazz, in hopes that I could enlist his collaboration in mixing and mastering the tracks. I first met Jean in Paris in 1974 during a student semester at the Musée de l'Homme. Originally a jazz drummer who had studied with Kenny Clarke, he was both the engineer of the Musée's prestigious record series on the Le Chant du Monde label, and also a well-regarded electro-acoustic composer working with the Groupe de Recherches Musicales (GRM) at the national radio studios. "Erda," one of my favorites among his compositions, includes a beautiful homage to Coltrane.[11] Although we had done some concerts together in the late seventies, it was a long-held dream of mine to work with Jean again. His jazz, experimental, and world music sophistication and his impeccable technical skills made him the perfect critical listener, and a week with him at his Paris home studio brought *Meditations for John Coltrane* alive.

Six months later, I returned to Accra again, and Accra Trane Station's 2007 work was documented on *Another Blue Train*, a project that marked the confluence of the fiftieth anniversaries of Ghana's independence on March 6, 1957, and *Blue Train*, Coltrane's 1957 classic LP of minor blues explorations.[12] Coltrane was well aware of the Gold Coast's independence and the birth of Ghana. But he didn't know that the country also quite literally had a Blue Train, a slow train of the night that connected the key cities of Accra, Takoradi, and Kumasi. It was Nii Noi's idea to make the connection with a musical train ride through the diasporic night called jazz.

This time the titles followed the narrative progression of a train ride, from "All Aboard" to "Up to Speed" (featuring a rhythmically expansive drum solo) and "Grooving North," then two long and moody free-meter improvisations titled "Topographies of the Dark" (one of them including a rendering of the melody to Coltrane's "Spiritual"), coming back to groove with "Blue Night Train," and closing with "Morning Light," a xylophone and bass duo recorded to the sounds of early-morning birds.

Later in 2007, Accra Trane Station performed in the United States, where we expanded to a quintet to work with the U.S.- and Europe-based jazz artists Alex Coke and Jefferson Voorhees. The quintet recorded *Topographies of the Dark* in the States, which was additionally a sound-vision dialogue with a series of Black Atlantic sculptural paintings of the same title, created in Accra by Virginia Ryan, the codirector of Foundation for Contemporary Art–Ghana.[13] The experiment was to pair and juxtapose Nii Noi's afrifones with Alex's sax and flutes, and Nii Otoo's APK with Jefferson's standard jazz trap set, my box bass playing its usual in-between part-bass / part-drum role where jazz meets Ghana. I didn't have a CD project in mind, just an encounter in the studio where Nii Noi and Nii Otoo could meet and play with two of my oldest musical collaborators, friends who were well aware and already quite sensitive to their sound. But a CD and then a joint concert resulted, and through them another set of possibilities to hear and imagine dialogue at places where jazz interiorities of African musicianship meet African exteriorities of jazz musicianship.

The third and fourth chapters of this book will go more deeply into Nii

9.1 and 9.2. Covers for *Meditations* and *Another Blue Train*. Art © 2006 © 2007 Nicholas Wayo.

10. Nii Noi performing with Ghanaba. *Photograph © 1995 Nii Yemo Nunu, Kotopon Afrikan Images.*

Noi and Nii Otoo's musical worlds, these recording projects, the Accra Trane Station video, and the contrasts and clashes between distinct yet overlapping vernacular cosmopolitanisms. But now let me rewind back to Accra and May 2005, for it was then, during early visits to Nii Noi's house to record our Coltrane conversations, that he opened two interlocking stories of jazz cosmopolitanism in Accra. The openings came as Nii Noi showed photographs on his walls of fame and spoke to my video camera about them.

"These pictures are by Nii Yemo Nunu, a good friend and local photographer," he said. "That's me playing with Ghanaba. I first connected with him in London in 1986, when he played the Royal Albert Hall together with Max Roach. He was supportive of what I was doing with Dade Krama, my African cultural group in the U.K. When I came back to

Ghana a few years later I went to see him at his library, called the Afrikan Heritage Library, and have worked with him on certain occasions ever since. I also recorded a very long interview with him in 1994 to document his history. My wife helped me transcribe it. I just wanted to take down some of his stories, but we ended up with two hundred pages! The man has a lot to say. His archive, his library, the way he arranged his collections from years in America, it's a map of his life and findings, and that really inspired what I've done here with my own collections of books and recordings. Anyway, I think Ghanaba is our most important connection to America and jazz."

As Nii Noi spoke I looked up incredulously at a wall of photos, a collage of side-by-side color blowups and black-and-white negative contact sheets. I was shocked. "This is amazing, Nii Noi. I mean, Ghanaba—Guy Warren—I didn't know he was still alive. I just hadn't heard about him in ages. Does he still play jazz drums or just specialize in this African drum setup in these photos with you?"

"When he returned to Ghana in the sixties, he used to play his jazz drums," he replied. "Right now, and since 1980 or thereabouts, he's been playing his own modified drums. He uses the African traditional drums in a jazz setting. In other words, he uses about seven drums and sets them up like a jazz kit. You have your snare drums and tom-toms and floor drums. He doesn't use a hi-hat. He uses two big *fontomfrom* drums as bass drums, and he uses foot pedals to control them. So, he hasn't lost his skills and techniques that he acquired on the jazz drums. What he has done is transfer all those techniques onto his African drums. And when he plays those drums, they don't sound like the jazz drums. They sound more like the royal drums of the Akan, of the Ashantis. Even then, he doesn't even play like the traditional drummers. He incorporates the traditional techniques and incorporates his jazz understandings and creates a whole new revelation."

"Wow. I heard some of his old recordings but nothing with a set-up like that. I listened to *Africa Speaks, America Answers*[14] after hearing Max Roach talk about the time Warren lived and played in the U.S., in the mid-fifties. Has he spoken to you about those times and his association with Max?"

"Yes, there's a lot in my interview with him about those times. Max Roach is very important to Ghanaba. They're still in touch to this day."

"I forget Max's exact line, but it was quite quotable, something like 'Warren was too African for bebop and too early for free jazz.'"

"Prof, do you actually know Max Roach? Man, Ghanaba will be so impressed, he'll want to meet you right away."

"Yeah. I must have seen Max last in 2000, or 2001, in New York, after a gig he played with brass at the Blue Note. That was before he took so ill. I hear he's not doing too well these days. Anyway, I know Max came here to visit, in the early seventies I think, when he was teaching at the University of Massachusetts. I read an interview, no, maybe it was something on the radio, where he talked about how teaching at the university made him realize that he had to gain more knowledge of African percussion, so he came here to rekindle his old friendship with Guy Warren."

· A few days later Nii Noi and I went to visit Guy Warren, now known as Ghanaba, at his Afrikan Heritage Library (Ghanaba's original and prefered spelling) in Midie, an hour and some from Accra on the Nsawam road. On the way, Nii Noi, somewhat sheepishly, said: "Prof, let me warn you. Ghanaba is going to ask you for something. I don't know what he will ask for. But he will ask for something. He will test you. That's how he is. He likes to challenge people. If it is something you can do it will likely be good for us all. If you can't do it don't worry too much, just tell him. He has worked with whites a lot, so he likes to be direct. Very direct. He might try to shock you, he does that with a lot of people."

Sure enough, after the basic exchanges about musical and personal connections, Ghanaba looked right at me and made his pitch.

"I'm told that you have professional equipment, that you know how to use it, and have trained Agazi."

"Yes . . ."

"OK, good. I want you to do something for me. Nobody has recorded my talking drums version of Handel's 'Hallelujah' chorus with a full choir. If I bring the choir here can you come and record us? This is my life's work. It's a document we badly need."

"Of course," I blurted out impulsively, feeling a wave of relief that the request was so easily fielded. Then the astonishment hit me: did Ghana's best-known drummer and jazz icon really just ask me to record his cover of Handel? What in the world is this about? My mind raced to the idea of "third stream music," a concept coined by the composer Gunther Schuller in the late 1950s to refer to an experimental blending of jazz and

European art music with an emphasis on new settings for improvisation.[15] Could Ghanaba possibly have come in contact with this idea during his late-fifties musical residence in the States? Was he consciously expanding it or commenting on it through the medium of African drumming? Or was this whole Handel thing coming from another set of motivations? The possibilities were totally mystifying.

I'd get the beginning answers to my questions three weeks later. That's when I arrived quite late (even by flexible local standards) to Ghanaba's place after several bumper-to-bumper traffic hours in Agazi's equipment truck with Nii Noi and Nii Yemo. As we walked into the house I could see he was fuming.

"*Tooo* much traffic," Agazi says, most apologetically, as we enter. Ghanaba snarls, stares him down, then goes for the jugular:

"How did you get your independence, boy?"

Duck and cover. It was the first of several instances of what I had heard about Guy Warren, that he had an explosive temper and could be mean and harsh.

Before things could get any worse I quickly told Agazi that we needed to get going, and we hurriedly set up the microphones and checked levels as the Winneba Youth Choir rehearsed and as Oko, Ghanaba's assistant, set up the drums. We tested everything by recording some hymns with the choir. As we were finishing our sound checks, Ghanaba's younger daughter, Mawuko, called "Sweetie" by her father, came out and said, "Professor, please, my father wants to speak to you, he's in the kitchen." As I entered, Oko was beginning to paint him in his customary white ochre. He turned and greeted me somewhat sternly:

"Are you ready for me yet?"

"Yes," I say. "We've set up and tested everything. And by the way, I brought my video camera. Will it be OK to leave it on during the session?"

As he looked back at me I could see his demeanor transform. His eyes lit up, a smile came over his face, and his voice opened up.

"Oh, that's woonndderfulll," he said, the vocal pleasure dripping off the lengthened syllables. "We'll make a *movie*!"

"Uh . . . well . . . let me explain," I follow, hurriedly, a bit worried. "I only have one camera. With the choir on one side and you facing them from the other with the instrumentalists I can't really make a movie because I can't record the two perspectives simultaneously."

Silence. Then he looked at me eye to eye, and as he got up from his chair I heard his voice go very far in the other direction.

"Steven, you told me you were a jazzman, *correct?*"

"Yes."

"Well *improvise* man, IMPROVISE!" he said, twice raising his voice, then cracking up and smiling. "Just *dance* with me."

And then as he turned back to Oko, he added my marching orders: "And get my footwork, I'm proud of my footwork."

I went back outside, and as I told Agazi that he'd record alone, that I'd be with the camera, the drums began to sound the rallying rhythm of *Ghana muntie!* "Rise up Ghana!" "Here ye Ghana!" "Stand tall Ghana!," calling the choir to move in from all directions and assemble. As they took their places a gunshot announcing Ghanaba's arrival led to his emergence through the side doorway of his house, his skin covered in white ochre, dressed in white robes and wearing a Ghanaian flag around his neck, led by fire-bearer Oko and accompanied by Nii Noi playing one of his afrifones. I had no choice but to walk with the camera from one location to the next to stay with the action. And thus the dance began, and continued, for another thirty minutes.

In a single continuous shot, moving with a wide-angle lens in the *plan séquence* manner Jean Rouch established for the intimate cinema of rituals in his numerous films in Niger and Mali,[16] *"Hallelujah!"* reveals Ghanaba's postcolonial staging of George Frideric Handel's "Hallelujah" chorus, joined by Nii Noi and the Winneba Youth Choir, a leading choir in Ghana and Africa at large.

What unfolds is Ghanaba's unique approach to the "Hallelujah" chorus as a mixture of African, Christian, Buddhist, and Islamic ritual together with formal European concert performance and Ghanaian ceremony. At the heart of the performance is Ghanaba's approach to playing Handel on seven ritual drums, arranged around him like a semicircle jazz drum set. The set-up includes two large *bomma* fontomfrom drums nontraditionally lying on their sides and played with jazz bass drum foot-pedals (those, I'm told later, a gift from Max Roach). He simultaneously plays the other five upright atumpani, apentemma, and small fontomfrom drums with traditional hooked sticks. Additional large upright ritual drums accompany portions of the performance, as do Nii Noi's sounds on the alghaita, a double-reed instrument associated with northern Africa and the spread of Islam. The choir of thirty-five voices is accompanied by a portable electronic organ.

Ghanaba's staging wraps the "Hallelujah" chorus into three other musical selections, in addition to instrumental introductions and interludes. During the opening procession to the drums, the choir sings the hymn "Lead, Kindly Light." Composed in 1865 by John B. Dykes with words from 1833 by John Henry Newman, this hymn has particular resonance in Ghana, as it is associated with the early 1950s formation of the Convention People's Party (CPP), and Kwame Nkrumah's leadership to Ghana's independence in 1957. The hymn was Nkrumah's favorite, but it was also a favorite of Mahatma Gandhi, whose nonviolent approach to political organization and anticolonial struggle Nkrumah admired and espoused. The song's folklore has other tragic historical and resistance resonances, as it was reportedly sung on the *Titanic* as the ship sank. But it is the powerful local connection to Nkrumah, the CPP, and Ghana's independence that is significant in how Ghanaba uses it to recast the "Hallelujah" chorus in both a cosmopolitan and national context, joining spiritual music and political history.

After a drum introduction and ritual evocation of ancestral spirit presences, Ghanaba and the Winneba Youth Choir conductor, Paa John (John Francis Arthur-Yamoah), lead the chorus into "Hallelujah." Considered among the most popular works of Western choral music, the chorus is part of Handel's oratorio *Messiah*, from a libretto by Charles Jennens. The piece was composed in 1741 and premiered in Dublin in 1742. Handel, a devout Christian, devoted the work to the life of Jesus Christ and its enduring significance. The libretto consists of sections of the King James Bible, much of it from the Old Testament, and is divided into three major sections: "The Birth," "The Passion," and "The Aftermath." The "Hallelujah" chorus is the conclusion to "The Passion" and its text comes from the New Testament book of Revelation.

Following a drum solo and before the choral conclusion, Ghanaba features Nii Noi on the double-reed alghaita and recites the Muslim call to prayer. Long a practicing Buddhist, but also a serious student of the Bible, the teachings of Mohammed, and many other spiritual writings, Ghanaba embraces in this staging a pluralistic vision of the political and religious in both Ghana's national culture and regional position, and the country's complex relationship to Islam, Christianity, and Western art music.

As the "Hallelujah" chorus finishes and he leaves his drums, Ghanaba segues the musical performance into the first stanza of the Ghana national anthem, "God Bless Our Homeland," written and composed by Philip Gbeho, emphasizing, through energetic recitative, its final phrase:

And help us to resist oppressors' rule
With all our will and might evermore.

At this point the joyousness of the "Hallelujah" chorus, reset in the context of Ghanaian independence, nationalism, and political and religious unity and diversity, yields to a more familiar local pleasure in the song and dance performance of Ghanaba's best known song, "That Happy Feeling." This song was first recorded on his 1957 Decca LP *Africa Speaks, America Answers* and was covered most notably by the German bandleader Bert Kaempfert on his 1962 LP *A Swingin' Safari*. Originally titled "Eyi Wala Dong" (literally "My Thanks to Him") as a song of praise to God in thanks for the birth of his two sons, Ghanaba accepted the English title suggestion from the director of Decca Records, Milt Gabler. The performance concludes with Ghanaba and the choir transforming the formality of the "Hallelujah" chorus into the party atmosphere of this African song.

The half-hour *Hallelujah!* performance video was followed, almost two years later, by a half-hour video conversation with Ghanaba about how he created this layered mix of Handel, jazz, Islamic music, the muezzin call to prayer, the Ghana national anthem, and "That Happy Feeling." By that time we knew each other well and had discussed the film and his career in detail. Joined together, the film's two sections reveal a vision of the "Hallelujah" chorus as postcolonial theater, an intertwined homage to Handel and Kwame Nkrumah as cosmopolitan and national agents of religious tolerance and pluralism.

The chapter about Ghanaba that follows reframes those issues through three years of our conversations about music, race, and jazz history. But for the moment, a brief answer to my initial wonder: how did Ghanaba end up playing Handel's "Hallelujah" chorus on talking drums with an African choir?

Born in 1923 and named Warren Gamaliel Akwei after the American president Warren Gamaliel Harding, the musician America knew as Guy Warren first came to the United States during the war, in 1943, from the then Gold Coast after enlisting in the U.S. Armed Forces Office of

Special Services in Accra.[17] He spent a brief time in Chicago training to be an OSS spy, and covertly was one when he went back home, overtly working as a journalist in order to gather British documents and pass them to U.S. intelligence. About that time he also became a founding member of the Tempos highlife band with E. T. Mensah. He also went to London to play in Kenny Graham's Afro-Cubists, bringing bongos, calypsos, and Afro-Caribbean concepts back to Gold Coast and fusing them into the emergent Tempos sound. But in 1950, before the Tempos recorded, Warren left the band and moved to Monrovia, Liberia, where he worked as a journalist, DJ, and drummer.

Changing his name to Guy Warren signaled his ultimate desire to come to America, to make it as an African American jazz drummer, and to separate from the man he often referred to as his "overbearing father." That man, Richard Allote Marbuor Akwei, was a sports star, then pro-

11. Guy Warren and Charlie Parker, Chicago, 1955.
Photograph © 2010 Afrikan Heritage Library Collection.

12. Guy Warren Zoundz at the Africa Room, New York, 1958.
Photograph © 2010 Afrikan Heritage Library Collection.

moter, administrator, educator, and school principal; central Accra's well-known Akwei Memorial School is named for him. Akwei relentlessly urged his son to do something "dignified." Jazz was not what he had in mind, and Warren was compared, unfavorably, to his junior half-brother Richard Maximillian Akwei, who later graduated from Achimota College, joined the civil service, and ultimately served as Ghana's ambassador to the United States, to Switzerland, and as the country's permanent representative to the United Nations.

In the United States from 1953, Warren lived first in Chicago and then in New York. He introduced African drums to American jazz musicians, specifically the under-arm pressure "talking" drum odonno, and recorded, first with Decca, then with RCA. He was the first Ghanaian to become a member of ASCAP (American Society of Composers, Authors and Publishers), and the first African to have a composition covered by American jazz artists—Art Blakey recording his "Love, the Mystery of . . ." in 1962, followed by Randy Weston, who adopted it as his theme song and recorded it three times, most recently in 2006. Warren became acquainted with key African American jazz stars of the 1950s. He met the likes of Charlie Parker, Max Roach, Sarah Vaughn, and Errol Garner, even rehearsed and hung out with Thelonious Monk. But his own first LP record, the 1957 *Africa Speaks, America Answers,* features a group of Chicago Italians. The following chapter explores the story of what that reveals about race, place, and power in 1950s America.

Two years later Warren recorded *Themes for African Drums*[18] with the African American hand drummer James Hawthorne Bey (later known as Chief Bey) and Lawrence Brown, the famous ultravocalic trombonist of the Duke Ellington orchestra. It was released by RCA in 1959. Bey also played with Warren's regular band at New York's African Room. Warren wanted *Themes for African Drums* to open a new conversation about drums, Africa, and jazz. But it didn't happen. Not only did RCA stick him with one of the most over-the-top exotica covers of all time, but Chief Bey was soon swooped up to be the fire power behind a Columbia Records project, Olatunji's 1960 *Drums of Passion.*[19] The story of why Warren's LP and his ideas of Afro-jazz dialogue tanked, and how the Olatunji LP established the American idea of African music and the commercial market agenda for Africa's place in jazz, will also be explored in the next chapter.

After leaving the United States, Warren made other recordings in the United Kingdom, inventing Afro-jazz, the term and concept that many people associate with a later wave of fusion and the rise of the Nigerian pop star Fela Anikulapo Kuti. But by the mid-1960s, Warren returned to Ghana and pretty much stayed home. He vigorously devoted himself to Buddhism, to spiritual study and meditation, to exploring his sensation of being divinely possessed, to experimental performances of the music of Ravel, Beethoven, and Handel on talking drums, to organizational work with the Ghana Musicians Union, to political involvements in the Nkrumah and Rawlings governments, and to cultivating the Afrikan Heritage Library, his large collection of print and recorded documents, which ultimately affiliated with New York University in Ghana.

Coming home to Ghana, he published in 1966 a bitter autobiography entitled *I Have a Story to Tell. . . .*[20] Filled with anger about the United

States, it vilifies white music producers and critics and club owners including John Hammond, Norman Granz, and Leonard Feather, excoriating them for what he saw as their refusal to take African music seriously. He also criticized African American musicians, including ones, like Max Roach, with whom he had direct friendships, calling them closed to the idea of renewed cross-fertilization with African music. He accused virtually everyone of being complicit in the wholesale exoticization of Africa. And he reserved some of his most outrageous and vicious words for Olatunji, calling him an exploited fake who joined the ranks of the exploiters.

A volatile man known in public for his harsh words and feisty style, "tough as Fela and almost always as high," in the words of one of his friends, he was finished with being Guy Warren, the African jazz drummer who passed for African American.

On July 1, 1974, Ghana's Republic Day, he changed his name to Ghanaba, "born of Ghana," and devoted himself to a spiritual-political-cultural triangulation of the binaries of jazz/America and drums/Africa through engagement with European art music and Ghanaian nationalism. The result of a cosmopolitics of listening broadly, the European classics portion of Ghanaba's knowledge was formed during years as a DJ both in Africa and Britain. From this foundation, his project to present the "Hallelujah" chorus created a unique, grand, and encompassing space to synthesize that spiritual-political-cultural commitment founded on music. As he told me when we first met, it was, indeed, his life's work.

Now it's back to Nii Noi's house in May 2005. And to another wall photograph that opened up a third story and a final contrasting arena of encounter with jazz cosmopolitanism in Accra. The photograph shows Nii Noi playing with a couple of men in red T-shirts honking antique brass squeeze-bulb car horns.

"That's another photograph taken by my good friend Nii Yemo Nunu," he said. "He's been Ghanaba's photographer for twenty years now, but he's equally the photographer for Por Por, the car horn band in La. They are all union drivers and they have a band with old car horns. Nobody knows about them because they only play for the local driver funerals in their community. It's a real workers' music, Prof. Nii Yemo introduced me to them a few years ago. He's part of the scene there because he's from La and his father was a well-known driver. I liked the por por music and had the idea to take them out into the street, to entertain the people

13. Nii Noi, left, playing his afrifone with the La Drivers Union Por Por Group.
Photograph © 2002 Nii Yemo Nunu, Kotopon Afrikan Images.

waiting for their *trotros* [public minibuses]. We did that a bit and then got a few gigs. That was the first time they played in the larger public, and that was just a few years ago."

Por por (pronounced "paw paw," with nasalization on the lengthened vowels) is the phonaesthetic name of the squeeze-bulb car horn and the sound it introduced to Ghana and its colonial Bedford, Austin, Oxford, and Morris vehicles in the late 1930s. Brought by traders from India, the horns were attached to wooden lorries that transported passengers, trucked goods, and opened up the timber and market roads in Ghana, first named Gold Coast, in the forties, fifties, and sixties. These vehicles were locally called *tsolorley,* "wooden lorry," and with public transport of passengers came to be known as *trotro,* from "three pence," the original colonial-era fee for inner city transport. Their English nickname came famously from the quality of the ride: "bone shakers."

In the township of La, one of the seven Accra residential areas of the Ga people, the city's original inhabitants, something unique happened with the coming of electric horns. The La drivers took the por por horns off their tsolorleys and with them developed a honking, squeeze-bulb horn music with the addition of struck tire rims, bells, and percussion. Their La-branch Drivers Union Por Por Group developed until formalized in the 1960s, actively performing for the memory of their departed union colleagues at their funerals.

Because the por por players are unionized drivers and not professional musicians and because the music was only performed at worker funerals, no recordings or documentation of their art existed. To commemorate the fiftieth anniversary of Ghana's independence on March 6, 1957, Smithsonian Folkways Recordings released the CD *Por Por: Honk Horn Music of Ghana*. I produced and recorded that project in collaboration with Agazi, Nii Noi, and his photographer friend Nii Yemo Nunu, son of the legendary La driver Ataa Anangbi Anangfio. *Klebo!*, a follow-up CD, focuses not on the band's historical repertory but on its contemporary fusion of Ghanaian dance music with international pop, jazz, and gospel sounds.[21]

On these recordings you can readily hear por por sound a multilayered story of regional history, colonialism, diaspora, and globalization. In the context of Ghanaian indigenous music history, por por obviously derives from *mmenson*, the multipart animal horn ensemble music of Akan origin.[22] There is also a clear articulation with later brass band music, indigenized from colonial origins to become central to the sound of highlife and combo jazz in the last sixty years. Horn to horn to horn.

The 1940s and 1950s brought well-remembered big-band jazz recordings, like those of Count Basie, to Ghana. The sound and choreography of big-band saxophone sections seen in popular film shorts also had a role in shaping the por por performance style, some players swinging their instruments in gestures typical of big band and rhythm and blues sax "honkers and shouters." As the music became ritually specialized, played by the La drivers exclusively at funerals for transport workers, another Black Atlantic connection was revealed, to the "rejoice when you die" musical performance of the New Orleans jazz funeral, the driver's road to heaven paved by road songs and the sounds of car horns parading through the streets, with community participation marked by dancers bringing up the second line.

Por por includes several local markers of global musical contacts with jazz. A Ghanaian television show of the sixties, *Show Biz*, used as its theme music a lively arrangement of a hit song by the Broadway "belter" Ethel Merman, "There's No Business Like Show Business." One of the

(a) Sax section vamp for Dizzy Gillespie's "Night in Tunisia"; (b) Por por honk horn variant of the vamp as heard; (c) Por por honk horn variant of the vamp as played

catchy saxophone section phrases in the arrangement, itself reminiscent of a background vamp to Dizzy Gillespie's "Night in Tunisia," was picked up as a por por horn riff. The result was a distinctive sound signature relating the honking of por por music to the modernity of both African American swing band jazz and Ghana's television service in the years immediately after independence in 1957.[23]

Back to May 2005. Shortly after I saw the red-shirted photo at his home, Nii Noi took me to the union office to meet Nii Yemo Nunu and the Por Por band. Coming into La town, our taxi was overtaken by the honking of por por horns, the drivers surrounding and escorting us down the final stretch of road to their office. We did the first round of brief greetings outdoors, with honked fanfares in between introductions and poured libations.

"Prof, you are welcome. The good Lord has blessed us with your visit, Prof, and we pray that you will be happy and come back to hear us blow." Those were the first words spoken to me by the man wearing white slacks, seen in the center of the photo opposite, the man everyone calls "Vice," the Por Por group leader and union vice chairman, Nii Ashai

14. Vice, Adjei, and the Por Por band greet me at the union office.
Photograph © 2005 Steven Feld.

Ollennu. To Vice's left stood Adjei, the group's lead instrumentalist. "Prof,"
Vice continued, "this is Adjei, our number one blowing por por man." As
our handshake slid toward finger snap Adjei smiled and with a soft chuckle
said, "Prof, you are welcome. Call me PARker . . . Charlie PARker."

I was still green, linguistically, that is. It wasn't until later that I learned
why the delay in Adjei's delivery had such playful value-added. In Ghanaian English everyone male is Charlie. Charlie is man, guy, dude. The
ubiquitous rubber and plastic flip-flop footwear is called Charlie *wotey*,
"Charlie, let's go!" But the name Charlie for generic "man" comes from a
Charlie famous for different footwear, the very well-remembered movie
star Charlie Chaplin.

Later I learned that it was Adjei, Parker, Charlie PARrker, who was hip
to the Dizzy Gillespie sax section vamp on the head of "Night in Tunisia."
He was the one who introduced new syncopations to por por, layering

them onto the metric grooves of the key Ghanaian dance rhythms in the group's repertory, *kpanlogo*, *gome*, and *kolomashie*. Adjei was the one in the band closest to Nii Noi, and the two really enjoyed mixing the sound of the por por horns with the afrifone, a musical rapport evident in Nii Yemo's pictures from the Por Por band's first nonfuneral gigs, in 2002, when Nii Noi took the group out to jam at the La trotro station.

But the story didn't start out quite so jazzy. Adopted by drivers of timber trucks working forest roads in the early days of the transport union movement, the squeeze-bulb horns were first brought together with tire rims and small percussion as a kind of ensemble noisemaking to ensure protection to drivers of disabled vehicles after dark. As punctured tires, a frequent occurrence on forest roads, were pumped back to strength, driving mates surrounded the vehicles and banged out encouragement on tire rims, bells, and frame drums while honking the por por horns to scare off dangerous animals and energize the pumping.

Likewise, the two-handed up-and-down motion of pumping the punc-

15. Traders on the "Fear Not" mammy wagon in La. *Photograph © 2006 Steven Feld.*

tured tires was turned into an enthusiastic dance of accompaniment. Today, the way you listen to por por is with your body, pumping along. It energizes the players and reembodies the music's origin story. The band always brings an antique pump to model the act. And at wakes and funerals they memorialize their driver mates by pumping an inner tube from start to finish in a swell of horn honks and exuberant dancing.

While much of the por por history is about men's work, it is also very much a women's story, beginning with the common designation "mammy wagon," from the way women's agricultural marketing dominated much lorry movement between village and city. Women shared widely in the creation of the stories, songs, and performances of por por, and have also always been in the band as vocalists and horn blowers, like Esther Tsotso Mensah, a key player in the present group. There is also the tale of a rare and legendary pioneer woman in transport, the driver and mechanic Matilda Afieye Lomo, deceased in 2004. She drove the Accra–northern Ghana tomato-and-onion route and was chairperson of the La Drivers Union for four years, itself an extraordinary event in the history of Ghana's Trade Union Congress.

The third film in the trilogy is *A Por Por Funeral for Ashirifie*. Nelson Ashirifie Mensah was a member of the group for twenty-five years, until his passing in late March 2008. The band, and Ashirifie's family, invited me to film his por por funeral. The film follows the band over a week of activities: libations and prayers, musical condolences at the family home, a trip to the mortuary to retrieve the body, parades through La town, to the union office and funeral home, performance at the wake, the funeral ceremony itself, and the trip to the cemetery graveside. The film concludes with Nii Yemo Nunu going to the union office to show Vice the book *Rejoice When You Die*, Leo Touchet's extraordinary photographic record of the New Orleans jazz funeral tradition.[24] As Nii Yemo and Vice look at the photographs the shock of recognition unfolds, flashes of astonishment becoming familiarity, familiarity becoming astonishment.

It's those flashes that bring into view the larger story of how por por funerals connect two critical dimensions of African urban modernities: motor vehicles and popular music. This not the American "jazz age" of F. Scott Fitzgerald and George Gershwin, but cars and music are locally critical media of cosmopolitan contact and imagination, of bodily and spiritual mobility, of pleasure and performance. In the por por chapter, I'll explore the coming together of these acoustic and visual materialities.

In brief, then, these are the three stories that have consumed me during five years of multiple Accra visits, and they are so musically and historically dense that any one of them could be the subject of a detailed monograph. But their overlapped connections, and particularly Nii Noi's central place in weaving them together, is the reason why I'm devoting a chapter to each before returning to their thematic and theoretical richness.

The intrigue of that richness of course originates with a simple question, one I've asked myself over and over, one you might have been asking yourself while reading these introductory descriptions. Namely, how do these stories relate jazz to the idea of cosmopolitanism?

Surely these tales don't quite resonate with what we learned in Western Civilization 101 about 350 BCE, Diogenes, and the ancient Greek ideal of combining *kosmos* plus *polites* into the "citizen of the world." Nor with what Diderot likely had in mind in 1751 when he defined the *cosmopolite* as "stranger no where in the world." Nor with the ethics of Kant, nor with what Goethe had in mind by translation as geographically transcendent resolution of difference.[25]

If the classical Euro-world references seem like a stretch, is it any easier to imagine these Accra stories as surface musical equivalents to another arena of cosmopolitan discourse: political projects of creating global networks outside of the stranglehold of nation-states? What about Seyla Benhabib's "rights of others," or Hannah Arendt's "universal responsibility"? Do these Accra bioscenes feel like the rights and responsibilities musical equivalents of "world citizenship," a notion presently rolled out in cosmopolitan settings from international diplomacy to postnational politics in connection with advocacy for human rights as a universal moral ground?[26]

We might ask how much more resonance we feel here with well-known multicultural cosmopolitanisms, like the world of W. E. B. Du Bois's "double consciousness," or Homi Bhabha's "in-betweenness," or of Trin T. Minh-ha's "modes of dwelling" as the motion between two? Are the connections closer? Closer, say, than those of a cosmopolitan life world for Edward Said, who devoted his final memoir to defending the preference to live "out of place"? Or of Daniel Barenboim, responding to Said with the assertion that he feels at home wherever there's a good piano? All told, does Accra's jazz cosmopolitanism come down to "multilocal belonging," the ground Paul Gilroy figures as a critical foundation to planetary humanism? Can these Accra jazz stories be read as reaching toward the cosmopolitanism of "universalism plus difference," in Kwame Anthony Appiah's pithy phrasing?[27]

Martin Stokes has it that "to evoke 'musical cosmopolitanism,' is to evoke a capacity of the musical imagination, and with that word 'imagination,' certain ideas about the powers, agencies and creativities of human beings at this point in time."[28] Let me start down that path, and particularly the bit of it that works on race and class, with stories that argue for jazz cosmopolitanism as the agency of desire for enlarged spatial participation. That agency plays out in performances and imaginaries of connectedness, detoured and leaped-over pathways storied and traveled from X to Y by way of Z. Let me make a case for why these performances of connectedness are necessarily erratic, uneven, and ironic. And from there suggest that they take us toward, and beyond, Svetlana Boym's notion of "diasporic intimacy," the uncanny closeness that unites dispersal and displacement with reclamation and replacement through surprising loops of material and echo feedback.[29]

In that spirit, let me suggest that Ghanaba's radical move, choosing jazz disruption instead of jazz mimicry, opens up a unique African critique of American nationalist jazz master-narratives. Let me suggest that Accra Trane Station offers a unique African respin of George Lewis's eloquent deconstruction of how "experimental" music came to be racially coded as "white" high culture while numerous forms of black experimentalism, no matter how radical or innovative, largely came to be coded by the lower designation "jazz."[30] And let me suggest that the diasporic intimacy of por por horns echoing the New Orleans jazz funeral performs just the kind of audible race and class patina of honked history that was so shockingly splashed in our faces in the aftermath of Hurricane Katrina. Let me suggest that jazz cosmopolitanism in Accra is about histories of listening, echoing, and sounding, about acoustemology, the agency of knowing the world through sound. Let me suggest that this acoustemology, this sonic knowing, is the imagination and enactment of a musical intimacy.

FIRST CHORUS, WITH TRANSPOSITION

Guy Warren / Ghanaba

From Afro-Jazz to Handel

via Max Roach

16. Ghanaba. *Photograph © 2010 Afrikan Heritage Library Collection.*

"Racists!"

"Excuse me?"

"You heard me, I said 'racists,' fucking racists!"

"Come on, who are you talking about?"

"Your people, so many of them. It's where I have to start the story with you. You said you wanted to talk today about my relationship to American jazz, jazz music, jazz musicians. And I'm telling you, in a word, what I think of all of that. They're racists."

"Why racists? Why use that word?"

"Because they thought we were incomplete versions of them. They thought that jazz was better than us, more sophisticated, that, you know, we stopped on the evolutionary ladder. That what we had to do with jazz was in the past, you know, that it was just about drums and the slave times. Well that's bullshit. And it's racist."

Ghanaba is in a feisty mood. He's chosen to start off one of our conversations with a punch. He's fond of boxing, and has used punching language often when talking to me about drumming. (His own boxing name was Kpakposhito, his name Kpakpo plus *shito*, 'red hot pepper.') He's also fond of being a tough guy who has for years enjoyed a public image as defiant, proud, rough, boisterous, and outspoken. He is well known for ruffling feathers by his use of crude speech in public. Offstage I've learned that it is just his fire, his passion for verbal sparring in English, mixing the language of the street with that of refined debate. He loves to get in the ring and work out with someone he considers a suitable partner. This is how it goes with us, and I like his candid honesty, even if it occasionally makes the conversation quite prickly.

Among artists and intellectuals I've met in Ghana, Ghanaba is surely among the most outspoken and articulate. He loves language, poetry, and literature of all kinds, and it shows on his bookshelves, his recording collection of many singers in many languages, and in his everyday

17. Ghanaba at home in his hallway. *Photograph © 1998 Nii Yemo Nunu, Kotopon Afrikan Images.*

speech. Friends tell me he is particularly eloquent when speaking Ga, his first language. And as you can hear in the *Hallelujah!* film conversation, his impeccable English is spoken with a distinctly North American accent, with nothing of the typical hint of colonial British or Ghanaian English pronunciation common to Accra.

Over the three years of our association, I sparred with Ghanaba's pugilistic side on quite a few occasions, particularly when I brought up names of people or specific historical incidents that irritated him. He could be brutally dismissive in his judgments and terribly tough on even his most loyal friends. But I also saw his remarkably soft side, contemplative, spiritual, and warm, as when I would show up at his far-from-Accra hideaway and find him deep in thought and meditation during and after reading his bibles, teachings of Mohammed, the Buddha, the Kabbala, and Khalil Gibran's *The Prophet*, his favorite book, the one he gives to friends, quotes often, reads even more often.[1] And while Ghanaba's playfulness is less known to the public, you can see it quite clearly in the last part of the "Hallelujah" chorus performance, when he clowns with the Winneba Youth Choir and mugs for my camera, encouraging me, behind the lens, to dance with him.

But in the conversation we just opened, I really want to understand how he is thinking about racism and a place for African music in relation to jazz. Back to him:

"Maybe it's not what *you* think of as racist, maybe you are just thinking about your own story, or how whites have treated blacks in America. But from the African side, I'm talking about racism. And it's just as racist when it comes from the African American musicians as when it comes from the white critics and record producers. You see, that's what they didn't understand about me in the fifties. That I saw through the racism, saw through THEIR racism, all of it, black, white, whatever, saw through all of their jazz bullshit. Jazz, Jazz, Jazz. They were talking all their American jazz bullshit. That's why they had no use for me, you see, that's why they said I didn't fit in. Because I wasn't part of that AMERICAN jazz *bullshit*" (his voice heightened, his emphasis delivered precisely). "I didn't want to sit behind a trap drummer with some congas, just playing some little African thing, what do you call them . . . huh? . . . 'fills' . . . behind the real drummer. That's what they wanted, that was how they wanted Africa to fit into jazz. They wanted 'fills.' They couldn't imagine our music as equal, as something that they should learn and have to meet. That's why I didn't fit in, that's why it's racist, that American *jazz bullshit*. It's racist."

Ouch. Ghanaba's narrative lands like a right hook, and its sting is more than a little complicated. As I came to hear versions of it over the years, I wondered what part was just bitterness verging on self-aggrandizement, and what part was a really serious challenge to the business-as-usual discourse on jazz qua pluralism, democracy, and race in America, like the much pilloried Ken Burns/Wynton Marsalis, PBS-sponsored, nationalist American jazz-gumbo master narrative.[2]

I occasionally brought up Ghanaba's ideas with Ghanaian friends to see how they played. In one instance the response was quite pointed: "Yes, he's got it! Why celebrate us as where something else came from?" The speaker was Nat Nuno Amarteifio, an architect, art collector and connoisseur, and former mayor of Accra, educated in the seventies at Howard and Pratt. What he picked up on and echoed was the dead-end cultural politics of celebratory citations of Africa as a place of origins with no further space for negotiating a truly historical presence. This is exactly what Ghanaba had been saying for a long time, that Africa was often reduced to a distant place and time in the American story of jazz. He

18. Ghanaba with his sankofa staff. *Photograph © 2005 Nii Yemo Nunu, Kotopon Afrikan Images.*

found that narrative to be an act of cultural humiliation, with no serious space for engaging with Africa in the present.

To discuss Africa and jazz with Ghanaba was always to become aware of the potency of history, of the vicissitudes of a music whose dynamic origins were overtaken, in terms of both acoustic and social complexity, by diasporic dialogues, global crossings, and transnational feedback. In some of Ghanaba's orations, I also heard a very local spin on a perspective associated with Marshall Sahlins, the "tradition is a mode of change" school of historical anthropology.[3] Ghanaba presented his version of it in our conversations around the concept of *sankofa*, of retrieval into presence (from the Akan word meaning "go back and take"). "If you want to go forward, go back to your roots" is the way Ghanaba put it in our conversation following the *Hallelujah!* film. The idea is iconized by the bird whose neck cranes over its shoulder to take an egg off its back, the proverbial Asante *adinkra* symbol you see topping Ghanaba's golden staff in the film.[4] Here as elsewhere, the past is not something fully finished and the present is not something fully immediate. History is the over-the-shoulder urgency to connect the past to now.

Before I dig further into his experience of jazz in America from 1953 to 1958, and into why Warren ultimately rejected it to return to Ghana, it is worth mentioning that there are other biographies in Ghanaian music that share some of this musical expansiveness. In writings on the interplay of jazz feedback in Africa and African roots in diasporic popular musics, the Ghana popular music historian John Collins also links the sankofa art movement to the outlook of the Kumasi guitarist Koo Nimo. He writes: "Despite basing his music on the old palm wine technique of playing guitar, he is able to blend that style with jazz and the bossa nova. As he explains: 'I am going to marry the traditional highlife guitar with Spanish and Latin American music; an Afro-Spanish style using traditional rhythms with arpeggio. I always use finger-picking, never the plectrum. Also I want to develop an Afro-jazz and use Wes Montgomery and Charlie Christian type chords in it.'"[5]

Koo Nimo's words here echo Ghanaba's long embrace of multiple fusions of popular genres and styles with African music, acknowledging that these diasporic forms have long had histories of expansion and contraction, breakdown and renewal.[6] This makes a lot of sense in the context of Ghanaba's biography. His childhood was shaped in the 1930s and 1940s by the sound world of bars and streets criss-crossing an extraordinary urban zone of migrations, Accra's Kadri Zongo, his mother's home place. The swing jazz he heard there, especially during the war years, when he encountered African American soldiers, overlapped with many layers of music from Ghana—Ga, Asante, and Ewe, plus music of Nigerian Hausa origin, Kru songs and dances from Sierra Leone, songs of multiple migrants and sailors coming and going. At the same time he absorbed the considerable presence of popular music and dance from American movies, from which he also learned to tap dance in the style of Bill "Bojangles" Robinson. And once he started with drumming, Warren's class position brought access to the best teachers in the Accra of his youth, and later teachers who imparted mastery of Western harmony, notation, and composition during his time at Achimota College.

All of these experiences were in play in 1943, when the twenty-year-old Warren Gamaliel Akwei changed his name to Guy Warren, dropped out of Achimota, and went to America for the first time courtesy of the wartime Office of Special Services, which trained him to return as a journalist while working covertly as a spy. By the time he got back to Ghana (then Gold Coast) to work as a journalist-spy, he was already sure that he would in time return to America to become a jazz musician.

In a 2007 autobiographical statement he remembers the moment like this: "By an interesting, if not miraculous coincidence at that point in time, I had read an article in an American show-biz magazine about one of the up and coming jazz stars of the period. He was Billy Eckstine, an excellent jazz musician. He had decided whilst he was at Howard University to take to the jazz world, and had dropped out of Howard and gone to jazz. Now, by another coincidence, Billy looked like me physically. He was my double!!! I decided firmly to drop out of Achimota and go jazz! And I did, bag and baggage! Just like Billy!"[7]

Right then, jazz was America and America was jazz, and part of the whole identification process for Warren involved rejecting things British as colonial and empire.[8] Warren was imagining a life of jazz in America, but his world of music was already a big world, of many musics that jazz touched. While drumming with the Tempos highlife band in the late 1940s, he went to London and played with Kenny Graham's Afro-Cubists, bringing back bongo drums and calypso experiences from his interactions with the early wave of London Trinidadians. By the time he left Ghana for Liberia in 1950, and then the United States, where he arrived in 1953, he was musically aware of South African *kwela* and township music, of *soukous* from Congo, *jùjú* from Nigeria, and perhaps *makossa* from Cameroon. The background to his African musical universe was seriously reflexive; he understood that African music contributed hugely to popular musics in the U.S. and the Caribbean diasporas. And he knew that the diaspora had fed back its own fusions into African popular styles, particularly in the case of Ghanaian highlife, through the influences of both jazz and calypso.

The dynamism Warren sought to explore in America was a matter of hybridizing the hybrid through rearticulation of roots. Thus, in 1973, when the historian John Collins asked him: "Why did you change from playing jazz to developing your own Afro-jazz fusions?" he replied: "It was a personal decision I made in my room in Chicago. I remember it very well. I said to myself, 'Guy, you can never play like Gene Krupa, Max Roach, or Louis Bellson. They have a different culture, and they can never play like you.' I had to make a choice between being a poor imitation of Buddy Rich or playing something they couldn't. I could play jazz well, but I possessed something that nobody else had, so I started to play African music with a little bit of jazz thrown in, not jazz with a little bit of African thrown in."[9]

Warren's idea was to give a more leading role to African creativity in the production of jazz music. But this hit a brick wall in mid-1950s America. Bebop was the rage. Africa's place was imagined to be long in the past, not in the present. The diasporic drive in bebop was Afro-Cuban, also imagined to be far from Africa.

Back to our jazz and race conversation:

"I read a newspaper account of a university lecture by Robin Kelley, where he referred to you as the 'Invisible Man' of jazz.[10] Are you comfortable being read through the metaphor of Ralph Ellison's book title? Of being known as unknown?"

"No, I don't like that. You know Robin Kelley, right?"

"Yes, we were colleagues at NYU."

"Well, he came to talk to me about His Grace, Monk. He said he was writing a book about him. And we talked about those stories, some you've heard now as well, about me and Monk. I was pleased that Robin Kelley wanted to record my version of that story, of His Grace and Nellie [Monk's wife].[11] I had never given those details to a historian, only a few bits to Nii Noi, he showed you, I think, right?" (Here he is referring to Nii Noi Nortey's lengthy 1994 interview with him, which records anecdotes about Warren's visits and conversations with Thelonious Monk.)[12]

"Yes, Nii Noi has shared that document."

"Well, I told Robin Kelley my story too, of course, I talked to him about the whole picture. What I wanted him to understand was that I was too African for the jazz people, for the African Americans who really didn't want to bend their bebop in the direction of my music. They wanted me to be a fake Afro-Cuban because Dizzy Gillespie was doing the Afro-Cuban thing with his bebop. How could I be Chano Pozo or Candido? They weren't Africans and their music wasn't African. But what they could play was African-sounding enough for the bebop people. I told him [Kelley] I was too African, but not African enough for America."

"Hold on, so you were too African because . . ."

"Well, I was too African because I told the truth about all this fake African drumming by so-called jazz or folk musicians like Olatunji. John Hammond tricked everyone. He sold Olatunji as a Yoruba, a Nigerian.

19. *Africa Speaks,*
America Answers,
LP cover, 1957.

But the music on his record was played by African Americans and Caribbeans who were mixing up all sorts of things. That's why I called Olatunji a false prophet who let himself and Africa be exploited for Columbia Records to make their millions."[13]

"And the 'not African enough' thing?"

"Well, I wasn't African enough because I wasn't tribal like that. I didn't fit their ideas of pure tribal Africa. It wasn't about me being a mutt with a half-white mother. None of them even knew that my mother's father was a British mining engineer. I played jazz with an African accent, to show that jazz could come to Africa and not just Africa come to jazz. And that was what they didn't like. I wasn't African enough because I wasn't tribal. I wasn't just playing tribal music. I wanted to play it all, jazz, Ga, Ewe, Asante, Nigerian, Hausa, West African, Central African, Congo, Watutsi, Masai, you name it. America wanted Africans to have a tribe, to talk a tribal language, to play their tribal drums. That wasn't me. Olatunji was willing to be sold as a tribal African, a Yoruba. That's what they wanted."[14]

The best-known Guy Warren composition is "Eyi Wala Dong," "My Thanks to Him" (God), from his first LP, *Africa Speaks, America Answers*, recorded in 1956 and released by Decca in 1957. The LP's front credit reads as Guy Warren with the Red Saunders Orchestra under the direction of Gene Esposito. Saunders was a Chicago drummer who worked a regular club job; he also played vibraphone and timpani, somewhat unusual at the time. At different moments in his career, Saunders played with Duke Ellington, Louis Armstrong, and Woody Herman, and recorded with Big Joe Turner. Esposito was a well-known Chicago pianist, arranger, and teacher who worked with, among others, Mel Torme, Art Pepper, Conte Candoli, and Woody Herman. Other sidemen on the sessions included the respected Chicago tenor sax player Tony Naponelli, the pianist Johnny Lamonica, bassist Jerry Friedman, and drummer Billy Gaeto.

"I used white sidemen because they have the ability to learn and be taught somebody else's thing. They have the basic training to absorb. We black people are not like that." That's what Ghanaba said to Nii Noi Nortey in 1994 when they discussed the background to *Africa Speaks, America Answers*, with Warren responding to Nii Noi's curiosity about how the band ended up featuring not African Americans but Chicago Italians, with a Hispanic and Jew in the mix.[15] Thirteen years later I read that quote back to Ghanaba in the course of one of our jazz and race conversations, resituating it like this: "Your response to Nii Noi seems pretty complicated to me. I mean, on the one hand it can be read as insulting to African American and African musicians. And on the other side it can be read as insulting to white jazz musicians. Another way to read it is that the insulted party is you, that the project was a trade-off, that racial pride and solidarity was less important than a certain musical control. You made that remark to another Ghanaian musician, a musical colleague. How do you feel about hearing it echoed back to you today by a white musician?"

"Well," he began, slowly, thoughtfully, "I've said openly for many years that my experience in America was hurtful. I went there knowing that I could play jazz well. But I wanted blacks there to be excited about the fact that I had something extra, that I could bring Africa into the music. Blacks rejected that, rejected the idea that Africa had any *new* contribution to make. On that front I experienced more openness from the whites. Maybe the whites were a little hung up about being less authentic, maybe they craved the idea of playing with blacks to become the real thing. I don't know. I didn't care if they, if they had a . . . had a jazz inferiority complex— can I say that? Hmm. Maybe they felt that getting close to Africa could deepen, or, shall I say, *blacken* their jazz a little bit? I don't know. I didn't go to America to be a psychologist. I went for jazz music. And the whites, at least in the beginning, were more open to what I had to offer. It didn't threaten their status to absorb something else. The blacks were busy being authentic with bebop. *Africa Speaks* threatened that."

"OK, I know you've said scornful things about black American musicians but have you considered how that scorn might be misplaced? In the mid-fifties, if I read the history and the biographies correctly, there were enormous obstacles and difficulties for black jazz musicians with the press, the clubs, the record companies, the police. All the same, tremendous experimentation was taking place, I mean black musicians weren't retreating musically just because of racism, on the contrary . . ."

"Oh!" he interrupted sharply. "Isn't it the whites who always remind us about Charlie Parker listening to Stravinsky!?"

"No, hey, that's not where I'm going with this. What I'm trying to understand is maybe the same thing that concerned Nii Noi, about your wanting to take the music in different directions to what black musicians then considered the critical horizons of experimentation."

"Well, I'll tell you the same thing I told Nii Noi, and that's that Gene Esposito was not trying to win Down Beat polls and come up with the next great bebop thing. So it was easier for him to take in what I had to offer. That's why we worked well together."

Gene Esposito worked on numerous projects with Milt Gabler, a producer and director at Decca in the 1950s. And, while it was principally Esposito who opened the way for Decca to record *Africa Speaks*, Warren could also have come up on Gabler's radar through the singer Billie Holiday. Holiday was a Columbia artist until 1939, when the label found her song "Strange Fruit" too sensitive to record. It was recorded instead for Gabler's Commodore Records, the first independent jazz label. Gabler simultaneously worked at Decca, where he became head of A&R (Artists and Repertoire) for three decades. Signed over from Commodore by Gabler, Holiday recorded as a Decca artist from 1944 to 1950. It is widely acknowledged that some of her strongest work was done in that period.

"Father, can I ask about rumors that you were briefly very close to Billie Holiday?"

"Whhh . . . what can I say . . . ," he replied, flashing me a soft smile, his at-the-moment atypically unsunglassed big eyes twinkling. "She was something else. She had the same skin color as my mother, and was as beautiful. Did I tell you that my mother had a voice like Billie Holiday?

It's really true. I remember her singing so well. She was a master seamstress and sang as she worked, or when she baked bread. I got the melody of 'Eyi Wala Dong' from my mother. She sang it so many times, with so many different lyrics. She was an improviser. That's the song I heard as she worked."

hiafo ji mi
mibe noko
awusako ji
mibe moko
ke ataale
ke mi Allotey
ni eha mi
mibi Alotei

I am a pauper
I have nothing
I am a beggar
I have no one
yet God [lit. "the father"]
gifts me with Allotey [first-born son]
and he gives me
my son Alotei [second-born son]

Ataa, mi nye oshi mada
mala, ma ajie oyi
majo, ma ajie oyi
makpan tetremantre ma ajie oyi

God, I can't thank you enough
I will sing to praise you
I will dance to praise you
I will blow the trumpet to praise you

O nuntso, ye obua mi daa
jen koojin fee ajie oyi
nguen borfoi fee ala onunyam daa
ohiafoia nunsto oyi wala dong

O Lord, assist me always
all creation praises you
all angels forever sing your glory
Lord of the poor, thank you[16]

The text of "Eyi Wala Dong" sings Warren's thanks for the birth of his sons. It was Milt Gabler who renamed the song "That Happy Feeling" and arranged for its instrumental publication[17] and rerecording as Decca's mega-hit of 1962, by the German arranger and popular bandleader Bert Kaempfert.

Berthold Heinrich "Fips" Kaempfert, was, at that moment, well known for "Wooden Heart," a big hit for Elvis Presley in 1961. His best-known composition came the next year, "Danke Schoen" for Wayne Newton, with whom he was also associated for the 1960s revival of "Red Roses for Blue Lady." But his best-known arrangement came in 1966, "Strangers in the Night" for Frank Sinatra.

Kaempfert's LP *That Happy Feeling* was released in the United States in August 1962; it went to number fourteen on the charts and then was released in the European market with the title *A Swinging Safari*,[18] the title that has stood in the LP's many reincarnations. Kaempfert's version of "That Happy Feeling" features flutes and piccolos; like the rest of the LP, there is considerable imitation of the pennywhistle sound from South African kwela, with other layers, like folky guitar, and Mantovani strings. The Kaempfert version drives a steam train over the fusion pulse of highlife, calypso, and jazz that Warren played bare-handed on hi-hat cymbals for the original recording, although not as mercilessly as the sheet music erases the song's intentionally gentle syncopation.

A Swinging Safari hit the international billboard charts swinging, and material from the LP, including "That Happy Feeling" was anthologized, republished, and rerecorded on at least six other Kaempfert LPs and CDs. The Kaempfert approach was picked up later by the James Morgan Ballroom Orchestra, and the song then moved into the world of ballroom dancing LPs. The current one in popular circulation on the fox trot circuit is published by Bruno Bertone's Strictly Dancing Laserlight Series. The Kaempfert version of the song was also picked up as background theme music for children's television programming by the announcer, actor, and comedian Sandy Becker, whose very popular *Morning Show* ran from 1955 to 1968 on New York's Channel 5, WNEW-TV.[19]

There is a profound irony in all of this, of which Ghanaba was painfully aware. As Guy Warren, he went to America to put an African accent in jazz and ended up recording his most famous song with a group of Chicago white ethnics. He was then well supported for forty years from royalty income deriving less from the original recording than from the song's whiter and brighter easy-listening versions, in the most prominent case, remade by a German apartheid sympathizer who recorded nostalgic songs of the *veld* and whose biggest safari hit was called "The Afrikaan Beat."

On the flip side of that record it is worth remembering that 1956, the year Warren was in Chicago working on *Africa Speaks, American Answers*, is better known for articulating a more popular narrative of the intersection of Africa and jazz. Following his *See It Now* visit to Accra in 1955, Edward R. Murrow made a CBS film about the European tour of Louis Armstrong and his All-Stars. The tour ended with a trip to Accra, where Armstrong was greeted by E. T. Mensah's Tempos playing their famous hit "All for You." Armstrong later said that he recognized it as a creole song from Louisiana. The two jammed at Mensah's Paramount Club in Accra, and the next day Armstrong played an outdoor concert in the presence of the soon-to-become first president of Ghana, Kwame Nkrumah, to whom he dedicated a performance of Fats Waller's "What Did I Do to Be So Black and Blue."[20]

Late 1956 and early 1957 in America was also a moment where a more powerful story of African diaspora entered the world of popular culture. As Henry Louis Gates tells it: "The album *Harry Belafonte–Calypso*, released at the end of 1956, ended up selling more than a million and a half copies, more than any single-artist album ever had before, and it remained on the charts for a year and a half. Elvis and Sinatra were big in 1957, yet Belafonte—the King of Calypso, as he was touted—outsold both of them."[21] And so, whatever the attention to Warren's *Africa Speaks, America Answers* in 1957 and 1958, it was massively overtaken on America's Africa and diaspora popular culture radar by the success of Belafonte's calypso, and the "Day-O" happy islands stereotyping that came with it.

Warren's second U.S.-based LP was *Themes for African Drums*, recorded in May 1958 and released on RCA in 1959. Here he was joined by Duke Ellington's legendary trombonist Lawrence Brown, and by three African American drummers led by James Hawthorne "Chief" Bey. Bey had toured internationally in the fifties with the Cab Calloway and Leon-

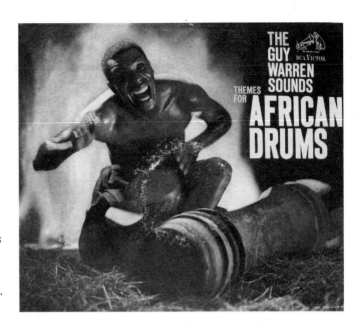

20. *Themes for African Drums*, LP cover, 1959.

tyne Price production of *Porgy and Bess* and then played with Warren regularly in New York.

Themes for African Drums includes Warren's song "Love, the Mystery of . . .," originally performed with Bey as part of a dance suite during their stint at New York's African Room. The song was covered in 1962 on *The African Beat* by the Afro-Drum Ensemble formed by the jazz drummer Art Blakey, which included Chief Bey, who introduced Blakey to the song. On Blakey's cover of "Love, the Mystery of . . ." Yusef Lateef's oboe powerfully reprises the role played on the original LP by the trombonist Brown. Later, Randy Weston, a pianist whose career has involved numerous engagements with African music, also began to perform the song; again, the introduction came through Bey. In time Weston adopted the song as his theme, and over the years has recorded it four different times.

But there's yet another irony in the criss-cross of Warren's song being covered by such widely respected jazz artists. Listen to Ghanaba talking to Nii Noi Nortey in 1994 (and echoing what he said in his 1966 book *I Have a Story to Tell . . .*):

"Art Blakey? You want to know the truth. Art Blakey bores me to death. After a couple of minutes I could go to sleep."

"Randy Weston? I met him only briefly. Chief Bey introduced him to my music. His version of African music is popular but he plays the bass all wrong."

In 2007 I reminded Ghanaba of these mean and dismissive comments. In my laptop iTunes library I had versions of "Love, the Mystery of..." by both Blakey and Weston, and I asked if he would like to hear and discuss them. He declined. I asked if he had anything to add to what he told Nii Noi Nortey in 1994. He snarled and demurred. But then, a bit later, after we had moved to another topic, he interrupted himself to tell me that he loved the Yusef Lateef oboe solo that opens the Blakey version.

"Lateef is a real musician," he said. "I would have liked to work with him. He was sincere in his study of African music. Maxwell [Max Roach] exposed me to him. His oboe work shows that he listened carefully to the alghaita and understands the Hausa presence in the music. I know they'll dislike me for saying this, but Blakey's playing on the song is awful. Loud and dumb. The Lateef section is the only worthy part of the recording."[22]

Back to *Themes for African Drums*: It was at the African Room, working with Warren, that Bey was likely heard by the influential Columbia Records producer John Hammond and then brought on in 1960 to be the fire power, with Taiwo DuVall and Montego Joe, for Olatunji's *Drums of Passion*.

Bey's work with Olatunji is particularly significant here. Arriving from Nigeria in 1950 to attend Morehouse College, Babatunde Olatunji was not a drummer or professional musician. Nor was he when he graduated in 1954 and moved to New York to study business administration. But he soon was teaching drumming to African Americans in the New York City area, and his first professional performance work was a nightly gig in 1958 at Radio City Music Hall in an exotica piece titled "African Fantasy." In 1959 he was contracted to Columbia, an association that produced five LPs between 1960 and 1966. The first and best known of these is *Drums of Passion*.[23]

From its popularity, regular work followed, including a shared bill in 1961 at the Village Gate with John Coltrane and Art Blakey. Coltrane, who had been exploring African names and sounds on a number of songs from the late 1950s, was particularly inspired by Olatunji and became a financial contributor to the establishment of his cultural center. There he recorded his last live LP, a few months before his death.[24]

In the introduction to *The Beat of My Drum*, Olatunji's posthumous

2005 autobiography, the ethnomusicologist Eric Charry writes: "The impact of Olatunji's first LP *Drums of Passion* can hardly be overstated.... It introduced hundreds of thousands and perhaps millions of Americans to African drumming, yet all of the other performers on the album were African Americans or Afro-Caribbeans from the New York area. Its songs and rhythms point to Nigeria, yet the performances on it are a hybrid of styles played on hybrid combinations of drums, many from Ghana. It established Olatunji as Africa's most famous drummer, yet he was relatively unknown as a drummer in his home country. And the three other drummers on it, Chief Bey, Taiwo DuVall, and Montego Joe—the ones responsible for much of its percussive power—not to mention the other vocalists, all remain relatively unknown outside New York's African American community."[25]

Accurately referring to the LP as "African-based music composed and arranged for an American audience," Charry nonetheless does not explore why this record was so much more popular than *Themes for African Drums*, the LP Warren released the previous year with Chief Bey. Part of the answer comes from something Charry notes: the tremendous marketing power of Columbia Records. The other part comes from something he doesn't note: that *Drums of Passion* was produced to appeal to an exotic and primitivist image of Africa in American popular culture. First, because it further entrenched the idea that African music was entirely drumming and chanting, quite contrary to anything in Warren's projects, and next because despite the hybridity that Charry articulates, the LP was promoted for its folkloric and tribal "authenticity."

As a musical concept and production, *Themes for African Drums*, like *Africa Speaks, America Answers*, represented a more cosmopolitan and openly hybrid and dialogic approach to points of contact and articulation between Africa (not just West Africa) and jazz, between Africa and African American as well as diasporic and Afro-Latin styles. Warren's LPs were experimental and in stark contrast to the folksy quaintness of the Belafonte and Olatunji recordings; his work insisted on Africa as fully present and contemporary in the world of jazz and diaspora.

Olatunji's 2003 obituary in *The Guardian* (of Nigeria) notes that despite popularity abroad, he was little known at home. The obituary also cites a 1997 interview for the same paper with Ghanaba. There Ghanaba stated, again echoing statements made in 1966 in *I Have a Story to Tell...*, that Olatunji was "one of the negative influences" on world knowledge of

Africa. Ghanaba is quoted as saying that Olatunji was manipulated to show that "African artistes are not intellectuals. That we are morons. That I refused to accept. But Olatunji accepted it because they know he is an illiterate man and he fitted well into their mindset."[26]

Here is where Ghanaba's bitterness and jealousy reached its mean-spirited low. Olatunji was neither illiterate nor a pawn of John Hammond and Columbia Records; a reading of his autobiography makes this very clear, and many who knew him have a different story to tell. In my own case, the story comes from August 1995. I happened to be working with the Grateful Dead percussionist Mickey Hart at his home studio the day his colleague Jerry Garcia died. In short order a number of events were being organized. One of Mickey's first calls was to Baba—Olatunji —asking him to colead a drum-line memorial procession for Jerry at Golden Gate Park. Baba agreed, marking the importance of his long association with the Grateful Dead, for whom he had opened, and with Mickey, with whom he had performed in the Planet Drum band, and who had served as producer for two of his records.

Although I'd briefly met Baba on a few occasions at Mickey's studio or Planet Drum concerts, I soon found myself in close proximity to him in very particular circumstances. His ability in that moment to radiate warmth, compassion, and solidarity was moving. It was impossible not to be charmed by his abilities as a communicator, as someone who knew how to be with people and bring them together musically at a very heavy time. An experience like that indicates to me just how much Warren's years of tirade and abusive rhetoric was no more than bitter polemic.

So, OK, at the time of *Drums of Passion* Olatunji was willing to make choices that Warren refused to make, ones Warren considered demeaning. Yes, he initially allowed himself to be marketed as a token of an authentic, folkloric type that Warren refused and rejected. Yes, quite the opposite of Warren, he was unaware of music laws and let Columbia take the copyrights on his music. As his book recounts, others were enriched at his expense for many years, and he waited a very long time to get back the rights to his work.

When all is said and done, perhaps Olatunji succeeded because he was both an inferior musician and superior border-crosser to Warren. And just as important, *Themes for African Drums* did not approach the necessary exotica threshold to be a commercial hit. Columbia figured out how to make a better marketplace recording, one that would seize Americans with an easier-to-manage image of Africa. *Drums of Passion* was that record.

But this drove Warren to over-the-top jealousy. "Back home he was never a musician!" he barked in a radio interview for *Jazz Weekly News* with Les Tomkins. "People think that just because you come from Africa you can play drums. No siree! Just because you come from America doesn't mean you can play baseball!"[27]

In the same interview Warren gushed over an issue of *Down Beat* with comments by the jazz flutist Herbie Mann, an early world music fusion proponent who worked with Olatunji in 1961. Mann said that Olatunji could solo but could not play backgrounds to a sustained groove in a swing jazz context. Warren delighted in this, twisting it into a statement of musical incompetence. But that is hardly how it was meant. Like many jazz musicians who have worked with African hand drummers, Herbie Mann was simply very aware of the difficulties of pairing African drums with jazz drums in the context of hard-swinging jazz. When the format involves ostinatos and vamps, more open-ended grooves and cycles, it is easier to match the horizontal push of continued off-beat phrased melodic accents and ties over bar lines with 4/4 or 6/4 Afro-beat playing. But in the context of twelve-, sixteen-, and thirty-two-bar song forms and hard-driving swing or bop, time conflicts abound in how African and jazz drummers might feel the "one," or feel the "and" before "two."

Thirty-some years after that *Down Beat* interview, Herbie Mann had become a resident of Santa Fe, and I once had an opportunity to talk with him, casually, about his history in the interstices of jazz and world music, beginning with his tour of Africa, sponsored by the U.S. State Department, in 1960. I found Herbie extremely respectful of the African, Asian, Middle Eastern, Latin American, and Caribbean musicians with whom he worked. I find it highly doubtful that he would have wanted any statement of his to seem demeaning of Olatunji.

But Ghanaba never would talk with me about this. Just the mention of Olatunji could make him ballistic. I can't take this story much further because, whatever Ghanaba's openness, this is one place he just would not go with me.

Anyway, the heaviest irony in the mix is that Olatunji would end up drumming for Max Roach on two tracks of the 1961 LP *We Insist! The Freedom Now Suite.*[28] This is one of Max Roach's most praised recordings, and the one that makes the move toward Africa that Warren had repeatedly encouraged him to make from the time they met in 1956. Roach was the drummer Warren most admired at that time, the one he most wanted to engage. But Roach was all bebop then and that engagement didn't come until Warren was out of the picture. This was the source of Ghanaba's greatest disappointment, annoyance, and agitation about America and jazz. Speaking about this with Nii Noi Nortey in 1994, he said: "It was in America that I came to the conclusion that the African American drummers were only trying to recollect their heritage. So I learned their approach, bearing always in mind that I was the original. That's how I came to play the African way. . . . The difference between me and the Jo Joneses and Max Roaches is that I can play their stuff but they can't play mine. . . . The one who perfected the style was Max Roach. He played smoother, and all the other drummers tried to play that way until Tony Williams came along. He was playing the same mould, but his accents were differently spread and it made his drumming more interesting. Elvin Jones played the ultimate in American style of drumming, very close to the African but not able to go across."

While the Warren-Roach relationship started off awkwardly in the United States and was recounted by Warren in a nasty way in his 1966 autobiography, what developed later was a long and deep friendship, with visits back and forth between the States and Ghana in the seventies and eighties and nineties. And most important, there was a joint performance, held in March 1986 at the Royal Albert Hall and titled *A Historical Concert in Dedication to Africa's Contribution to the World*.

After a visit to Ghanaba in 1973, Roach wrote an open letter, both a gracious embrace and a statement of solidarity: "In this letter I would like to record that Ghanaba was so far ahead of what we were doing [in the fifties] that none of us understood what he was saying—that in order for Afro-American music to be stronger, it must cross-fertilize with its African origins. Ghanaba's conception, like that of Marcus Garvey, George Washington Carver, etc., was beyond our grasp. We ignored him. Seventeen years later, Black music in America has turned to Africa for inspiration and rejuvenation and the African sounds of Ghanaba are now being played all over the United States, wherever Afro-American music is played."[29]

In 2007, I tried to pick up the story, like this: "I want to tell you about a conversation I had with Max Roach. I asked him about your fifties presence in the U.S. Max said you were too early in 1956. He was likely talking

21. From right, Max Roach, Ghanaba, and Mawuko Ghanaba, New York, 1998. *Photograph © 2010 Afrikan Heritage Library Collection.*

about bebop but more directly talking about politics. He said that everything would have been different if you came in 1960, or later, that the black pride that swept through the music would have opened a different dialogue with you, musically and politically. Perhaps he was also thinking about 1961 as the year he released *The Freedom Now Suite*. Do you feel anger toward Max for using Olatunji and not bringing you back over for that recording date?"

"No, I'm not angry," he said. "By then I was gone. Maxwell did what he needed to do. I was angry in 1956 and 1957. He was interested in the odonno [talking drum] but just as something on the side. Bebop, bebop, bebop. Anything else was a distraction. And he was busy being king, winning all the polls and being the best. That's the way the magazines like *Down Beat* and *Metronome* controlled the whole jazz thing, with their dumb-assed polls. Yeah, Maxwell is right that 1956 was the wrong time for him and me. But then, in time, he came here, we talked, he showed his openness to what we have and where we have taken the music. And I went to see him at home in New York. I rate him a great friend."

Ghanaba said those words to me while seated in a special room in his house, a kind of private study, where his usual chair is placed in front of a poster for Haile Gerima's acclaimed movie *Sankofa*, filmed in Ghana in 1991.[30] Ghanaba had a critical role in the film as an actor, musician, and informal but contentious advisor to Gerima's script. His penultimate trip to New York City was for the film's 1993 premiere, to which he invited Max Roach. After the screening Ghanaba gave Max the film's poster, with his image on it. But in the moment, Roach signed it in dedication and gave it back to him. The inscription, which I could read clearly sixteen years later, was just above his head as we spoke: "Ghanaba, You are one of the Greatest." Next to his signature there, Max drew a three-piece drum set. While many pictures, awards, and signed notes of praise fill a long public hallway at Ghanaba's house, the presence of this poster, the only thing of its kind, in his inner sanctum, indeed marked a special relationship.

After five years in America, Warren changed his name again, to Guy Warren of Ghana, signaling his concern to be known as an African, and not mistaken for an African American. The change marked a movement away from America, despite the fact that by 1958 a few things were going better for him. He wrote about the moment in his last autobiographical statement, in 2007: "At this point in time my fortune had turned around. Marie Antoinette Wilson Howells, whom I affectionately called Lady Marie, a millionairess, and great-grand-niece of John Quincy Adams, the sixth president of the U.S.A., had become my mistress. I had also become fairly popular in America after I had launched my first music album, *Africa Speaks, America Answers*. It was also at the time when the Black Consciousness movement was at its peak with Kwame Nkrumah and Ghana's independence shining on the world scene in 1957–1958."[31]

But the *Themes for African Drums* versus Olatunji's *Drums of Passion* debacle soured Warren. Decca released his *African Sounds* in 1962, a solo drum-centric LP also featuring the vibes and marimba player Ollie Shearer, who had worked with him at the African Room, and the brilliant bassist Richard Davis (perhaps the only jazz musician whose resume includes recording with Eric Dolphy and Elvin Jones, as well as with Igor Stravinsky and Leonard Bernstein). Three other U.K.-recorded LPs followed in the sixties as well, each one with mostly white musicians but more and more African emphasis and accent. The last of these was the landmark LP *Afro-Jazz* in 1969. Then he retreated.[32]

Once back in Ghana, Warren was sought out by many musicians. One of the frequent visitors in the early 1970s was Ginger Baker, drummer

22. *Afro-Jazz*,
LP cover, 1969.

from the rock bands Cream and Blind Faith, who, influenced by the *Afro-Jazz* LP, temporarily relocated to West Africa and built a multitrack recording studio in Lagos, immortalized in the world of rock by *Band on the Run*, a hugely successful LP released in 1973 by (ex-Beatle) Paul McCartney and Wings. At that Lagos studio Warren recorded the song "Blood Brothers 69" for Baker's 1972 LP *Stratavarious*. Other tracks on the LP featured Fela Anikulapo Kuti. It was Baker's *Stratavarious* that became the point of enunciation for Warren as the spiritual father of Afro-jazz, the concept more obviously developed by Fela, with support of the Nigerian drummer and Warren protégé Tony Allen.[33]

This was also the moment that Warren participated in the *Soul to Soul* music concert in Ghana that led to the movie of that name. A fourteen-hour show held in Black Star Square on Independence Day, March 6, 1971, the concert featured Wilson Pickett, Ike and Tina Turner, Les McCann and Eddie Harris, the Staple Singers, Santana with Willie Bobo, Roberta Flack, and the Voices of East Harlem. Warren headed the Ghanaian contingent of performers, which also included the Damas Choir, the pop singer Charlotte Dada (famous in West Africa for her 12/8 regrooved cover of the Beatles hit "Don't Let Me Down"), the highlife guitarist and palmwine pioneer Kwa Mensah, Kumasi drummers, and Accra's best-known rock band, the (Psychedelic) Aliens. Aside from a brief moment where the Ghanaian calabash player Amoah Azangeo sat in with McCann and Harris, there was no soul-to-soul crossover, and none of the Ghanaian performers appeared in the film, although the Damas choir and Kwa Mensah briefly make it onto the reissue of the CD soundtrack.

In his 1994 interview with Nii Noi Nortey, Ghanaba was damning about the *Soul to Soul* concert, and what he saw as the lack of interest in real dialogue or balance. Here's what he said: "Came time for the show, the Damas Choir did their poor man's imitation of the American Negro spiritual, you know, the 'Lawdy, Lawdy, Have Mercy Upon Us Swing Low Sweet Chariot' kind of shit. They did a poor man's version of it, and the other little combos which were imitating the Americans imitating us were also allowed to play their stuff, and I went to lay down mine. As I came on stage, I saw from the corner of my eye one of the American producers waving to the cameraman not to shoot. He was criss-crossing his arms like that. I saw it and I was wondering why he was doing that. It didn't occur to me that he was referring to me. I thought he was saying hold it, so I played like thunder that night. After Wilson Pickett, I was wild. We were waving and flying Ghana colors: red, gold, green. But my sequence wasn't shot. It was prohibited."

I read those lines back to him but Ghanaba never wanted to talk with me about what he told Nii Noi in 1994, nor to watch any of the video. His ultradismissive one-liner, the last time I tried to bring up the event with him, was: "*Soul to Soul*? They were paid one hundred times more than us. Did they have one hundred times more soul?"[34]

On July 1, 1974, Ghana's Republic Day, the man known as Guy Warren and Guy Warren of Ghana said goodbye to both and changed his name to Ghanaba, "born of Ghana," in a total embrace of African identity. Through the seventies, his distance from the United States and United Kingdom ironically led to increased applause from the diaspora. In August 1981, Aklowa, the African Heritage Village at Takely, near London, bestowed on him the honorific title Odomankoma Kyerema, Divine Drummer. And that was the public persona he adopted and developed to the end, and the one seen in the *Hallelujah!* film, a drummer standing between the spiritual world and the people, playing drums that speak, *kasa!*, a divine praise and voice of remembrance for Ghanaians to hear and give response.[35]

"Can we move to diaspora and Pan-Africanism?" I asked. "In your archive the other day, I read an issue of *Ebony* magazine with an article on the reinterment of W. E. B. Du Bois in Accra, at the Pan-African research center where he lived, declared a national shrine by the Ghana government. In the article there is a picture of you with your fontomfrom drums playing at the ceremony. A couple of other references come to mind too: you performed both as a musician and actor in Ethiopian filmmaker Haile Gerima's movie *Sankofa*, set at the Cape Coast Castle slave fort. You also participated in Panafest at the Castle. Nii Yemo showed me his pictures of you there with the Jamaican dub poet Mutabaruka, who also appeared with you in that film. Could you speak about these connections, contemporary African music and art, Pan-Africanism, and this remarkable site in the history of slavery?"[36]

Well, sometimes it didn't matter how much room to move I tried to offer. Questions could go down in flames, and fast. This was one of those times.

"Yeah," he snarled, "well, all that may be great for the African American tour groups and the travel agents and the promoters but what the hell does it do for us? These places are ugly and should stay that way. In fact, I protested strongly against all the preservationists, all the people who wanted to whitewash the castles to make them pretty for the tourists. I couldn't believe this. It's just a cynical money-making scheme. These places need to crumble, they need to rot. We need to watch them rot and record our pain and distance. You told me your family comes from all over Eastern Europe, right? Well, let me ask you something. Did Jewish travel agents lobby to make Auschwitz comfortable for tourists? Of course not. The idea is horrible, completely horrible. Who wants to make evil pretty? So why are the African American tourism promoters lobbying us to lime-wash the walls of Elmina and Cape Coast every year? I can't believe African Americans want to drink their cokes at tables in the courtyard of a slave castle. I think it's disgusting. Let these places crumble as the concentration camps should be left to crumble. They aren't museums, they are places where torture and rape and brutality were practiced each and every day. The equivalent of the ovens. Let them vanish."[37]

When Ghanaba was in a cranky mood he'd alternate between bitterness about America and statements of relief that it was there that he received his Buddhist awakening about returning to his African roots. When he was exhausted, he could just revert to bravado, stuff like: "I am to jazz music what Kwame Nkrumah was to modern African politics" (a line likely originated by a journalist, but one he became fond of issuing like a personal calling card). When he was too cantankerous for deeper conversation I'd just throw him a bunch of slow balls.

"So who are your favorite drummers?"

"First of all Baby Dodds, then Big Sid Catlett, Maxwell [Max Roach], Elvin Jones, Tony Williams."

"And your favorite composers?"

"Beethoven is my number one, then Ellington, Handel, Tchaikovsky, Ephraim Amu, Jerome Kern."

"What about favorite recordings?"

His list began with "Across the Track Blues" by Duke Ellington, and passed through items by Frank Sinatra, Billie Holiday, Count Basie and Lester Young, Jimmy Lunceford, Glenn Miller, then circled back to Duke Ellington, the "Money Jungle" trio with Charles Mingus and Max Roach.

"But," he concluded, "my all-time favorites, and I don't mind if you say this, my all-time favorites are Beethoven's Symphony number 9, by the Paris Conservatoire Orchestra conducted by Carl Schuricht, and OF COURSE, Handel's *Messiah*, by the Huddersfield Choral Society and Royal Liverpool Philharmonic conducted by Sir Malcolm Sargent."[38]

It was probably sometime in the late 1970s or early 1980s that Ghanaba began to develop his idea to stage Handel's "Hallelujah" chorus using his African drum kit of seven ritual drums, arranged like a jazz drum set. He tried this out with police band, orchestra, different singers, and over a long period settled on the format you experience in the film, with the "Hallelujah" chorus preceded by procession and Nkrumah's favorite hymn, and at the end by the muezzin call to prayer and the Ghana national anthem. But what makes it all so terribly unique is the finale of "Eyi Wala Dong," "My Thanks to God," also known as "That Happy Feeling," performed as a "welcome to Africa" handkerchief-waving spiritual coda to Handel.

A key filmic moment in the unfolding festive atmosphere comes when Ghanaba acknowledges the choir's organist, and shouts out, "*Obroni wo awu!*" This phrase refers to European-style second-hand clothes, and its utterance produces smiles, giggles, and cracked-up laughter all around

23. Ghanaba at the drum set he used to perform *Hallelujah!*.
Photograph © 2005 Nii Yemo Nunu, Kotopon Afrikan Images.

from the choir. It comes as a playful jab at the organist, whose monotone button-down suit and tie set him apart from the rest of the choir, all dressed in colorful African cloth. But the words "obroni wo awu" literally mean "the white man is dead." And while everyone knows that "the white man" in direct reference here is the one who once wore the organist's suit of clothes, Ghanaba opens up another interpretive possibility in this moment of joy: that the dead white man is Bert Kaempfert. Because here, laying his praise for God on top of Handel's, he repatriates his mother's song, resetting it in the fully dignified musical context of a mixed European, African, jazz, Christian, Islamic, Buddhist spiritual music theater, powerfully burying the cumulative insult of the *Swinging Safari*.

We launched the *Hallelujah!* film at Accra's Goethe Institut in late April 2008, a few days before Ghanaba's eighty-fifth birthday. The Winneba Youth Choir came to sing Ghanaba's praise, his son Glenn's band came to drum it, the embassy diplomats spoke compliments, and I presented him with the published DVD and a video player system as a birthday gift.

Before the film showed, I joined Ghanaba in a small group of dignitaries, Ghanaian filmmakers, and academics. In a moment of introduction, Ghanaba presented me as "Sir Galahad" to the newly arrived German ambassador, Dr. Marius Haas, whom he had met just moments earlier. In response to the strange look he (and I) immediately received from the ambassador, Ghanaba quickly said that he was choosing this occasion to knight me for pulling a sword from stone, for aiding the distress call that his *Hallelujah!* project be documented.

On the surface this was a generous gesture of praise toward me. But what Ghanaba more seriously accomplished in the moment of that verbal gesture was to profoundly and intentionally insult the Ghanaian filmmakers present. Later I learned that each had histories of either blowing off requests to film his "Hallelujah" chorus project by telling him it wasn't really African, or of not finishing films of his work that he previously helped them start.[39]

Now it is May 4, 2008, Ghanaba's eighty-fifth birthday. Nii Noi, Nii Yemo, and I have gone to greet him at home. Nii Noi and I have brought our instruments to give him a little fanfare. But his mood and the presence of Nii Yemo's camera leads him to grab an odonno drum to jam with

24. Me and Nii Noi with Ghanaba on his eighty-fifth birthday.
Photograph © 2008 Nii Yemo Nunu, Kotopon Afrikan Images.

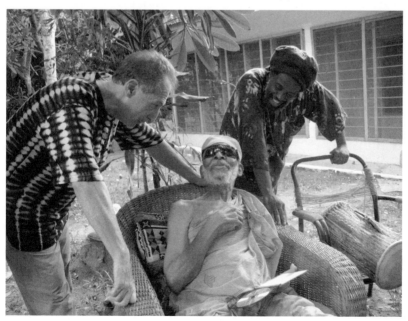

us. On his eighty-fifth, Ghanaba is still a man of the stage, not of the audience, and he wants the camera to record him exactly the way he wants to be seen.

After playing, I give him a birthday packet of CDs, with some music of Grieg and Sibelius that I selected at his request during a recent trip to Scandanavia. I also brought him a fusion CD featuring a Sweden-based contemporary African group, as well as the most recent CD by Accra Trane Station together with American jazz musicians, and a solo jazz piano CD by my father. He thanked me for this last one in particular, and I tell him that my dad will also be eighty-five this year, and is still playing. He opens it first, and begins reading aloud down the track list, stopping at the first Ellington tune. Without speaking the title, he immediately begins to growl-scat the melody, "bah bu du bah du bah," looking up to Nii Noi and me for the response, "bu du du dah," and proceeds to get us into a scatting round on the head of "Don't Get Around Much Anymore."

"Oh yeah, I'm gonna love this," he purrs. He continues to read down: "Midnight Sun," "I Remember Clifford," "On Green Dolphin Street," sighs "Oh, yes," and begins to scat the next Ellington track, "Prelude to a Kiss," encouraging us to join, then citing more titles until he comes to the last Ellington piece, "Take the 'A' Train." But instead of scatting he goes silent, with a tense look in his face. Nii Noi and I, standing behind his chair, glance back and forth to each other until the pause is too pregnant —could he possibly have forgotten it? We start to scat the line only to be loudly and immediately interrupted: "WHAT! Do you guys think I don't know it!" And within seconds he's bent over, damn near rolling out of his chair and onto the lawn in convulsions of laughter about so mercilessly catching us out.

I visited with Ghanaba occasionally over the following months until I left Ghana in August. By that time he had noticeably lost some weight and was clearly nervous about his health, asking me to help with the cost of some medications. I didn't return to Ghana until December 2008, and planned to visit him soon after, as we had arranged and reiterated in our monthly phone conversations. Nii Yemo was out of town, so I made my appointment for the weekend after he was to return. But just before that, Ghanaba was struck by pain and taken to the hospital.

After listening to his lungs the attending doctor asked if he was ever a smoker. "Oh, no," he whispered innocently, with a long pause as the doctor continued to fix the drip in his arm. "Only *wee* [marijuana], every day, for as long as I can remember," his most soft and serene voice greeted in kind by the doctor's smile. Then he closed his eyes.

A few days later, Nii Yemo and I were in a taxi heading out to Anyaa to see Nii Noi. The runoff in Ghana's presidential election was coming on, and talk-back radio, a grand national space of passionate public participation, was overflowing with debate, speculation, and strident declaration. Our driver's radio was blaring, as they often are in Accra cabs. A relatively soft but all the same forceful voice came over the airwaves, a woman, middle-aged and educated by the sound of her intonation and choice of words. The opinion she had to offer was that the news of Ghanaba's death was a herald of victory for the opposition NDC (National Democratic Congress), the political party with whom he was closely linked, particularly through his friendship with the former president J. J. Rawlings. She reasoned that this outcome was assured because Barack Obama, a black man, was elected president of the United Stated immediately following his white grandmother's passing. Such a loss, she reminded listeners, could be a spiritual sign that a special sacrifice will be followed and rewarded by deliverance. Even in death, it seemed, Ghanaba couldn't escape the discursive grip of America's racial politics.[40]

Seven months earlier, I was trying, another time, another way, to really be sure I understood his angle on jazz. "Look," I said, as we made our way through a box of his fifties jazz memorabilia, "I want to be sure I've got this right. Are you really saying that jazz, American jazz, is provincial? And how can you say that, I mean, how can you dismiss things like fifty years of groups from the Modern Jazz Quartet to the Classical Jazz Quartet, all the 'Third Stream' experiments, and the many ways jazz hooks up with European art music? And what about the way jazz musicians have drawn from and entered into fusions with improvised, written and oral musics from all over the world, including Africa, for a very long time?"

"Well, what I'm saying is that the Americans were happy to take Africa into jazz, to make it serve jazz. But it was the name 'jazz' that was always on the marquee. It was JAZZ up there in the Broadway lights. My *Hallelujah!* uses Handel and jazz but the spotlight is on Africa. I'm putting the African accent in European music and jazz both, showing that this music can equally serve Africa. That's what I'm trying to change, the view that Africa is here to serve jazz or European music. I'm saying that if people are open they will recognize that our contribution can extend European music and jazz both."

"So can I call you a jazz cosmopolitan?"

"Well," he said, "to me the cosmopolitan label implies an ability to be at ease in many places. And I wasn't at ease in America. At times I was more at ease with the music, or certain people. But I also came to see that the music could divide people. I went for jazz, but jazz is what kept me out. It kept me out, but that led to my Buddhist awakening and rebirth. Here I am happy. Many people visit me. Many drummers come. Lots of Americans, Steven, you *inquisitive* Americans!! [Big laughter.] Do you know Royal Hartigan? He came with his Ghanaian teacher, Godwin Agbeli, a good drummer who has made it in America. We talked and played. Royal took down my story and wrote an accurate biographical review for an American book.[41] Robyn Schulkovsky came too; do you know her? She lives in Germany. We improvised together. She had all her big crazy drums and gongs and I had mine and we had a good time. Santa Klaus made a movie of us.[42] Robyn liked to jump around barefoot and was very energetic. Some people questioned me playing drums with this kind of wild white woman and I told them to fuck off! I play with anybody I want to play with. If I only played with the local village illiterates where the hell would I be today?"

"Some of our people are so small-minded," he continued, after allowing a pause for his rhetorical question to land its punch. "This country lacks leadership and vision. That's why people have small-minded ideas. Their lives are ruled by fears and all their little village quarrels. I tell them it's good to have people come and challenge us. That's why I told Nii Noi that it was good for him to play music with you. I always say this and people here still go behind me and say that I'm a madman who got these crazy ideas from whites. I don't have time for such foolishness. If whites are musically curious about us, we must be equally curious about them, I have always stated that . . ."

"You said a moment ago that you weren't at ease in the U.S. even though you knew musicians and knew jazz music. Can I ask you how was it later, when you returned to visit, with Max for example?"

"You see, when I first went to America I wanted to be a Negro. But I found out that I didn't belong to that society, that I was an African. When I went back to visit America in the seventies and eighties, I was more at ease there because I had found myself. And what I found is that I am a man of HERE. Someday you'll see it in my will, that when I die I want to be cremated and have my ashes placed just outside, over there where my

25. Nii Noi Nortey blows for Ghanaba's funeral viewing.
Photograph © 2009 Nii Yemo Nunu, Kotopon Afrikan Images.

chair is, the place that is so serene, where I meditate most days. That's where I want to be. But I want the tombstone to read 'Africa Speaks, America Answers.'"

When I returned to Accra six months later, I was consumed for days with people catching me up on the many stories of Ghanaba's state funeral. I already knew from emails and phone calls that the event had been wild. But no verbal account could compare with the first photograph Nii Yemo put in front of me. It's a scene from the private viewing at Ghanaba's home, repeated more publicly the next day at the National Theatre. In the image Ghanaba is not "lying in state." He is upright, dressed regally in his victorious white, and towering over a pair of atumpani drums. The morticians managed to sculpt him upright and holding his sticks to the drum skins as if in repose after full play. And to his side, there's Nii Noi, cheeks puffed, circular breathing his way into an afrifone, intoning the absence of Ghanaba's silenced drums in the auditory glow of his heralding horn.

Getting together with Nii Yemo to hear his stories and look through his meticulous and loving documentation of all the events, I was most struck by the short videos he shot of the cremation. I guess nothing should shock me after three and a half years of talking to Ghanaba. But I was, all the same, stunned by the theatrical images of a group of black African Hare Krishnas with flowing clothes, finger bells, and hand drums circling around the outdoor cremation platform chanting "Hare Krishna, Hare Hare, Hare Rama" while the fire swelled and consumed Ghanaba in his fontomfrom drum–shaped coffin.

"The cremation ceremony was amazing," Nii Yemo said. "Rawlings came to say a few words, and shed a tear, and that was very moving. But the strongest moment was when they lit the pyre. Poom! Pra! Pra! Pra! It just went up like a flash, it was really something to see. And the man in charge of the crematory there told us, 'You see, his spirit really wanted to go, it just shot forth.' That was really something, Prof. He told us that it often takes some time, there is smoke, or the flame stalls or something else makes the process take some time. He was really impressed that the fire just torched up like that. He said, 'This man was really powerful, he was ready for fire, there's no other explanation.' "[43]

A few weeks later, the Ghanaba stories a bit deeper in the background, Nii Yemo and I were back at work on our por por research.

"Prof, look at what I found in my things." From his bag Nii Yemo produced a 1961 hardcover second edition reprint of M. J. Field's classic 1937 ethnography, *Religion and Medicine of the Ga People*.[44]

"Do you know it?" he asked.

"Only about it, I know it's an anthropological classic, but I haven't read it, may I borrow it?"

"Well, I thought you would be interested to see this copy because the notes by hand inside are by Ghanaba. The book was his; he loaned it to me to make some copies for him but never collected it back. Look at all he says here. He had many opinions! It's too bad, Prof. There were *soo* many things you and Ghanaba didn't get to talk about."

Indeed. How I wish I could have asked Ghanaba why the "Witchcraft" chapter of Field's book is the sole one that received his underlining and commentary. As I was thumbing through, the pages seemed to naturally open to 146 and 147. And there my eyes scanned to a place where next to an underlined sentence Ghanaba had written, in his largest capital letters, "TRUE!" Looking more closely I saw that his margin comment sits alongside these lines by Field:

"It may be that one 'compulsion neurotic' can recognize another, for [and Ghanaba's underlining starts here] *it is quite certain that many Africans have far more delicate powers of observing others than Europeans have.*"

Yes, that is one of the many conversations I'm sorry to have missed.[45]

SECOND CHORUS,
BLOW FREE

Nii Noi Nortey

From Pan-Africanism to Afrifones

via John Coltrane

26. Nii Noi Nortey. *Photograph* © 2005 *Steven Feld.*

"We could hear our struggles when Coltrane screamed. We could hear the other side when he played so cool and meditative, reflective. He captured the extremes of our struggles as African people. I'm sure he didn't go out to do that, but that's what struck us. This is somebody whose music is relevant to all that we're doing. This is a music that will strengthen us. It's like a hymn, you know, for Christians they have their hymns, and for other people they have their devotional songs. For me, who was just a pedestrian of some sort, not really religious, I found in Coltrane a real alternative to received religions and received practices. Coltrane offered me a whole new musical world."

That was how, in May 2005, Nii Noi Nortey opened the first of the video conversations we recorded over the course of three years while working on Accra Trane Station projects. Principally about John Coltrane and diasporic music history, the conversations also cover his times based in London in the seventies and eighties, his life in Accra since 1989, his travels in Europe and Africa, the invention and practice of his afrifone instruments, his sound sculptures, and his thoughts on connections between music and art. And through these topics, what was always evident was Nii Noi's constant concern with the culture of politics and politics of culture in Ghana. We also talked about his experiences working with Ghanaba, with Nii Otoo Annan, and with the Por Por band, musicians and musical worlds close to his own, and those into which he led me. Clips from some of our video conversations, along with clips from rehearsals and recording and performance sessions in Ghana, Italy, and the United States, comprise the film *Accra Trane Station: The Music and Art of Nii Noi Nortey*.

Now juxtapose Nii Noi's opening video statement with one from the tail end of our very last video conversation. That moment is Nii Noi's response to me, asking, in May 2008, just as I had recently asked Ghanaba: "Can I call you a jazz cosmopolitan?"

"Yeah, I think the word "cosmopolitan//s//m" . . . cosmopolita*nism* was introduced by you because it's so so big a word for me to use! [Laughter.] But at the same time I think that it embraces the same concept, you know, of going beyond your little horizon. And hoping that outside of that little horizon of yours there's still sense and meaning. And I think in that respect the music we play is cosmopolitan, you know, cosmopolitan because it borrows from many traditions and experiences and people.

"If Coltrane came alive today, he will see aspects of his music in our music, definitely, that's being cosmopolitan, I think. If Beethoven—I don't know much of his music, but because, you know, he's one of the most famous classical musicians—if he comes today, and hears our music, I think he will recognize certain fragments here and there, melodically, you know, which we probably didn't borrow directly from him, but they probably came through Coltrane and from somebody else and through somebody else, you know, that way I think, too, he will recognize the music that we're doing. Now if Osei Tutu, the great Asante poet and

27. Accra Trane Station, DVD cover painting.
Art © 2009 Nicholas Wayo.

drum composer comes today and listens to our music he could also recognize certain aspects of his legacy. And I think that is also extending this very tradition of this century back into the seventeenth century; that is showing a certain common linkage which is universal, you know.

"Because we borrow from these various traditions and we tend to extend this borrowing into the future, I think we are really premised to call ourselves a cosmopolitan musical group, you know. We travel around the world and the effect of our music in Italy or in the States or in Accra or in London is almost the same, the effect is the same. We may not play to a very large audience in Accra and we may not play to a largely African audience in Accra, but still we get a good appreciation from the little African audience that we get, you know. Because they may be artists, they may also be aspiring musicians, they may probably have copped out of that because it's not commercially viable, so they decide to be something else. So when they hear your music, it rings a bell, you know, it rings a bell, they see the approach you're taking. In our music we're using resources and ideas that the artists too may be using in painting their things and conceiving their concepts, you know. We're all sharing the same things, both as musicians and artists, you know."

In the *Accra Trane Station* film, that comment is book-ended by clips from musical performances. What you see and hear before and after Nii Noi's answer are segments filmed live during concerts at Albuquerque's Outpost Performance Space in October 2007, when Nii Noi and Nii Otoo Annan came to the University of New Mexico for a teaching residency.

The segment before Nii Noi's cosmopolitanism riff comes from the opening tune of the evening's first set. The piece is titled "All Aboard," and it originally appeared as the first track on *Another Blue Train*, the Accra Trane Station CD project we recorded as a trio in the first half of 2007 to coincide with local celebrations of the fiftieth anniversary of Ghana's independence. Nii Noi had long been struck by 1957 as both the year of Ghana's independence and the year of John Coltrane's classic LP *Blue Train*. His CD idea was to improvise a train ride, one whose acoustic moods could evoke new links between Coltrane's 1957 LP of minor blues explorations and the sound world of Ghana's freedom. Nii Noi's train ride through the blue diasporic night called jazz exploits titles for narrative mood, following Coltrane's practice in his later period.[1]

The instrument you see Nii Noi play in that initial moment is uniquely his own and homemade, built up from a *shenai* purchased from an Indian

28. Nii Noi playing his soprano afrifone.
Photograph © 2007 Steven Feld.

merchant in Birmingham, England, later retuned, its double-reed re-
ceiver modified to accept an American clarinet mouthpiece, homemade
ligature, and modified plastic reed. The body was then leathered in
northern African style by a Hausa craftsman in Accra, the added bell said
to be Tibetan by the London pawnshop owner who sold it. Nii Noi calls
this his "soprano afrifone" and the sound he strives for evokes that of the
Afro-Islamic Sahelian double-reed alghaita, an instrument equally con-
sonant with the northern and southern Indian shenai and the *nagasvara*
and the *zurna* of Ottoman and Romany crossroads. This sound arrives
through the intermediary voicing of John Coltrane's soprano saxophone,
whose shenai- and nagasvara-inspired timbres derived from his mid-
1960s engagements with Indian music.

Nii Noi's idea for this "All Aboard" piece is to suggest the West African
train station as a place of multiple cultural goings and comings. He put it
this way: "The train station proper in Accra is a rallying point for market
traders and travelers, people traveling different ways for hundreds of
miles, going to specific market centers on specific days. It means there's a
lot of traffic when you go to train stations in the mornings or in the

evenings. The interaction of buyers and sellers also is very, very interesting at a train station. It's just like the audience and a performer. What you see on a concert stage, the interaction between performer and audience, is what you see between sellers and buyers and travelers and drivers, and that type of thing. And also, it's interesting that we use a train station, because early in the sixties, when they phased out the steam trains, they were replaced by a new type of train called a 'blue train.' "

Nii Noi's train ride is articulated temporally through the rhythm locally called Afro-Beat and associated with Fela Anikulapo Kuti, a rhythm package built from percussion layers of fifty years of interchange in Nigerian and Ghanaian popular dance musics. It is articulated spatially through the soprano afrifone sounding an African North reaching South, and a jazz West reaching East. These cosmopolitan space-time routings are crystallized further by suggestion of the high-priest ancestors Fela Anikulapo Kuti and John Coltrane meeting down by the sonic crossroads where music simultaneously embodies spirituality and an ethical politics of rights.[2]

In one of our later video conversations, also in the film, Nii Noi mentions how impressed he was by the way Coltrane's *A Love Supreme* put together what he called "the torrentials and the sublimes." For Nii Noi the "torrentials" refer to the timbre of passionate cry of Coltrane's late period, what many listeners and commenters heard as the searing voice of wrenching anger and reaching hope in 1964–67 black America. It was the voice that took the saxophone to new acoustic heights and depths, to new multiphonic and microtonal interiors. That is the voice that Nii Noi studied seriously, learning circular breathing, altered embouchure, and extended fingering techniques both on the saxophone and on his own afrifones, all to reach for the "torrentials."

That's the sound of the second piece book-ending Nii Noi's comments, taken from a later Outpost set where Nii Otoo's African Percussion Kit was juxtaposed to Jefferson Voorhees's trap set and Nii Noi's afrifones to Alex Coke's saxophone. The piece is called "Black Heat" and its CD version appears on the quintet release *Topographies of the Dark*, seven pieces in dialogue with sculptural paintings by Virginia Ryan, a visual artist who promoted Nii Noi's sculpture during her tenure as codirector of the Foundation for Contemporary Art–Ghana.[3]

Ryan's *Topographies of the Dark* are fashioned out of thousands of pairs of washed-up flip-flops collected from Accra's beaches. Machete-cut and sculpted into triple layers, they are covered with a gluggy mix of glue, sand, bitumen coal tar, and dull and shiny black paints. Inspiration for this work came equally from the local aesthetics of working with recycled materials, from a *New Yorker* article by the architect Rem Koolhas describing aerial viewings of a Nigerian coastal oil slick, and from the power crisis that gripped Accra in 2007, when residents experienced twelve-hour electricity blackouts every second day.

"Black Heat" is the hottest track on *Topographies of the Dark*. The video clip from the live version offers a sustained swell over densely driving percussion, the late Coltrane torrential outpour of extended-range multiphonics intertwined on tenor sax, played by Alex, and by Nii Noi on tenor afrifone. Nii Noi's instrument is a hepta-retuned and leathered bell-optional PVC breakdown of a Rajasthani flute to which a tenor saxophone crook and mouthpiece are affixed. The sax and afrifone voices disappear into each other, leap out and become distinguishable momentarily, then burst back into Trane Station embrace.

This enactment of cosmopolitan aesthetics across the bridge of Coltrane's "torrentials" takes us to Nii Noi's thoughts about cosmopolitanism as a way of "going beyond your little horizon." Nii Noi first cites John Coltrane, moves to Beethoven, then comes back to Africa and Ghana through Osei Tutu. In each case he suggests that if they came alive today they would recognize a thread connecting Accra Trane Station's music with theirs. In less than three minutes Nii Noi's cosmopolitan imagination sews up his own work with the spatial thread of diasporic black America, Europe, and Ghana, and the temporal thread of twentieth-, nineteenth-, eighteenth-, and seventeenth-century musical, cultural, and political legacies. Big. I'll start where Nii Noi ends.

Osei Tutu was a founder of the Asante empire, ruling as Asantehene, the king of all Asante, from 1701 through 1717. Through conquest, expansion, and revenge he tripled the empire, consolidated its power base in Kumasi, and gained equal reputation for diplomacy and militarism. He established an annual celebration, Odwira, a festival for all Asante, a grand articulation of poetry, music, dance, costume, and theater, bringing festival into political process along with religion. As the largest group of Akan, or Twi-speaking people, the Asante were at the center of trade and dominant in gold and kola. From 1701, military prowess brought the inland Asante to the serious attention of Europeans on the coast, increasing potentials for trade alliance.[4]

29. *Topographies of the Dark,* CD cover. Art © 2007 Virginia Ryan.

Here's Nii Noi: "Osei Tutu's legacy is celebrated and admired as disciplined rule," he told me, "but also as caution. He died in battle due to arrogance, leaving his amulets behind, because he miscalculated the deviousness of his enemies. So, you know, just when he let the spiritual lapse, his political astuteness failed him." And the enduring lesson of this, as Nii Noi emphasized, is that there can be no exercise of political skill without concomitant attention to spiritual practice. This story is at the heart of the narration of the greatness of the Asante nation, and also at the heart of contemporary culture in Ghana, where prayer and spiritualism pervade political action and every dimension of its interpretation. This is not, as knee-jerk Western liberal journalists would have it, about a failed separation of church and state. It is about a historical distillation of political agency that is informed and performed spiritually at the level of everyday *habitus.*

Nii Noi was only four years old in 1957, when Ghana became independent, but he said that the moral of the Osei Tutu story was presented directly to him as a child and has stayed with him all his life: watch your back spiritually; vulnerability accompanies the exercise of all strength and power. Growing up in Ghana in those years as the middle-class son of a nurse administrator and distinguished economist-accountant who was also marketing advisor in the first Nkrumah government, later to serve twice as a member of parliament, Nii Noi described himself, modestly, as a "bookish" child; his father more proudly recalls him as having a youthful gift for mathematics. Sending Nii Noi to London, his father imagined that his son would return as a nation builder, a college-degreed economist, ready for government service or a post with the World Bank.

Nii Noi recalled his 1972 move to Britain, aged nineteen, this way: "I went there to study economics, but I did more politics, more sociology than economics. . . . I was good in public policy and special economics, the more human-related things. I wasn't too much into the finance. Later, I realized music was more liberating than going on to do economics. So I had no option, you know, because I noticed the liberating factor in the music, because I became more informed about the cultures of the world through music than through economics."

A moment later he elaborated:

"We used the libraries a lot because we were all discovering ourselves and because it was a period not so long after the sixties and black power; there was still enough energy in the youth community which I went to meet. I think that formed me a lot and affected my direction, socially speaking. My consciousness, I think, was heightened by the many books that reflected the struggles of African people around the world at the time. I stayed there in London for a little while and then moved on to Birmingham for about two years. And there too, because it's provincial, you had a lot of time for yourself. There was enough time there to read and use the public libraries extensively. And they were well equipped. There were books on African culture. There were books on jazz. There were books on history and politics, the whole body of works that influenced the social struggles of the sixties and the seventies."

During the period 1972–79, Nii Noi read ravenously about the struggles of African people on the continent and in the diaspora. This is where he first seriously encountered jazz music, reading Pan-African history and politics.

"Yeah, man, I was never a musician at home, never did anything musical. I was just into my Jimi Hendrix, you know. But I was impressed when

I read Malcolm X, how he knew his Charlie Parkers and Billie Holidays and John Coltranes. That really said something to me."

So Nii Noi began listening to jazz music in the context of Pan-African political conversation with East, West, and South Africans, and with people of Caribbean origin, first in London, and even more after he moved to Birmingham. His love for Coltrane's music led him to work in a factory long enough to get the money to pay for a saxophone and lessons.

But Nii Noi's musical world was not limited to nor principally centered around jazz. Jazz was part and parcel of a larger set of Afro-diasporic dialogues and experiments, and his percussion and instrument work with the Pan-African poetry group African Dawn[5] brought him into contact with diverse East, South, and West African conversations routed through the black British experience. Another refinement developed through Dade Krama, a contemporary African cultural group emphasizing interplays of ancient and contemporary musical, political, and poetic knowledge. And while Nii Noi's Pan-African politics percolated through Coltrane and these converging African conversations, he also took note of the more obvious populist synthesis that was taking the black British community by storm: reggae.

"What was so strong," he told me, "was how reggae music popularized all the history and politics that we were reading and debating. I liked books more than dancing, you know. I liked Jimi Hendrix and John Coltrane's music because they were the intellectual equivalents of Malcolm X and Kwame Nkrumah. But I had to find a way to bring my high-minded Coltrane-type music into the story. You know, I had to convince people that I could hear in Coltrane what they could hear in Bob Marley."

Nii Noi found his opportunity in an opening for a saxophone player in the black British reggae band, Misty In Roots.[6]

"I joined in 1982 just as they were due to travel to Zimbabwe," he reminisced. "They had been invited to play at Zimbabwe's first independence anniversary. The reason being, the group had played many benefit concerts for Zimbabwe during the liberation struggles. After independence, they saw it fit to invite a group to play in Zimbabwe. And it was good. It was well supported by the government and we traveled widely. We played stadiums, to packed capacity. We were taken care of. We were also initiated into the culture of Zimbabwe. But it was just after the struggle. So, there were energies, you know, ancestral spirits were still

30. Nii Noi (right) performing in Zimbabwe with Misty In Roots, 1982.
Photograph © 2010 Anyaa Arts Library Collection.

lurking around. [Laughs.] They had come from the shade to see the fruits of revolution, and we partook in that. It was nice. We associated with the fighters who had just come from the bush. They were settled in Harare, and that was where we all met. It was good to interact with people who had just fought for their independence and who could articulate to you intense things that happened on the battlefield, first hand, and that affected one's growth."

"Yes, the Zimbabwean experience was eye-opening," he continued after a reflective moment. "I mean, sometimes I felt very Zimbabwean because I was there at a very crucial time in their history, when they were forging their identity, and that also rubbed off, because we were also there searching, and to be in the midst of a searching people, you can't help but be affected. So we also took some of that grace, some of that whatever-that-is that came from the ancestors. For me, personally, it was my most spiritually intense time, because I wasn't very particularly spiritual. My political understanding of things didn't make me very spiritual. I was an ideologue, you know, dogmatic. I didn't spend too much time reflecting on the spirit. It was in Zimbabwe that I was struck that there was need to reflect more on the spirit, because there was a spirit of a nation assessing itself, a whole nation was assessing itself spiritually, so how could you as an individual not be affected? So I think from then on, I realized my music was going to be more serious and important, because it was going to have a strong spiritual base."

Apart from its critical place in his ideological and spiritual development, what was most musically remarkable about Nii Noi's years of work with Misty In Roots is that he managed to get through them barely playing a lick of straight reggae sax riffs as accompaniment to the band. Rather, during rhythm breaks and specifically during down times for the singers, he would accompany the rub-a-dub riddim drumming and bass on alto sax, playing in a free jazz improvisation style that went from boiling to explosive on the Coltrane-Ayler vu meter,[7] working the crowd up to a frenetic and exuberant dance high for ten or twenty or thirty minutes at a time before the refreshed singers would come back onstage and take over with their next round of songs.

"That was all I could do," he said. "I could do it on top of the reggae beat, and it was exciting. And the people with me didn't know about the Albert Aylers and the John Coltranes, they just knew their reggaes. So when I started blowing those things, it freaked them out! [Laughs.] It was good. All of us, in Zimbabwe, Zambia, into Europe, it was that summer. I think it was my contribution to Misty In Roots. I think my brothers in Africa identified with the group, because we were African-minded. I always wore my African clothes, talked my African talk. I wasn't too much into the Jamaican thing. But we coexisted nicely. We were all friends and comrades. And I was accepted in the band like a real member."

Nii Noi's early association with black British reggae royalty produced lifelong friendships. While he did not adopt Rastafarian religious or speech practice, he became associated in other ways with its package of style and consciousness, like his adoption of dreadlocks and associations with the strong community orientation in the Rastafarian dimension of Misty In Roots.

Situating himself in that milieu, he reflected: "Personally, I'm not a Rastafari, I'm not of the faith of Rastafari. But I have been influenced culturally by the movement, because I live in a small closed environment and am surrounded by Rastafari. And to identify yourself in your community it means specifically that you have to embrace currents in your community. So embracing Rastafari or Rastafarians doesn't make me especially Rastafari, but I've accepted the community around me. I think they influence our cultural consciousness, they offer an alternative to the white mainstream. They underlined black consciousness, basically."

"How did that connect with what you were reading at that time," I asked, "with the ways you were bringing the music and books together?"

"What reggae did really was to popularize the consciousness that was in books, you know. Those of us who had access to books and read African history and Caribbean history and African American history had a lot of information at our disposal. But it was reggae, really, that made this information available to people who didn't have access to books. In which case, consciousness flooded the African community more after the reggae thing, yes. And it affected everybody, because you could see your people changing as a result of new information. So, whether or not you were Rastafari, you were affected by Rastafari culture, because it's your people. Whether or not you liked reggae, you were affected by reggae."

But it was more than reggae that drew Nii Noi into black Caribbean and diasporan discourse; he became personally more intertwined when he married Paula Efua Grant, a teacher from a family of distinguished educators who came to Britain from Guyana in the mid-1960s. Efua's father was the schoolmaster and writer Eric Grant, whose works include the biography of his son, and Efua's brother, Bernie Grant, a trade union-ist who rose to become one of the first black British members of parlia-ment. Bernie Grant was a well known if much contested thorn in the side of British politics, foremost a champion of workers, and an advocate for dignity in civil rights and cultural diversity. An arts center in Tottenham, his London constituency, is named in his memory.[8]

Telling me the story of meeting Efua, Nii Noi connected it, through Misty In Roots, to another key aspect of his experience of Zimbabwe, introduction to and study of the Shona mbira: "My wife comes from Guyana, and I'd given my mbira to a friend who had lived in her house. My friend was now living in Zimbabwe. So when I asked him for my mbira, he said, 'Go to this address, I left your mbira there.' I remember it was on Easter, Easter holiday. And I thought, 'OK, on the Easter holiday I'll go pick up my mbira.' And I was given the name of the person who had the mbira. I spoke with that person on the telephone, 'I'm Nii Noi.' 'Hello, I'm Rosemund.' 'I spoke to Bupe, and Bupe says my mbira was with you, and I'm coming to pick up my *mbira*.' 'Okay, come pick up your *mbira.'* So off I set to pick up my mbira. Just when I got on that main road where the address was, I noticed there was a woman coming towards the same address from the opposite direction. And I thought, 'Oh, this is a woman I'm going to see.' And we all slowed down a little bit to see whether in fact we were going to go in the same house. But she entered before I did. So she went into the alley, opened the door, didn't shut it, just stood at the door, thinking I was going to come in there. And then I walked in, knocked on the door and she opened and said, 'Yes, who do you want?' I said, 'I want Rosemund.' 'How do you know Rosemund?' (Because she's the junior sister of Rosemund and she thinks she knows all Rosemund's friends.) 'Where are you coming from? You're not Rose-mund's friend.' 'Well, I've been sent to collect something from Rose-mund.' And then she opened the door for me.

And I sat, waiting for Rosemund to come. Then a friend of my wife-to-be came and they were all studying economics, I think. So they got into some argument about economics. And I thought, well, let me wield my old economic ax. [Laughter.] I spouted out some theory which was convincing, you know, and probably struck them, 'Oh, he's an intelligent guy too.' Anyway, later Rosemund came, we spoke, I got my mbira, and I'm done. And then later I phoned the house, you know, 'Thank you for my mbira. Hi to your little sister!' And it started from there on. So mbira has been kind to me. It's given me a wife and two beautiful boys."

Circling around his Ghana-Caribbean-U.K. stories, or making points of connection between them, Nii Noi always came back to Coltrane in our conversations, consolidating intersections first announced to me in his family shrine, the little globe with his sons and Efua, positioning his own travels, readings, listenings, acquisition of knowledge, and experience on a Coltrane time line.

"Myself, I came to Coltrane from the tail end. I came to Coltrane focused on his last years, and what I heard in that listening was more of the rhythmic things, the way he was playing with Rashied Ali and just before that with Elvin Jones, when Elvin was still with the quartet. That musical period attracted me more, because I could hear the interplay between Coltrane the saxophone player and all the drummers."

Nii Noi's plural phrase "all the drummers" here relates to the way he hears Coltrane's classic middle period quartet, roughly 1961–65, with the pianist McCoy Tyner and bassist Jimmy Garrison and drummer Elvin Jones, as a rhythm section of interlocked drummers. The more we listened to those recordings together, the more he suggested that the music was a multilayered percussive ground against which one heard the voice of Coltrane's saxophone. He expanded that idea when referring to Coltrane's last two years, 1965–67, and the groups that included Alice Coltrane on piano, Garrison on bass, and Rashied Ali on drums.[9]

"And the drummers, all them drummers, were playing something nearer to what I heard in Africa, in terms of complexities and tonalities and all kinds of things. I heard more of the African things in these drummers. I heard the drums overlapping and hooking up like our drummers do, and over that I can hear Coltrane as a drummer playing the saxophone, working his rhythms too. I heard more of the African things in these drummers. So Coltrane's music for me is just a sound he projects and the image that we get of Africa in his music, first and foremost, before the sheets of sound. I hear the sheets of sound rhythmically. Others may hear it harmonically. I hear it as the drums overlapping each other, I see Coltrane as a drummer playing the saxophone, in which case I see him shifting his rhythms. Some may say harmonic progressions, I say that's rhythmic progressions. Because all rhythms have their melodies, and kinds of harmonies, too. Once you approach your music rhythmically, then all these things follow. So I think the basis of Coltrane's music to me is rhythm, not so much the many chord changes he brought into the music. He stopped playing all those chord changes and reduced them to one or two, which also is very African, because we tend to work more at that level of keeping the music simple."

It was that way of hearing the sound and the rhythmic power of Coltrane's concepts that animated additional dimensions of Nii Noi's conversations with his own Ghanaian musical heritage and the larger study of musical instruments on the African continent. From the Western saxophone and flute, he first went into the study of Ghanaian percussion, flutes, and winds, then strings. The trip to Zimbabwe with Misty In Roots in 1982, which got him hooked on the Shona mbira dza vadzimu, later brought him to look into other forms of *sanza* (lamellophones) in West Africa. And to put his African musical experiences together not just through instrumental but also intellectual exploration, he took up the self-study of African music and wrote about the symbolism of instruments and the insights of music ethnographies like Paul Berliner's *The Soul of Mbira* and Charles Keil's *Tiv Song*.[10]

"Reading those books in particular was revelatory," Nii Noi told me (well before he knew that their authors were both personal friends and professional colleagues). "I knew that Africa could bring out the best in anyone searching for music's power. But those two books really impressed me, you know, because they showed the complexity of how Africans thought about music, made it clear that we too had our Beethovens and Coltranes, even if they were living in villages."

A few days later, taking a pause from our recording sessions for Accra Trane Station's *Tribute to A Love Supreme* recording project, Nii Noi and I watched a DVD, *The World According to John Coltrane*,[11] on my laptop, together with Nii Otoo Annan, Agazi, and Nii Yemo Nunu, respectively drummer, engineer, and photographer on the project. The DVD features a studio performance of Coltrane's commemorative piece "Alabama," originally recorded on the 1964 LP *Coltrane Live at Birdland*.[12] For Nii Noi it revealed an explicit link between Coltrane and contemporary Ghana.

"What we all saw on that video was a man from our own definition, or from our own perspective. Here is a man playing a horn, playing a funeral dirge, and behind this funeral dirge, there was a man playing his atumpani drums. And these are cultural references in Ghana that I'm making, because when somebody dies here, if it's a great person, a king or a chief or a noble, you know, some great person who's achieved much in society, when he dies, it may be accompanied by flute and horn dirges with drum accompaniment, not unlike what Coltrane and Elvin Jones did on 'Alabama.' And as I explained to my people, this was a case where some four black girls were bombed in a church in 1963. Once they got the story as to how the whole thing unfolded, then the music becomes even clearer. From then on, we could even hear voices in Coltrane's playing, we could even put in Ghanaian words in his playing: 'Oh, how sorry, man. How sad that all these little children have been bombed.' It was a lamentation, and lamentation is universal, I think. And we could hear the lamentation in his playing. So I'm so aware that we could even substitute African mourning styles into that playing, and it's not so far-fetched, really, because Coltrane was doing what an African dirge player would do, and Elvin was doing what an African ceremonial drummer would do on occasions like that."

Interestingly, the "Alabama" introduction is played not by Coltrane's tenor sax and Jones's drums but by sax and piano. Elvin Jones lays out on the head of the song; the percussion sound that accompanies Coltrane's dirge-like spiritual recitative melody is a rolling left-hand piano drone played by McCoy Tyner. I asked Nii Noi if this made any difference to his comment that "Coltrane was doing what an African dirge player would do, and Elvin was doing what an African ceremonial drummer would do."

"Oh! You see!" he responded, excitedly. "It's just like what I told you before. It could have been any of the drummers or all of them with that rolling sound. It could have been Elvin with his mallets on the tom-tom or Jimmy Garrison with his bow on the bass or McCoy Tyner on the keys. They are all drumming, all drummers, and it is that sound, that way of linking up the horn to the drums, you know, that way of accompanying the voice of the priest or voice of the conch shell or voice of the *atenteben* flute or the voice of the saxophone. That is the universal side of lament, that way there is some thunder sounding under and all around the sad, crying voice. So in Coltrane's case, it makes his approach more African, yes, more African that he can use any or all of his drummers to bring out that sound. He is really speaking an African language that way."

"Tell me about the language part," I asked. "Are you hearing the melody like African dirge melodies and the sound of wailing voices here, with special language or poetic phrases?"

"In Coltrane's music you can hear the various African language groups," he said. "And it's not surprising that when Coltrane vocalizes, it seems to fall in this language group area here, because first and foremost it was probably taken from here, all his ancestors were taken from here to the Americas, or also probably he studied African music in the libraries, listened to it in the libraries. So obviously he was making a conscious attempt to do what an African would do. So even if he couldn't speak an African language, he tried as much as possible to vocalize it in his instrument. I think Coltrane was speaking an African language. Coltrane leapt from the American language idiom into an African idiom, and I think he did it very, very successfully, because of his understanding of history, because of his understanding of music from other parts of the world."

Nii Noi returned to Ghana to live full time in 1989. Since then, in addition to twenty years of musical association with Ghanaba, his work is documented in the progression of three successive groups, Mau Mau Muziki (1990–97), African Sound Project (1999–2004), and Accra Trane Station (2005–8).[13] Each group was of different size and instrumentation, but the percussionist Nii Otoo Annan, whose story follows in the next chapter, was a constant in them all. While Nii Noi principally played

31. Nii Noi playing
his bass afrifone.
*Photograph © 2007
Steven Feld.*

saxophone in the 1990s, he devoted more time in the African Sound Project and Accra Trane Station years to developing his six self-made afrifone instruments.

"The afrifones have liberated me from the saxophone," he explained, "because they are much easier to play than the saxophone, easier to blow, not as difficult to get your notes and your sounds as the saxophone. They don't require the long hours spent on saxophone practice. Because they are limited in a way, they don't have the range of the saxophones. But they have the voice of the statements we want to make, so it makes our music, it simplifies our music, makes it more direct and relevant. It makes our music more African than African American when we play with the afrifones. And that's what I want, like Ghanaba, not to be an African playing what people think of as jazz on standard jazz instruments, but playing African music on African instruments that are informed by the history of jazz and especially the spirit of Coltrane, and the politics of those times."

For Nii Noi "those times" speak to the confluence of Coltrane's music and Nkrumah's Pan-African politics, writ large in the story of Ghana's independence. A critical role model and collaborator in that story was Ghanaba, both because he absorbed jazz but always put the emphasis on African idioms, and because he emphasized the significance of performing in one's own community.

I asked Nii Noi about his participation in Ghanaba's *Hallelujah!* project, how it related to his own approaches to the Africanization of jazz sources and references, how it created a spiritual and political arena through music. After telling me about his years of rehearsing and recording various duets with Ghanaba, and developing those concepts through Mau Mau Muziki and African Sound Project, he answered by coming back to the topic of instruments.

"Ghanaba prefers my alghaita to my saxophone, because that fits into his definition better. The saxophone brings in more of the jazz element, which he is trying to sidestep, which also means that when I am playing the saxophone, I repeat myself because I am influenced by great masters, great traditions. It doesn't always fit into the context of his music. But when I play the alghaita, which is the oboe, then it brings something alive, and that is when he features me more prominently. . . . So my role in his music is quite important to me, because I create an atmosphere of an ancient past, which is also good for him because it creates an aura in which he can settle and project what he wants to say. So the accompaniment is offstage onto stage, and once we're onstage, I follow the direction as to what the music demands: if I'm to stay on my alghaita, or if I'm to change to another instrument. But mostly it's alghaita when I play with him. And I think, when we do that, for both of us, there's the addition of a new instrument and the creation of a new tradition, because fontomfrom drums normally don't usually go with the alghaita horn and the alghaita horn doesn't often go with the fontomfrom drums. But we utilize rhythmic principles which are common to both musical traditions, so when we combine that, it extends the parameters of the music by many thousands of years, because drums and horns go back in time. And when we play them free like we do, it evokes an ancient past."[14]

"And why evoke an ancient past, I mean, how does that relate to the Pan-African aspect of your project?"

"The ancient past means that the sound has traveled and survived in the present, and that gives it more power, I think. Through Morocco the alghaita sound came all the way across to Nigeria, and it is also very common in Chad, and Niger, and also a very prominent instrument in many parts of Asia and Europe. Obviously, it is an ancient instrument because it has traveled many, many miles. Maybe that's what attracted Coltrane, too, the idea that one sound had touched and joined so many cultures, religions, ceremonies, you know, that one sound traveled that long, that much, that one sound could take you so deeply into the history of all of these African and Asian and Middle Eastern and European cultures."

In addition to these years of music, sculpture, and attending to Anyaa Arts Library, his collection of books, recordings, and artifacts modeled on Ghanaba's Afrikan Heritage Library, Nii Noi also engaged briefly in journalism, mostly, he told me, as a way of staying in touch with people from his seventies and eighties black British Pan-African circle. But it was also a way of expressing his support and deepening his connection to the Pan-African Kemetic spiritualist, healer, and traditional priest from Burkina Faso, Naba Lamoussa Morodenibig, founder of the Earth Center and *The Firefly*. From 2001 to 2003, Nii Noi contributed fifteen columns to *The Firefly*, a magazine of Pan-African culture and philosophy and spirituality based in Chicago. His topics included Ghanaba, Kwame Nkrumah, the Mau Mau, Patrice Lumumba, Ambuya Nehanda, Carmen Perreira, Miriam Makeba, Amilcar Cabral, Frantz Fanon, Pitika Ntuli, and John Coltrane. He started the last piece in the series with the line "Song titles are important indications of a composer's world view," and went on to discuss Coltrane's many African titles and references.[15] Without knowledge of Norman Weinstein's book *A Night in Tunisia: Imaginings of Africa in Jazz*, Nii Noi developed parallel thoughts on the sequence and significance of Coltrane's many African place and history references.[16] Arguing for a spiritual unity in themes, he wrote: "It is precisely this that colors the voice Coltrane bequeathed to the saxophone, the voice of the African high priest/ess."

Discussing that concept with me, he said: "Coltrane essentially is a spiritual person for us, and this is something that any African will relate to, like the way any African or Pan-Africanist will relate to Coltrane's covers and art and song titles. And because he's a spiritual person, he definitely projected that in his music. So for me, spirit possession is one of the highlights in his music, because he seems to be possessed himself when he plays. And if he's possessed, then the idea is to project that possession onto us, the audience, too. So the possession element in his music makes it feel very African, to me. You know, because he's there in the role of a priest, trying to invoke or exorcise or that kind of thing, and he doesn't do it passively, he really goes into it and takes you along. He tries to pull you into it, to get you involved in the whole music. That's his strength, he's a whole lot like the traditional priests, trying to work charms on you."

Sculpture is the concretized material incarnation of Nii Noi's synaesthetic unification of visual and musical art as Pan-African cultural and spiritual politics. In January 2006, when I returned to Accra for my first long stay, Nii Noi greeted me with his exhibit called *Accra Trane Station*, an installation of twenty related sound sculptures, each named for Coltrane compositions. In the *Accra Trane Station* film you see my first tour of three of them, "Africa Brass," "Naima," and "Giant Steps." Over the first six months of 2006, Nii Noi made refinements to these pieces during the time we recorded the trio material for *Meditations for John Coltrane*. When I left Accra, Nii Noi went to London to see his wife and college-age sons. Unbeknownst to me, he did a major reorganization of the twenty Coltrane sculptures before departing, reassembling them into a train and station, and parking the entirety in his studio space. When I returned to

32. Nii Noi's "Freedom Float" sculpture. *Photograph © 2007 Steven Feld.*

Accra in January 2007 for a second long visit, he was back at work there in preparation for the coming fiftieth anniversary of Ghana's independence. He was critical about the elitist tone of the national celebrations, and explained his tribute, titled "Freedom Float," as a populist and oppositional act.

"I prefer the word 'freedom' to 'independence,'" he began. "The man at the helm of the Freedom Float is Kwame Nkrumah, the chief architect of the float, he's the driver, the chief driver. And he's sitting in the front holding the steering wheel with Africa as a centerpiece. And the steering wheel also happens to be a car horn, typical of the La trotro drivers. And that is also to suggest the joy of the moment, and of movement, and the loudness and the triumphs of those times. In this culture there are always pennants of Ghanaian colors, red, gold, green, and black that go with the noise. There are also flowers, which suggest celebration. And there's a number plate, A.D. 1957, the year of independence. In the float proper, we may find both ordinary folks and politicians, those who are attuned to the aspirations of the people and have made themselves into capable leaders. So we have for instance Marcus Garvey, the pioneer of Pan-Africanism as we know it.[17]

"Also in the float you have ordinary musicians and dancers, you know. That's part of the celebration too, ordinary folks going about their ordinary business with their various transportation forms. Like here we have a trotro as a popular form and you know it's part of the independence spirit. So the independence spirit, freedom spirit, is more a popular expression of the people. Also, in the float we highlight the role of children in the development of the continent, so here you find children in all endeavors, trying to make something meaningful out of their lives. And that also becomes part of the freedom celebrations, the liberation of the children from mundane things into more creative things.

"Also in the float we have a representation of musicians . . . jazz musicians, Lester Young, Billie Holiday, Thelonious Monk, Charlie Rouse, Ghanaba, Sonny Rollins, Dexter Gordon, Charles Lloyd, Duke Ellington, some bluesmen too, Lightnin' Hopkins, Junior Wells, and more jazzmen, Coleman Hawkins or Benny Carter, Randy Weston, Milford Graves, the drummer. You'll see also the symphony orchestra, our very unsung symphony orchestra, one of the very first established on the African continent. And here they play a combination of Western and African musical forms. So everyone is here, musicians, ordinary folks, representations of

33. Nii Noi's *Accra Train Station* installation. *Photograph* © *2007 Steven Feld.*

ancient civilizations, children, you know, politicians and leaders, everybody that joined the process of freedom."

"Last year," I say, as we head inside, "last year everything was out, and now it is all in the station. Why?"

"Yeah, it's parked," he replies, "because *Meditations* is playing. Now that the soundtrack is done, it's playing, so the train is parked in the station. Look at the train, man, and you're hearing *Meditations,* and you can see the work is done, it's well done."

Compared to the way stories of Osei Tutu were brought into Ni Noi's consciousness as a child, or the way John Coltrane and the musical worlds surrounding his legacy were a critical inspiration linking almost twenty years in the United Kingdom to almost another twenty back in Ghana, Beethoven might seem a less likely citation here. But he's here for an equally significant, if unanticipated, reason. Namely, Nii Noi, like many Africans and diasporans, embraces the belief that Beethoven was black. Nii Noi first encountered this idea in the 1970s, a time of particular popularity of books by Joel Augustus Rogers.

Born of mixed-race heritage in Jamaica in 1880, Rogers migrated to the United States in 1906 and became a naturalized citizen ten years later.

He lived in Chicago and then in Harlem during the renaissance. A journalist and self-trained historian, he devoted his columns for black newspapers and his numerous self-published books and pamphlets to neglected legacies of African and diasporic achievement. His foremost agenda was historical vindication, and he placed his work firmly in the line of battling racism. *The World's Greatest Men of Color, One Hundred Amazing Facts about the Negro, Nature Knows No Color Line*, and *Five Negro Presidents* were among his many titles. Between 1941 and 1944 he published his three-volume magnum opus, *Sex and Race*, his most sustained attack on myths of Aryan racial purity and superiority. It is hard to underestimate the subversive and radical quality of his title for that time, not to mention his subtitles: *Negro-Caucasian Mixing in All Ages and All Lands*, and *The History of White, Negro, and Indian Miscegenation in the Two Americas*.[18]

While Rogers was close to Marcus Garvey, whom he knew in Jamaica, and once praised by W. E. B. Du Bois, even his ardent supporters were aware of serious gaps between his ideological commitments to humanist antiracism and the historical accuracy of quite a few of his assertions. After his death in 1966, some of his claims, including ones whose historical plausibility had long been questioned by both black and white intellectuals, were nonetheless uncritically circulated in Afrocentric circles.

This returns us to the site of Nii Noi's apotheosis, the 1970s black British United Kingdom, where he was surrounded by African and Caribbean students and artists. It was in this milieu that Nii Noi first read, with amazement, he reports, these lines in Rogers's booklet *One Hundred Amazing Facts about the Negro*: "Beethoven, the world's greatest musician, was without a doubt a dark mulatto. He was called 'the Black Spaniard.'"[19]

Rogers argued that Beethoven's mother was a Moor, descended from the Africans who made Spain their home for centuries. His commentary was focused on the designation of "Spagnol" or "Spanish" to refer to what he called Beethoven's "dark" or "swarthy" or "blackish-brown" or "mulatto" skin complexion, and his "flat thick nose."

These days one can find numerous Afrocentric cyber-echoes to Rogers's arguments and their particular attention to physiognomy. An often-quoted writer on this topic in the black-and-proud blogosphere is the African American pianist Deborah D. Mosely, and the most often cited part of her Internet article "Beethoven, the Black Spaniard" draws attention, like Rogers, to characterizations of Beethoven's physical appearance. In *"Beethoven by Maynard Solomon, p.78,"* she writes, "he is described as having 'thick, bristly coal-black hair' (in today's parlance, we proudly call it 'kinky') and a 'ruddy-complexioned face.' In *Beethoven: His Life and Times* by Artes Orga, p.72, Beethoven's pupil, Carl Czerny of the 'School of Velocity' fame, recalls that Beethoven's 'coal-black hair, cut a la Titus, stood up around his head' [sounds almost like an Afro]. 'His black beard . . . darkened the lower part of his dark-complexioned face.'"

An additional repeated focus for Mosely is the Viennese residence subsequently called "Schwarzspanierhaus," the "house of the Black Spaniard." Another is the essentializing claim that Beethoven's syncopation practices were so radical for Western music in his time that they had to derive from an African sensibility. Using language that again recalls Rogers's frequent emphasis on vindication, Mosely protests the "academic theft" of Beethoven's ancestry and calls for "academic justice for the people whose great and noble past was stolen and hidden from them."[20]

That these ideas have long been in popular circulation called musicology into the controversy early on, at least as early as 1949, in a *Musical Quarterly* article by Donald MacArdle, Beethoven scholar and extensive annotator of Anton Schindler's *Beethoven as I Knew Him*. Setting the trend for most subsequent discourse, MacArdle gave no credence to the "black Moor" theory of Beethoven's ancestry. Most later refutations cite him, and some grow much more dismissive. Yet after reexamining Rogers's fifteen sources, and numerous others in seven languages, the virtuosic Africana music bibliographer Dominque-René de Lerma concludes his *Black Music Research Journal* piece with considerable nuance: "Beethoven is united with the African concept of the community and the spiritual, like John Coltrane, but we are richly blessed by authentic Black heroes. Having Beethoven as an in-law is quite sufficient."[21]

That comment notwithstanding, it's probably fair to say that musicology's talk-back on this story has cumulatively involved somewhat more positivist commentary defending "the facts" or "the truth" of Beethoven's whiteness than pursuing the historical and ideological significance of the many assertions and reassertions of his blackness.

A subtle interpretive space for such a reading was recently opened in an allegorical story by one of our great witnesses to anxieties of racial dignity, the South African Nobel laureate Nadine Gordimer. Her short story "Beethoven Was ¹⁄₁₆th Black," also the title to her most recent collection, lets an imaginary white radio announcer's "Beethoven was..." become her space to explore the fraught dialectics of confusion and desire. "Once there were blacks wanting to be white. Now there are whites wanting to be black. It's the same secret," she begins, on the path, again, to examining intertwined South African hopes of restitution and reclamation in the ruins of racial history.[22]

But as in the case of De Lerma, what makes Nii Noi's discourse distinctly fascinating is the juxtaposition of Beethoven's name with Coltrane's. Here's Nii Noi: "People might confuse John Coltrane with a Scottish man because of his name," he said. "Just like Beethoven's name is German, and people don't see his African background, because Beethoven is embraced by the German culture, and everybody knows him to be a German. But in terms of race, Beethoven would be called an African in this time because he's of mixed race. But, you know, you can't claim his Africanness alone. He's part of the world community. Like Coltrane. And the more Coltranes, the more Beethovens, the more peace there will be in the world. Because you can't make music that is that great and that universal without a deep spiritual component."

Nii Noi appropriates Beethoven, including the presumption of his racial heritage, into a universalizing consolidation of just the suspicious sort that the musicologist Nicholas Mathew exposes in his critical review of tendencies to unify Beethoven's voice against pluralist possibilities. Nii Noi seems to be tapping into exactly that default vein where, in Mathew's words, "Beethoven is the home key of the musical canon, so to speak."[23]

Nii Noi uses Coltrane as the equally universalizing relative minor of that canonic home key of Beethoven. And in doing so he performs a sweepingly essentialized narration of Coltrane as Africa, that is, of Coltrane as the unification of rhythm and spirituality. But of course, speaking as an African, and speaking in Africa, it is all made considerably more complex by the way Nii Noi simultaneously universalizes and Africanizes both Coltrane and Beethoven, and in the same sentences.

"Coltrane is Africa," he said—again. "It's like it was his dream, because he recorded so many African titles, and in a conversation he had with Olatunji, he expressed the desire to visit Africa. He didn't, because he died. But I think our train can bring him back—he can visit spiritually on our train. Future generations in Africa, when they study music, will have to study jazz as an art form. And because of the African references John Coltrane made in and through the jazz art form, he will end up being studied in the future by African students, on the same level as Beethoven or Bach or Mozart, or great African classical musicians. We've had ours, too, of course, on the continent, traditional composers on a level like Beethoven and Bach. But I think Coltrane is a modern figure, and I expect his contribution to African music, or music in general, will reflect that kind of modern parallel between him and the European greats. Africa could be in the vanguard musically if we taught Coltrane and Beethoven together, you know, put them on exactly the same level as we put our African music."

I know what you're wondering now. Is Nii Noi aware that he might be skating on thin ice, alternately freezing difference and melting universalism in this confluence of Osei Tutu's spiritual/political empire in West Africa, Beethoven's porous Europe flowing into and out of northern Africa via Spain, and Coltrane's fluid voicing of Black Atlantic spiritual rhythm?

Maybe. But how about reading this another way, by asking if Nii Noi is using different language to imagine a deep cosmopolitics, a progressive philosophy of history, one that could dress Kantian universalism in the kente cloth of Nkrumaist African socialist humanism? Imagine Nii Noi harmonizing the voice of Jürgen Habermas, the philosopher who theorizes postnational patriotism in the context of new plural-multicultural presences within old nations. Imagine Nii Noi pumping bass to Kwame Anthony Appiah, the philosopher who grooves on the reconcilation of postmodern multiculturalisms with enlightenment ethics. Contemporary cosmopolitanisms are transformative, Habermas and Appiah argue, if justice is similarly understood at national and supernational scales. Indeed, cosmopolitanism is thus fundamentally a necessary ethical response to all forms of injustice.[24]

Could Habermas's or Appiah's visions of cosmopolitan ethics be equally revealed via Nii Noi's reading/sounding of the 1950s to 1970s as a confluence of cultural, spiritual, political moments that link African histories of decolonization to diasporic struggles for civil rights and multicultural recognition? And what does it mean that this confluence is so musically marked and historicized through the creative assertions of reggae, free jazz, and Afro-experimentalism?

Nii Noi is surely on a parallel path here with Ghanaba. Slipping Beethoven in between Coltrane and Osei Tutu, Nii Noi reprises Ghanaba's triangulation of the interaction of African and African American or Afro-diasporic musics with the necessity to cite and engage Europe. And in that context, Nii Noi's performance of Afro-centric self-essentialism is surely an energetic search for the broadest source of connections—explicit, implicit, overt, covert, partial, fragmentary—that create an Afrocentric cosmopolitics of world musical citizenship.

Some help with imagining that emphasis on connections, the "from X to Y via Z" routings of my chapter titles, and Nii Noi's Trane tracks, comes now if I momentarily return to Ghana's fiftieth anniversary of independence and the contrast between the remoteness of Nii Noi's homemade and parked-at-the-station "Freedom Float," and the over-the-top competitive displays of cultural largesse performed in the independence anniversary moment by European embassies in Accra.

I don't think anyone who experienced Accra in the month of March 2007 would dispute the fact that the hands-down winning performance in the contest of conspicuously excessive independence anniversary showmanship was staged by the Italian Embassy. At a cost of over $500,000, they airbused Daniel Barenboim and the 160-member-strong La Scala orchestra and chorus to Accra for twenty-four hours to perform Beethoven's Ninth Symphony at the fourteen-hundred-seat National Theatre. Forget the fact that the evening opened with some local drumming. Forget the fact that there were two black faces in the chorus (one African American and one African Canadian). Forget the fact that the house was partially filled with African listeners because the fifty-dollar tickets were all gratis even if the who and what of attendance was very tightly and politically controlled. Nobody really noticed these things.

What was locally stunning was that under the surface, pockets of Accra, most of them not in attendance for one reason or another, knew that this was Black Beethoven Comes Back to Mother Africa, even if the homecoming took place amidst complete cluelessness on the part of Barenboim, La Scala, and the Italian Embassy. Moreover, what moved people in Accra, what was very much noticed, was that the whole presentation was spiritually divined, that is, outside of typical political process. And that's because Beethoven was invited to Accra by a personal appeal to La Scala's music director, Daniel Barenboim, from Kofi Annan, the former U.N. secretary general and Ghana's most high-profile international citizen.[25] While ultimately paid for by the Italian government and city of Milan, the event was received locally as a gift of angelic cosmopolitanism, beamed down to Accra over the rainbow of a New York handshake.

34. Portrait of Kofi Annan. *Art © 2008 Sheff.*

But here Beethoven's discursive currency as the "home key of the musical canon" wasn't just transposed up a notch to that key of elite cosmopolitan diplomacy. It got modulated to the even higher key of celebratory black political capital in the United States. Because the entire BBC wire-service story of the Barenboim–La Scala performance of Beethoven's Ninth at Accra's National Theatre was placed into the United States Congressional Record on May 1, 2007.[26] It appears there as the appendix to a brief speech of fiftieth-anniversary congratulations to Ghana from New York's Fifteenth District (Harlem and Upper West Side), whose representative of more than twenty years, Charles Rangel, was the first African American head of the House Ways and Means Committee. A phone call to the staff associate in Representative Rangel's office informed me that yes, the congressman was proudly aware of Beethoven's black ancestry.

A few months later, by way of both unrelated funding and different diplomacy, Accra Trane Station was invited to tour in Italy. By chance, our itinerary included Milan, where Nii Noi and Nii Otoo taught a class at the university, and where the Music Conservatory sponsored a trio concert at the hall of the Circolo Filologico Milanese, right next to La Scala. Just before the performance, we found ourselves relaxing down-

35. From left, Nii Otoo Annan and Nii Noi Nortey in Milan.
Photograph © 2007 Steven Feld.

36. Accra Trane Station performing in Milan.
Photograph © 2007 Lorenzo Ferrarini.

stairs at the Circolo bar with our host, Nicola Scaldaferri, ethnomusicologist at the University of Milan. Nii Otoo nonchalantly requested a glass of gin from the bartender, then proceeded to pour it onto the marble floor as libation to accompany prayer for spiritual strength in the performance to come. As we left to go upstairs and play, a journalist stopped us to ask our impressions of Milan. With a nonchalance topping Nii Otoo's libation, it took Nii Noi just a few words to tell him that as Maestro Barenboim and the La Scala orchestra and choir had recently brought Beethoven back to Accra's National Theatre, he felt that as a Pan-African group it was equally important for us to bring Coltrane's African legacy to Milan's La Scala annex.

The video LCD tells me that there is but a minute left on this, our last Coltrane conversation cassette, and I say, "Thanks, Nii Noi, I'm still thinking about how you link up Accra Trane Station from Coltrane to Beethoven and back to Osei Tutu."

"Well, Prof," he responds, drawing deeper into his professorial voice than I did to mine, "it's no different than linking Malcolm X to Karl Marx then back to Kwame Nkrumah. It's all the same, like, maybe it just seems more obvious when you put it on the musical level, when you can hear it in our music. That music's strength, I think, the way everything can come together politically and spiritually, without reading books."

"Yeah, I'll think about that," I say, just as the video cassette runs out. I'm still thinking about it.

THIRD CHORUS,
BACK INSIDE

Nii Otoo Annan

From Toads to Polyrhythm

via Elvin Jones and Rashied Ali

37. Nii Otoo at the Sam Ash Drum Shop, New York. *Photograph © 2009 Steven Feld.*

Ghanaba and Nii Noi Nortey's stories feature tales of youthful rebellion and adventurous travel, stories of well-educated and high-achieving sons of distinguished fathers at different key moments in Ghana's formative times. Coming from families of accomplishment, education, financial resources, and elevated class position, they came to make radical and innovative political and cultural statements through unique artistic careers. In both cases the access to travel, book and recording resources, and international inspiration led to intercultural interactions that shaped diasporic consciousness, a jazz consciousness applied locally to political and artistic participation in over fifty critical years of a global Ghana.

In striking contrast, there is no class privilege, elite family achievement, or deep educational accomplishment in Nii Otoo Annan's story, and the role of travel there is indeed of a much later and very differently class-inflected variety. Rather, Nii Otoo's tale speaks first to how the choice of a traditional musical path, of spiritual empowerment through ritual drumming, came to be intertwined with less traditional paths, featuring multiple engagements in popular, church, jazz, and experimental musics, as well as international travel to play traditional drum-dance ensemble music in cultural groups, and later to travel with the Accra Trane Station and *Bufo Variations* projects.

When he was quite young, perhaps ten or eleven, Nii Otoo was locally acknowledged to have a musical gift. In the deep-Ga Accra he inhabited, this acknowledgment took the form of a shiny chief's sedan pulling up to the family house to whisk him off to villages for a day or two at a time to join the chief's drummers for various ceremonies. By the end of his primary school years, the vehicles came more and more often. As a result of this and his family's working-class position, the drumming door that opened closed the school door behind him.

"Everyone was working working from early early, I tell you; my mother cooked plantains in the market every day like still today with my sister, all of us helping."

Otoo is the second-born child of ten, with seven sisters and two brothers. His father, born in 1924, was a soldier, one of the sixty-five thousand Ghanaians recruited into the British army. He served in the Burma war in the 81st Division, which defeated the Japanese at Myohaung.[1] In later years he worked as a draftsman at Accra's 37 Military Hospital workshop, until his eyes failed him. Otoo stopped school at age fifteen, at (British system) form 4, roughly tenth grade, although from the age of eleven he was playing professionally in churches and villages and by thirteen was more consumed by music than school and had performed poorly in his classes for several years.

After Otoo dropped out of school to work as a musician, his father encouraged him to learn an additional trade and arranged for him to be part of a carpentry training program at the military base. Well into the course a six-week music gig came up in the north and Nii Otoo wanted to travel. He didn't tell his father, only the overseer of the course, who agreed to cover for him at roll call. When Otoo returned from the gig he found that his name had been scratched off the class list and he was barred from the program. He went to see his father in the office down the hall to ask his help, but his father became enraged and threatened to have soldiers drag him off the base. Later, Otoo's mother told him that he was sacked directly by his father, who feared that Otoo's irregular class attendance might jeopardize his own job.

"So Prof, you see, I didn't learn English properly, I wasn't in school, I was in the villages. They gave me drums to play, cloth to wear. I came home with my belly full, they paid my father some small money too. You know, I don't speak correctly like Nii Noi. I didn't learn reading well. There was nothing to read at home."

Home was Korle Gonno, a fishing and commercial beach area (particularly populated by bars) on the coastline just west of Central Accra, whose people ranged from mixed working-class to impoverished. There today, just as when Nii Otoo first walked the streets as a child in the early 1960s, days and days go by when the only language one hears is Ga, the little bits of intermingled national Twi or international English or street pidgin, mostly emanating from the radios or TVs of numerous small kiosk shops or overflowing in hymns from evangelical corner churches.

Four marriages, eleven children, and increasing responsibility for his parents and upkeep of the family compound have kept Nii Otoo challenged to make ends meet. He often must supplement music with stonemasonry jobs. And despite the generally very low pay and long travel times to work even longer hours at music, he takes everything he can get. Seasonal cycles of rituals and festivals and weekly Saturday funeral performances provide one source of drumming work. As an electric guitarist or bassist, he performs with several highlife and community dance bands when the work is available. As an electric bassist he also has a longstanding Sunday morning and Wednesday night gig leading a group at a local church. On occasion, the preacher calls on him to drum sermons of praise on either the trap set or the underarm odonno "talking" drum.

Nii Otoo's relationship to musical work has always been uncomplicated with regard to commitment and passion for learning and performing. It is considerably more complicated at all levels of finance, compensation, and the uneven lifestyle of just making it from day to day with unreliable work schedules and low compensation.

"You see, Prof," he explained, "in Ghana here there is only one boss. When you work it is always like that. That is the way in Ghana here. When they make a group there is one boss. And he is the one getting everything and chopping [the money]. So even if you are a master and can play play everything everything you must sit down and just take what the boss gives. You can't say nothing. No. Me, I can't say 'no' to work, even if it is five cedis, two cedis, even if it is food money and transport. We take the work because we have no work. What can we do when we have no work? We must take it. The bosses are doing fine fine. The rest don't know what the money is, just take something small, what the boss wants to give."

So despite his established status as a master of diverse instruments and styles, Nii Otoo has always been a sideman and never a leader, playing for hire, and erratically at that. And that position freezes him financially in terms of regular payment in any way commensurate with his artistic skills.

Quite in contrast to all this in terms of prestige and potential recognition, for almost twenty years Nii Otoo played in experimental groups instigated and lead by Nii Noi Nortey: first Mau Mau Muziki, then African Sound Project, then Accra Trane Station. Things didn't start off easily. Speaking of the earliest group, Nii Noi recalled: "We realized there was a need for a more versatile drummer. . . . The xylophone player in the group knew someone who knew Otoo. So he went to Korle Gonno and asked after the whereabouts of Otoo, the legendary conga drummer, or so I'd been told. So one day at rehearsal Otoo comes to demonstrate his skills, only to antagonize the earlier members!! [Uproar of laughter.] So from there on there was a lot of friction in the band, you know, people coming to rehearsals disgruntled knowing there's a new drummer, you know, that kind of thing."

But despite those internal band frictions, Nii Noi realized that a drummer with Otoo's locally unique abilities could help him realize his own musical vision, to Africanize the jazz drum kit differently from Ghanaba's innovations. So Nii Noi cultivated Nii Otoo's understanding of the free jazz canon, exposing him to photographs and recordings of contemporary avant-garde jazz drummers like Elvin Jones, Rashied Ali, Andrew Cyrille, Sunny Murray, Paul Motian, and Milford Graves. And as group leader he experimented by having Nii Otoo play different mixes of hand drums, typically four to six of them, kpanlogo, djembe, odonno, brekete, together with jazz drum kit hi-hat and ride cymbals. This was Nii Noi's "APK" or "African Percussion Kit."

A version of Nii Noi's APK idea is the instrument I first heard Nii Otoo play, and it is the instrument I got to know by playing with him over three years in the Accra Trane Station band. But to open my musical conversation with Nii Otoo about that work, as well as the larger story of encountering the uniqueness of his jazz cosmopolitanism, a long detour is necessary, back to my earliest anthropology of sound research, in the Bosavi rainforest of Papua New Guinea.

It's 1976. I'm in a two-seater single-engine propeller plane, flying low, beginning descent over a rainforest in Papua New Guinea. Having devoted the last four years to graduate studies in African languages and arts, I'm on the way to visit friends doing fieldwork in Papua New Guinea. The place I'm about to land will consume the next twenty-five years of my life.[2] But I don't know that yet, indeed, have other plans, envisaging a quick visit and then a move to Africa. As we descend through the cloud cover I take my first picture. It records a vast and densely tree-topped expanse of primary rainforest. The picture taking is but a momentary distraction from the airplane engine noise, and from the voice speaking inside me. I open my diary notebook and write my first words: "I'm being hurled into broccoli. The pilot has a map open on one knee and a Bible open on the other. He's an evangelist, I'm a heathen. He has a Cessna, I

38. Bosavi rainforest aerial. *Photograph © 1976 Steven Feld.*

have a Nagra. He's doing the Lord's work. I'm cargo, revenue. We can't speak. It's too loud and we have nothing to say to each other. I have to deal with his noise and he has to deal with my silence. His ears are covered with headphones and he says things into a microphone at his lips. He's tuned into God and missionary shortwave radios. Roger. Is this why Lévi-Strauss starts *Tristes Tropiques* with how he loathes travel?"[3]

Another half-hour and I'm on the ground. My ears unclog and the travel now seems more than worth it. And while I perhaps have a few too romantic 1970s ideas about the acoustics of ecology and the ecology of acoustics in a rainforest environment, I've nonetheless come to a remarkable place to listen in to a deep and complex history of human listening and eco-acoustic coevolutions.

Settling into a Bosavi village alongside my colleagues and their five-year-old son, I found the intimate audibility of everything both immediate and overwhelming. But there was one problem. I wasn't prepared for the visual claustrophobia. How to hear through the trees? How to hear the relationship of forest height to depth? Where is a sound when you can't see more than three feet ahead, and looking up only takes your senses into the impenetrable density of the canopy? How to acquire expert ears onto the world?

The answer came more quickly and easily than I imagined. Passing by the village longhouse on many late afternoons as I headed to the forest to listen and record, I'd encounter groups of children. Invariably they insisted on joining and guiding my forest walks. We'd play a simple game. I'd attach a parabolic microphone to my recorder and enclose my ears in isolating headphones. Standing together in the forest, I'd point the parabola in the direction of unseeable forest birds. That would be the signal for the children to jump up, take my forearm, fix, and anchor it. Sure enough, as they made their move, a bird was in all-of-a-sudden sharp acoustic focus in my headphones. Then the kids would burst out laughing, meaning it was time for me to come up with something more challenging.

What a forceful daily lesson in listening as *habitus*, in routinized, emplaced hearing as an embodied mastery of locality. It's only a matter of seconds before a twelve-year-old Bosavi kid can identify a bird by name and tell quite a bit about its location. How does this happen? The lesson was bodily, powerful, and gripping. Whatever else they are, human histories are histories of listening, fabulously local eco-acoustic ways of place making that come from the routine business of sensuous human copresence with what Donna Haraway calls "companion species."[4]

So, rather quickly I realized that I was traveling into a forest of relational ontologies and their acoustemologies, their acoustic ways of knowing, tracking orientations to the world through sound.[5] The key questions were immediate and palpable: what are the linguistic, musical, and aesthetic consequences of humans and companion species making place by acoustically coinhabiting the rainforest ecosystem? What is the enduring significance of selfness in/through otherness relations that develop over time in the bond of lived interactions between humans and nonhumans, humans and environments? Indeed, where do these divisions collapse? What are the refigured boundaries of all overly binarized, overly anthropomorphized divisions of nature and culture? Can we move on to grasp a local territory of coliving, a convivial ethics of coeval and intertwined presence?

In Bosavi I had some exceptional teachers to guide my introspection into such questions. One was Yubi. For years, every encounter with him made me wonder, why were Bosavi's most prolific composers also its most accomplished ornithologists? Yubi taught me to hear acoustically adaptive knowledge as coaesthetic recognition. He taught me how each natural historical detail had symbolic value-added.

Listening together to fruit doves, he first taught me how birds sound simultaneously as ancestral spirit presences and as time-space clocks. Over the years he demonstrated how the local invention of song reprises that transit with poetic texts that map avian spirit movements through the forest. He taught me how ceremonial dancers become spirit presences when heard and seen as birds at forest waterfalls. He taught me that the figure of a spirit bird emerges when the singer's voice flows out-and-over in the same waterfall way.[6]

Ulahi was another guide to how songs sung in a bird's voice link the living and dead, present and past, human and avian, ground and treetops, village and forest. She explained that songs don't sing the world as experienced by travel on foot, but move through watercourses, following the flight paths of forest birds. Through her compositions and her own regular singing at the Wolu creek, Ulahi taught me how water moves through land as voice moves through the body. She taught me how songs are the collective and connective flow of individual lives and community histories. Just one creek and its flow from her local home and to the gardens and land beyond mapped dozens of poeticized names of birds, plants, shrubs, trees, sounds, intersecting waters, and all of the activities that magnetize them to the biographies of lives and spirits in her local social world.[7]

Over twenty-five years, with the help of Yubi, Ulahi, and many other singers, I recorded the trajectories of about one thousand of these Bosavi bird-path songs. They contain almost seven thousand lexical descriptors, names of places, of flora, fauna, topography, as well as sensuous phon-aesthetic evocations of light, wind, motion, sound qualities. These songs constitute a poetic cartography of the forest, interwoven by layered biographies of social relationships. This poesis of the ordinary details of the everyday is vocally and locally emplaced by what is called *dulugu ganalan*, "lift-up-over sounding." The idea conjoins the sonic layers of alternation, overlap, and interlock that characterize the interactions of all forest sound presences, with all of the ways they are met and mimicked in copresent human inventions of voice, text, and motion.[8] The chronotopic historicity of sounding these songs is thus inseparable from their environmental consciousness. As knowledge productions, Bosavi songs are machines for cohabitation, an archive of ecological and aesthetic coevolution.

That archive is also a repository of memories about powerful sounds that define contacts and imaginaries. Another of my local guides and teachers, Kiliye, was a young man in the era of Bosavi's first contacts with outsiders, and he was fearless enough to run away with one of the white men's axes. In Papua New Guinea's remote monolingual places like Bosavi, the local word for "ax" often became the first term for "government." But later "government" was signified by *bikmaus*, "big mouth," the word for "shotgun" in *tok pisin*, the pidgin lingua franca. That's because a common first-contact pacification ritual for remote villagers was to watch a colonial officer put a shotgun to the head of a pig and blow it to bits. "Government" meant the ultimate power to silence with noise. Kiliye didn't have to read Jacques Attali's *Noise* to understand visceral confrontation with acoustic terror. When colonial pacification patrols arrived in Bosavi, the explosive surprise of the first bikmaus blast to a pig's head made him involuntarily pee down his leg.[9]

Thirty years later, in the mid-1980s, the dawn of the era of rainforest logging and mining, a newly dramatic sound emerged as large helicopters staging oil production could be heard through the skies, occasionally landing for the first time in a remote Bosavi village. The sound was shockingly loud, even compared to the already familiar sounds of small airplanes. And ten years after that, in 1996, Kiliye's grandson Odo, leader of Bosavi's newly emergent string band scene, composed a guitar song mapping those years of helicopter flight paths into the rainforest. He named it *Nupela bikmaus*, "New Shotgun."[10]

In 2000, as mining and logging activities made it more complicated for me to return to Bosavi, Charlie Keil, my oldest friend in the scholarly world of world musics, invited me to northern Greece as he, his partner Angeliki, and the photographer Dick Blau were finishing *Bright Balkan Morning*, their photographic and oral history project about Romani instrumentalists.[11] They commissioned me to create a companion CD for the book. In the course of the collaboration, Charlie and I drove and walked though countrysides that indexed generations of layered histories of ethnic interactions in which the Romani story was situated. Wandering around, we would often find ourselves listening to visible and invisible cascades of sheep and goat bells, and in the mix, a herd dog's hostility overlapped by a shepherd cursing the dog's kin back to the beginnings of antiquity.

Listening in to all that ringing—near, far, above, below, in sight, out of sight, soft, loud, stationary, moving—powerfully brought back the soundspace of the rainforest. And that's when, in the immediate overlay of auditory recall, I began to wonder if bells might stand to a thousand years of European village acoustemologies as birds stand to thousands more in the New Guinea rainforest. That's when I began to wonder if animal bells sonified the boundaries of common and private land, and with that, sonified histories of class, wealth, labor, and struggles over land ownership. That's when I began to wonder if there were pastoral parallels to what was so audible in the Bosavi rainforest, an acoustemological triangle linking sound to ecology and cosmology.[12]

Those questions impelled me to ten years of listening and recording animal, church, festival, and carnival bells in villages, towns, and cities in Greece, Italy, France, Finland, Norway, and Denmark.[13] And what I've continued to hear is how time and space fuse as bells ring, patterns of immediate resonance simultaneously sounding a *longue durée*. Bells, like rainforest birds, resound simultaneously as natural historical clocks, as place markers of the ecosocial niches that define communities, and as spiritual beacons mediating heaven and earth. Every aspect of their acoustic immediacy recalls, as in the rainforest, the daily, seasonal, and long-term acoustic cycles in which life takes place. And something else: like the newly minted euro performing the late capitalist fantasy of an integrated European economy, bells ring a common acoustic currency, transnational imaginations of a patrimony and heritage called Europe.

These are not unique revelations, and in this new rainforest of acoustic puzzles I have found myself walking down paths blazed by historians and artists and other teachers, like shepherds, blacksmiths, bell ringers, and carnival participants. Alain Corbin's *Village Bells*, for example, opens many lines of inquiry into the audibility of struggles between the church and civil authority in nineteenth-century France. Imagine bell ringing as a performance that asks who owns time. Imagine bell ringing as a performance that asks who controls the space and time of labor. Imagine bells as the ringing of contested rights to announce the calendar of births, deaths, marriages, festivals, gatherings, and dispersals. Imagine bells as the sonic history of ambivalence over the regulation of habitual village space-time. That's where Corbin takes the conversation.[14]

Likewise, Jean-François Millet's famous 1859 painting, *L'Angélus* relates the visual and acoustic space-time of prayer and work to the defining character of rural French class and community. In his rendering of extreme depth, a muted and miniatured church steeple is acoustically amplified outward to the looming spatial scale of an image dominated by bowed peasant workers in the field. The acoustic space-time of the *angélus* ringing, and the silent or softly vocalized praying, is set against the visual space-time of the sky's hazy glow and the distance that separates the spheres of peasant work and domesticity.[15]

Maybe it's obvious that pastoral church bells connect time, class, labor, and community, and that animals are given voice, distinction, difference by bells. But why do humans both become and other that difference in carnival garb? Why does carnival noise invert or abandon time, and thereby play with and subvert hierarchies of class and power? Why do fools and outcasts wear bells? What does this ringing signify on the body of the clown or reveler, the prostitute or criminal?

Carnival disrupts civility because belled noise making rewrites the rules of space and time, of who and what can or can't be heard, of who and what can or can't be controlled. Carnival denaturalizes quiet and articulates struggle in and through belled noise. In the *mundus inversus*, it is the thundering of bells that most often renders impossible ordinary hearing and speaking. It's only a ding-dong away to bells controlling the noise of criminals and fools by ringing their alterity. Marginality sounds with each move, but the punishment is equally poignant in the imprisonment of quiet stillness.[16]

39. Thundering bells of Skyros carnival, Greece.
Photograph © 2004 Dick Blau.

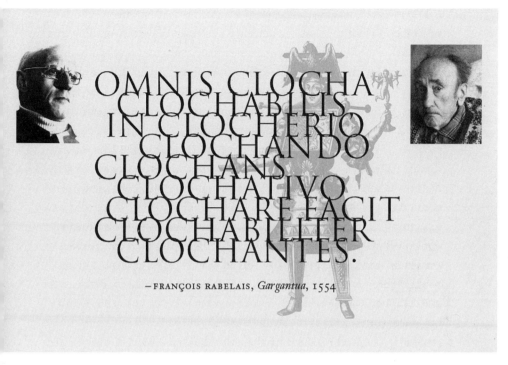

OMNIS CLOCHA
CLOCHABILIS
IN CLOCHERIO
CLOCHANDO
CLOCHANS
CLOCHATIVO
CLOCHARE FACIT
CLOCHABILITER
CLOCHANTES.

— FRANÇOIS RABELAIS, *Gargantua*, 1554

40. *Clochando* collage. Art © 2010 Steven Feld and Michael Motley.

Just like the bird flight paths of Papua New Guinea rainforest songs, then, the ringing paths of European bells made audible to me how the world sonified is the world known, the world felt, the world performed. What became audible was how agents and audiences were listening to the production and reproduction of categories, listening to the ordering of things through ten centuries of European pastoral histories.

The idea takes us right to central issues in critical theory as well. Imagine Michel Foucault lecturing on how bells govern time through the authority of controlled space. Imagine Mikhail Bakhtin reminding him how bells disrupt space through the time of noise. Imagine me listening to them in stereo. Imagine Foucault detailing how bells discipline space through the time of domestication. Imagine Bakhtin reminding him how bells obliterate time through the space of the carnivalesque. Imagine me listening to them in stereo. Imagine Foucault riffing on how church bells order the time of work by marking the spatiality of prayer. Imagine Bakhtin reminding him to listen to belled cows grazing. Imagine me listening to them in stereo.[17]

Those were the sounds and sound-thoughts that had been filling my ears when I went to Ghana, a detour occasioned in part by reading that bells played the "timeline" in ensemble music, a phrase I first came across in writings by the distinguished Ghanaian musicologist J. H. Kwabena Nketia, who was referring to how single, double, banana-leaf, or thumb and finger bells repeatedly ring the common pulse of drum and dance music. I was equally influenced, later, by John Miller Chernoff's reference, in *African Rhythm and African Sensibility*, to this bell "timeline" as the "heart beat" of ensemble music.[18] Listening in Europe made me wonder how Ghanaian bells might differently index or musically mediate experiences of cyclic, linear, multiplex, and cumulative time. So the idea was to pause from the campanological curiosities of the Old World to check out how local musicians and blacksmiths might present a contemporary yet much older-world perspective on bells, musicality, and space-time.

But before I heard a single bell, or met a single musician or blacksmith in Accra, I encountered a different chronotopic index of terrific acoustic presence: the late-night croaking by common toads, identified from my recordings as *Bufo regularis* by the Swiss biologist Mark-Oliver Rödel, whose *Herpetofauna of West Africa*, volume 1, *Amphibians of the West African Savanna* is the authoritative tome.[19] Emanating from two-foot-deep concrete sewers flanking city roads, the toads' voices are intensely amplified by the cement walls of their fetid amphitheaters, the ratcheting sounds broadcast far and wide. Do the concrete sewers turn the toads into rock stars capable of attracting massive numbers of groupies? Does evolutionary success equal sex excess brought on by the power of amplification?

Intriguing questions, but this acoustic bufology intrigued me less for the extreme amplification factor than for the rhythmically complex sonic interactions I could hear when walking alongside the sewers, heightened when listening from the center of the road to the criss-crossing of simultaneous toad vocalizations from either side. Recording these sounds late one night, my mind raced ahead to the possibility that I could someday play them back locally to open a conversation about sensing place in Accra's urban acoustemology. I wondered, did city residents hear the toads as a series of acoustic street-lamps sounding the trajectory of the road? Did toads have any relationship to ritual, as bells did in Europe, or to rhythm, like birds had to melody in the Papua New Guinea rainforest?

That's the long-winded back story that takes me to my first meeting with Nii Otoo in 2004, hearing him play with Nii Noi Nortey, then returning to Accra in 2005 to study bell playing and rhythm principles with him while recording his and Nii Noi's tribute to John Coltrane's *A Love Supreme*. When I returned to Ghana a year later to play with the band and resume lessons with Nii Otoo, I asked him to listen in to a *Bufo* soundscape I had created a few months earlier for a concert in New York. Taking his headphones off, he spoke a short but revelatory dot-connecting statement that I'm still trying to unpack. "You hear, Prof, it is like what I have been showing you in our music. The crickets are sounding everywhere like the bell with very strict time, and the kɔkɔdene [the toad's name in Ga, Nii Otoo's first language] are master drummers, making many rhythms that cross on top and sit below."

"Sounding everywhere," "crossing on top," "sitting below": how might the metaphoric space-time concepts that Nii Otoo used be shaping forces of musical imagination? A first revelation was the way Nii Otoo complicated my listening. I was focusing on the left-to-right, foreground-to-back, immediate-to-deep layers of rhythm that I could hear in the toad interactions. But he was juxtaposing all of that to the additional height-depth layers of the cricket pulsation. In effect his listening blew up a larger 3-D acoustic picture, making clear that the figure-ground relationships that I was discerning could all dissolve into another figure against another ground.

A second revelation was the spatial use of "crossing on top" to signify side-to-side changing rhythmic motion. "Crossing on top" is drummer-speak for additive improvisation, pattern embellishment or ornamentation layered as a topping or upper auditory layer onto the "sitting below" ground of intermediate and lower-level rhythm-defining pattern repetitions. "Sounding everywhere" took me into something both familiar from the rainforest and European pastoral, as well as the study of African percussion, namely, sound filling and thereby defining space as a density of simultaneous height-depth, foreground-background, side-to-side interplays.

Over time I considered and queried Nii Otoo's thoughts on "sounding everywhere," "crossing on top," and "sitting below," both as we were listening, and as we were playing. My desire deepened to communicate something about the intricacy and richness of his listening, his sonic knowing, his companion species ears-onto-the-world acoustemology. But I knew how much Nii Otoo felt in the background around Nii Noi's intellect and articulateness in English, knew the linguistic limitations of our interactions, knew how words were not the main medium of our exchange. And I knew too that other than playing and improvising, what Otoo most liked to do with me was listen to music. So I proposed that we collaborate on an experiment in listening and playback, one that might more directly and sensually listen in on his listening-in to *Bufo* toads, and with that, to use playing and recording, rather than verbal interchange, to represent the beneath-the-surface complexity of our acoustemological dialogue.

We started by listening together to toads, live and recorded, including sped-up and slowed-down versions of the recordings. Then I created a six-minute *Bufo* piece from my field recordings. The piece uses a real-time baseline while mixing multiple height and depth layers. It starts with the body-time metronome of me walking into the spatial surround of the *Bufo* sound-field and proceeds to allow numerous rhythmic interaction patterns to emerge in the density of repetitions. From the sounds of the crickets and my footsteps and breath, the recording thus opens up with metronomic pulse, that is, with grounds against which acoustic densities of the *Bufo* interactions can be figured.

Nii Otoo then listened in to this audio toadscape on headphones, feeding back his musical responses by overdubbing it ten distinct times, each overdub an original variation on a different instrument or set. What is revealed by this listening-in acoustemology is the relational epistemology of how Nii Otoo uses the toads simultaneously as a metronomic click-track, stimulus, calculator, and companion species musical interlocutor. His overdubs feed back the polyrhythmic math that reveal a simultaneous hearing in patterns of three against two, four against three, and six against four. They feed back the articulateness of hearing space-time interplays as "crossing on top," "sitting below," and "sounding everywhere." Some detail is required to make clear just what is at stake.

Nii Otoo improvised each variation in a complete take, without additional edits or overdubs. Variation 1 is performed on tenor and bass gyil xylophones. Variation 2 is performed on the gome, a seated bass drum played with heels and hands. Variation 3 is performed on a brekete, a snared bass drum played with palm and curved stick. Variation 4 is performed on the odonno, an under-arm pressure drum played with palm and a curved stick. Variation 5 is performed on gome, brekete, and odonno drums. Variation 6 is performed on electric guitar. Variation 7 is

41. *Bufo Variations,*
CD cover. *Art* © *2008*
Nicholas Wayo.

performed on an ashiwa, a seated rhythm-box bass with three metal keys. Variation 8 is performed on a mix of gome, two kpanlogo, and two apentemma drums, played with mallets and hands. Variation 9 is performed on the "gangofone," Nii Otoo's experimental rack of seven gangokui double bells, played with mallets and sticks.

Variation 10 is different. For our last session, Nii Otoo set up an APK combination of kpanlogo, gome, and brekete drums, hi-hat and ride cymbals, and with jazz brushes played not to the toads but to a previous overdubbing of the same toad track, played by the saxophonist Alex Coke, vocalist Tina Marsh, and myself on ashiwa rhythm box bass. For that trio recording Alex, Tina, and I simultaneously improvised to playback of the toad piece, but each in different rooms, and with no eye or ear contact, hearing only the toads in headphones, with no clue as to what each other was playing. Only afterward, at the recording console, with the toads removed, did we hear the live interplay of our collective conversation, and mix it into a trio track for the CD *It's Possible.*[20] Nii Otoo's overdub of that track listens in and feeds back on our trio composite track, adding an African free-jazz overhearing.

For the *Bufo Variations*[21] presentation CD, we begin with unaccompanied *Bufo* soundscape, continue with Nii Otoo's ten variations, and end with *Bufo* again, in a slightly different mix. On nine of the ten overdubs, the toad tracks are taken away so that Nii Otoo's total musical response is fully exposed. But to clarify the process midway, and heighten the listening experience, his Variation 6, for electric guitar, retains the ambient Bufo track so that you can hear him playing along with what was in his headphones.

Nii Otoo's improvisations sound the generative math of many rhythm families. They also map his histories of musical absorption, linking national, ethnic, regional, and over-the-border patterns that reach from Ghana into Nigeria, Togo, and Burkina Faso. They also head in the direction of jazz. In this way, Nii Otoo's cosmopolitan listening feedback speaks to how numerous Ghanaian rhythm families sound the historical and musical space and time of place, nation, and the interpenetration of international musics.

Consider some of these dimensions track-by-track through Nii Otoo's playback annotations and comments as we listened together to the composite recordings. His attention to detail reveals much about the complexities of his listening practice and how it feeds back into performance.

In Variation 1, for two gyil xylophones, Nii Otoo says the introduction has "the left hand walking" to my footsteps, and the right "coming in" to trill like the crickets. After the introduction, the left hand states patterns and the right embellishes. Playing the left with two mallets and the right with three, Otoo uses echoing and mirroring in a musical mimesis of the left-right, forward-backward sounding space of the frogs and the up-down sounding space of the crickets.

Listening to his composite, he called his playing "Kakraba Lobi" after the famous Ghanaian northern master player who was a frequent performer on national radio and much noted teacher in residence, 1962–87, at the Institute of African Studies, University of Ghana.[22] Nii Otoo never studied with Kakraba but said that after seeing him play he wanted to take the energy of his left-right hand interactions and do something less traditional with the technique, where independence of the hands can be spread to multiple instruments and improvisations against ostinatos played with a jazz touch. He credits his use of volume dynamics on this track to Nii Noi introducing him to the drumming of Elvin Jones and Rashied Ali. Ghanaian instrumentalists more typically play at one dynamic level start to finish.

In Variation 2, for gome bass drum, Nii Otoo begins with a Shai East rhythm associated with the inland Ga-Adangme, but in a jazz-inflected form. (Adangme is a language closely related to Ga, with both coastal and inland dialects and populations.) This transforms to *otofo*, another Ga-Adangme rhythm. Otoo notes hearing the bell pattern in his head throughout (in 12/8 the count is 1111323). Slowing down at two points, Otoo brings in rhythms of Bamaaya, the social music of the Dagbamba, widely heard at funerals and festivals in northern Ghana. While describing these rhythm morphs, Nii Otoo talked frequently about "topping it" in relation to all rhythms, meaning playing all the interacting dance parts and adding what jazz drummers call "fills" both connecting implied beats, and rhythmically underlining overt and nonovert connections.

In Variation 3, for brekete drum, Nii Otoo again uses Dagbamba rhythms from the North, *takai*, a royal dance for festive occasions, and *bamaaya*, and uses drum-speaking to interject phrases, "Turn yourself!," "Stand!," "Wave!," "Bless you!," "Strut like a king!," all in relation to rhythms associated with kings and princes.

In Variation 4, for odonno "talking" drum, Nii Otoo simultaneously plays drum, bell, and rattle parts from *tikali*, again from the North, music for the gods, a ceremonial style, mixed with sounds from Ipala, a Nigerian sounding of drums talking to gods, telling how to dance. The ending swells back to Ghana, with the familiar rhythm call of *Ghana muntie!*, "Listen Ghana!"

In Variation 5, for gome, brekete, and odonno drums, Nii Otoo uses *sisala*, another northern rhythm, which usually involves four drum parts. Here he plays five drum parts on three drums, no bell part, with the rhythm keyed to the timing of the dance. When I asked, at this point, why so many of the rhythm package choices came from the North, Nii Otoo said, "They are heavy, more heavy, spiritually. We feel them reaching down to us here. They are more heavy. Nigeria too, they are more heavy with spiritual music, dance music. We must take from them."

In Variation 6, for electric guitar, Nii Otoo plays off the metronomic pulse of crickets, using them as a background timeline bell. He calls the first song, an original for himself, "Otoo *kwao*," *kwao* short for *kweku*, the day name for those born on Wednesday. He calls the second song "Ɔdɔyewu," and says it is a re-versioning from 1960s guitar band rhythms he associates with the famous Kumasi guitarists Koo Nimo and Kwa Mensah.[23]

In Variation 7, the ashiwa box bass is played in the style of *otoome*, typically a large *tamalin*-type frame drum played by stick and hand.

42. Nii Otoo recording *Ghana Sea Blues*. Photograph © 2010 Steven Feld.

But Nii Otoo transfers the typically right hand on frame skin and left hand on frame shell pattern to alternations of hands on wood and hands on metal keys.

In Variation 8 for gome, kpanlogo, and apentemma drums, Nii Otoo begins with sticks on wood on the drum shells to indicate walking and shuffling sounds in the night, and then moves to a rolling and tumbling "thunder" sound that he says he picked up by listening to Elvin Jones and Rashied Ali from the late Coltrane period. Then he goes into fast *waka*, in a jazz form fusing elements of kpanlogo, with common pulse bell pattern (in 12/8 the count is 22323) and then develops a solo with different speed alternations, but coming back constantly to phrases that reference the underlying bell pattern.

In Variation 9, for gangofone, Nii Otoo uses (southern Ghana, Togo, and Benin) Ewe *atsiagbekor* rhythm, mixing two and three bell parts. Atsiagbekor is a well-known social dance form, its dance movements closely keyed to drum motifs. To shifting middle ground parts new "tops" are added in the form of what Nii Otoo calls "speaking" parts, with evocations of the phrases "Come here," "Stay here," "Where are you going?," "Just stay, don't move!," "I'll come back and see you!," "Stay on it, I'm with you!," "I'm going and coming!" Here Otoo plays with tympani mallets. The second half of the piece shifts from mallets to curved sticks and to Ga *kple*, a stately rhythm of spiritual songs, playing both bell and drum parts and "speaking on top."

While these improvisations speak to how Nii Otoo utilizes musical geography as a listening topography and history of ethnic-national-international cosmopolitan dialogues, they also take us into a distinctive musical conceptualization of variation and its basis in rhythm weaving. Could this be an intimation of musical infinity? Trying to speak more deeply with Nii Otoo about variation, I found myself playing different musical examples to elicit his thoughts as well as playing along with him on ashiwa box bass. While a respected master of both traditional Ghanaian percussion and popular and jazz musics, Nii Otoo has had little exposure to concepts of variation in Western European art music. As he had never heard the name Johann Sebastian Bach, I made the introduction, by way of *Goldberg Variations*.[24]

While completely self-taught, Nii Otoo has considerable knowledge of Western harmony and melodic motion from playing guitar and bass. Not surprisingly, he noticed the repeating patterns of Bach's bass line motion from one variation to the next, and at one point, stopped to sing the down and back line, G–F♯–E–D–B–C–D–G. But listening in to the density of Bach's keyboard music, Otoo's main auditory focus was on something more familiar in West Africa, the interdependence created by independent yet interlocking left and right hands. Nii Otoo asked me to pause the recorder several times to relisten to the left-right and front-back play on the double manual keyboard. He greatly enjoyed much of what he heard. All the same, it was the harpsichord's shimmering timbres that he responded to most immediately while hearing Bach's music, qualities he likened to the snare of the brekete drum, the rasping interplay of crickets and toads, and the buzz of his xylophone's resonators.

Take a moment to fantasize what the *Goldberg Variations* might sound like had Bach been born in Ghana, gone to sleep each night listening to *Bufo* toads, and devoted himself to the mastery of polyrhythms with the same dedication he showed to harmony. One of Nii Otoo's variations addresses this fantasy in a rather good-humored way, using tenor and bass gourd-resonated gyil xylophones in a G major pentatonic, the instruments tuned G – A – B – D – E, Nii Otoo realizing G major as *Goldberg*'s home key. Nii Otoo plays the left one-octave bass xylophone with two mallets and the right three-octave tenor xylophone (one octave overlapping) with three. As in the other variations, you'll hear his interdependent interlocking as a "crossing on top" and "sitting below," both in the ways he separates and links the two instruments, and the ground-to-figure ways ostinato layers and rhythmic phrase repetitions intersect fragments of newly emergent melodic improvisation.

Nii Otoo has never touched or even seen a double manual keyboard, but Bach's extensive use of hand crossing was intuited by him solely on the basis of the performance recording.[25] You can also hear a great deal of play between three and two in Otoo's rhythmic parsings, and as is well known, *Goldberg*'s grand ternary form, with canon in ascent every third variation from numbers 3 to 27, is matched by contrastive binary symmetries on the multiples two, four, eight, sixteen, and thirty-two.

In his *Bach: The Goldberg Variations*, Peter Williams[26] notes many of the work's recurring patterns, and some of his phraseology stands in perfectly in a descriptive lexicon of Nii Otoo's improvisational playfulness: angular lines and inversion (page 56), anticipation in the bass (57), "cascading" and disappearance becoming reappearance (61), "patterns crossing, chasing and coming together" (68), "lines appear to go their own way" (74), "many tied notes over the bar-lines" (re Variations 18 and 19, 75), "bubbling lines testing the player's hand-positioning" (76), and "lines tumbling over each other, answering or running against each other, both up and down" (79).

Through the additional detour of Western art music variation, *Bufo Variations* thus collaboratively engages two overlapping histories of listening in and feeding back. The history that connects Nii Otoo's listening feedback to my interspecies Papua New Guinea rainforest and European bell research underscores ways numerous musical practices and styles around the world have been, and continue to be, inspired by rhythms and textures of the natural world. The other genealogy relates such inspiration to possibilities for complex audio-environmental mimesis in lineages of Western and non-Western musical experimentalism.[27]

Beyond this, Nii Otoo and I have, often at his urging, listened to many different kinds of music together. Like Ghanaba and Nii Noi, Nii Otoo is a voracious listener to recorded music, these days totally connected to his iPod. I asked him how the habit started.

"My father loved music," he said. "Yeah, always always we had music, wind-up power first, then valve [tube] radiogram with turntable, then reel-to-reel, four-track, cassette. He bought Ghana music, Tempos, Ramblers, King Bruce, Koo Nimo, and international, Jim Reeves [he sings a bit of melody from 'I Love You Because'], jazz too. You know, Prof, one day I brought Nii Noi to the family house to meet my father. And you know what he says? 'Hey, wow, I know you, I used to see you in the record shop!' True! Before he knew the man's face as my father, Nii Noi had seen my father. So he knew him. I'm telling you, my father loved having records very much. Now he is blind. When I am at the house and I play Ghana music from my iPod he is yelling, 'Hey, what are you doing with my records?' and I say, 'No, it is not your records, the white man has these songs in his computer and we study them in our work.' And he says, 'You lie, Otoo, you have my records now and are selling them! Come and play them for me!' " (Huge laughter.)

In sessions of listening together, Nii Otoo has asked me most about the music of John Coltrane, whose drummers, Elvin Jones and Rashied Ali, have brought him much inspiration. A piece Nii Otoo adores is Coltrane's "One Up, One Down," in the thirty-minute live version that features a ten-minute-long, rhythmically ferocious duo by Coltrane and Jones.[28] One time, as we were listening to this, the recording came to the place just before the band comes back in with the final head. Just then Nii Otoo said, "I'm hearing him sweat, Prof, I'm hearing him pour libation on the drums."

Nii Otoo is familiar with sweat. He takes it to be a deep expression of the spiritual merger of a drummer and his drums, the workout libation that seals their bond. You can see this in the video sequence of Nii Otoo sweating onto his drum skins in the *Accra Trane Station* film. Sweat, of course, indexes the energy and bodily engagement of work, the exhibition of its passion, its seriousness. Otoo told me that the sight of sweat was also part of his first encounter with Elvin Jones, when Nii Noi showed him some magazine and LP album photos of Jones at play. What he saw and heard, in effect, was a synaesthetic image of the bodily authenticity of the drummer's spiritual transport. And among iconic images of jazz drummers, on LP and CDs and in magazines, Jones is most often depicted equally dripping with sweat and with some portion of a cigarette drooping from his lips.[29]

Elvin Jones joined the John Coltrane Quartet in 1960, and for about five years played with the group that included the bassist Jimmy Garrison and the pianist McCoy Tyner. Among many highlights of that period, the musicality of the drums was a critical part of the Coltrane quartet sound, increasingly shifting the concept of drumming from accompaniment to constant conversation. Jones's playing was marked by an exuberance and sustained stamina rarely seen or heard in jazz drumming. His approach to polyrhythm, sound mass, and timbral dynamics, and his virtuosic use of sticks, brushes, and timpani mallets became grand dimensions of the quartet's swelling reputation.

The Coltrane quartet not only developed 3/4 time far beyond its historical antecedents in the so-called jazz-waltz genre; on songs like "My Favorite Things" they simultaneously played 3/4 with and against 4/4 in intense and at times overwhelmingly dense ways never heard before in jazz.[30] The pianist McCoy Tyner, who started as a drummer, brought formidable left-hand rhythmic vitality to the practice of chord comping, interlocking with bassist Jimmy Garrison's thick and stringy percussive attack. But Elvin Jones was the engine whose steam took them all way beyond the swing-time of forward-propelled ties-over bar-lines and endless dotted quarter notes. His multi-gestalt three against two and four against three laid mesmerizing polyrhythmic carpet for Coltrane, whose spiritual search reached into searing and soaring acoustic highs during their duos.

The sweat that captivated Nii Otoo in Jones's playing indexed this intersecting aesthetics of density and intensity. Over and over again, this is what brought expression to Otoo's face and words into his mouth. Listening one day to Elvin's brush-work behind the bassist Richard Davis and the tenor saxophonist Frank Foster on "Shiny Stockings," from their record *Heavy Sounds*, Otoo burst into exclamation: "You hear it! The guy is terrible! I tell you, Prof, the guy is terrible terrible! Wow! He will mess you up! He has so many things going just on snare. He is taking you this way and that way [at the] same time. Oh! This man is too much, terrible terrible, I tell you!!"[31]

What Otoo was so terribly excited about was the complex and ever-densifying layers of textures, rhythmic figures, and interactive patterns connecting the movement of the brushes across snares and toms and

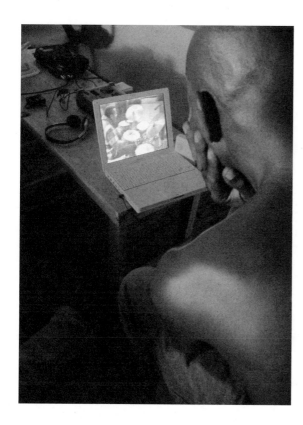

43. Nii Otoo watches video of Elvin Jones with John Coltrane. *Photograph © 2005 Steven Feld.*

cymbals. The practice is parallel to Otoo's own xylophone playing or drumming, where independent but interlocked hand and foot combinations create dense gestalts in which new multiples or divisions emerge over underlying cycles. It was while listening together like this that Nii Otoo's richest and most engaged responses would come to the fore, zeroing in on something poignant about his way of listening.

"Otoo, tell me about those first times listening with Nii Noi to Elvin Jones."

"He worked hard to make his drums speak, Prof. You know it, our word *kasa*, to speak, that's what drums must do, they must speak to people. You know our mobile phone company, the one called Kasapa? Their symbol is the bell gangokui. When the phone rings it is the bell sounding [sings the bell ringtone: low-low-high]. Drums are like mobile phones, they are for speaking. So that's what I heard, the way Elvin Jones was speaking, working the drums, working to make his drums speak."

Nii Otoo's sense of a work-and-sweat connection to Elvin Jones devel-

44. From left, Nii Otoo Annan with Rashied Ali at the Outpost Performance Space, Albuquerque, New Mexico. *Photograph* © *2007 Steven Feld.*

oped over years of drum-speak interanimation in Nii Noi's bands. But it became amplified, indeed locally mythologized, when Nii Noi and then others, remarked on Nii Otoo's uncanny physical resemblance to Jones.

"Yeah, I can see that, I can see that," Rashied Ali said to me, as I told him my story of first meeting Nii Otoo, introduced to me by Nii Noi, with a hearty laugh and riff about him looking like Elvin Jones. "Goose bumps came over me," I told Rashied. "That's sweet, man, that's really sweet," Rashied said, as he signed a copy of *Interstellar Space*, his 1967 duet record with John Coltrane,[32] over to Nii Noi for his Anyaa Arts Library. "It's a beautiful thing," he said, lifting his head and looking up at the three of us, "the way we're all connected, you know, the way we come together in music. I love that, having Africa that close."

Nii Otoo and I also spent considerable time listening to Rashied Ali's 1965–67 recordings with Coltrane. Nii Otoo's favorite track is the duo "Jupiter Variations" from *Interstellar Space*, which features plenty of multidirectional "crossing on top," "sitting below," "sounding everywhere." Sitting next to Nii Otoo during the performance by Rashied Ali's quintet at the 2007 Outpost Coltrane Festival that brought us all together in New Mexico, I could feel his excitement. After the first set, he gushed:

"Prof, he's giving us strength. He is pouring libation as an elder, opening the road. He's giving me strength to follow."

This way of connecting drum work in sweat and libation as fluid strength now takes us to the liquid site Nii Otoo claims as his spiritual source: the ocean. I got a taste of this sensibility in regular visits to Nii Otoo at his family home in Korle Gonno. Walking the beach there one day to see some fishing boats, we came upon a ramshackle fragment of a building. There we encountered its superintendent, a man known as Ataa Jata, "(elder) lion," and his shrine, Mɔ Bɔ Bɛ, roughly, "don't even think about feeling sorrow."

Ataa Jata explained that he had erected the shrine several years earlier when he began serendipitously receiving light-skinned dolls, doll parts, and animal toys from the ocean. He introduced us to each one, well propped up in its place atop a stack of old car tires, by name, from the first one he received, the one-armed blue-eyed plastic doll torso "Hello Sir," to some of the most recent, like the terry cloth rag dolls he called "Ginger," and "Mr. and Mrs. Brown."

45. "Hello Sir" at Ataa Jata's seaside shrine, Korle Gonno.
Photograph © 2007 Steven Feld.

Nii Otoo told Ataa Jata that we would be walking, and on our return would meet him at the bar to make an offering to the shrine. But Ataa Jata insisted on joining us, and did. Walking down the beach together at the water's edge, and just fifteen minutes later, by amazing chance, he was gifted, just before our eyes, with a washed-in white-faced terry cloth doll from the ocean. Ataa Jata told us that the water spirits were aware of our visit and had signaled by sending this messenger, whose name was evidently "Mr. Steven." I was then called upon to open my wallet and send one of the young boys accompanying us back to the bar for an appropriate portion of *akpeteshie*, the local gin.

When we returned to the shrine, the small bottle was there, and Ataa Jata emplaced "Mr. Steven" with his other dolls and performed a rite of cleansing and acknowledgment, pouring libation, reciting rhythmically, and spitting streams of gin to anoint the dolls before drinking himself, and pouring the last of it on the ground.

But I could tell that Nii Otoo wanted to get going and was uncomfortable with the way the shrine keeper was trying to hang on to us, as when he insisted on coming on our shoreline walk. As we left the beachfront and walked down the road toward his family compound, Nii Otoo told me that Ataa Jata was a legendary local thief, that I should protect myself spiritually and otherwise when in his presence, and never go back to the shrine unaccompanied. When, the next year, I asked Nii Otoo if we might visit the shrine again, he told me that it had been burned down. And just six months later, Nii Otoo told me that in the course of an attempted robbery Ataa Jata had been beaten and cut within an inch of his life. He lay near death for three months and only barely recovered.

But later Nii Otoo explained how offerings like the libation for "Mr. Steven" renew and reinvigorate spiritual and material connections. They repay old favors and gifts while signing the contract meant to ensure future ones. Such rituals are a way of holding the world in the balance, performing for renewal. This was when Otoo first told me that one goes to the water "to get an answer." Indeed, he and others later confirmed that spiritualists often tell their clients to go and sit at the water and the answer will come as their mind clears with the sounds of the water coming in and out. When one is confused, needs guidance, it is by going to the water for some time that the answer will come.

The water provides, Otoo told me, but one must obey to receive. If you are always disobedient and making trouble, the water can take you, can finish you. In fact, he was sure this is what happened to Ataa Jata, that the ruin of his shrine, and ultimately his own ruin, was brought on by a series of repeated offenses at the site and in the presence of powerful water spirits, until the transgression was just too much.

This encounter led to conversations about various powerful experiences, some of them gifts, some of them tests, that have touched Nii Otoo at the ocean. One was the arrival, in 2008, of twins, his last-born children, a boy named Oko and girl named Akwele. After their birth, Otoo, a Christian, did not follow custom, which demands a consultation with a "fetish priest" to learn where the children had come from. Life became tense, and he had disturbing dreams. Nii Otoo's mother, also a Christian, felt that custom must be respected lest some deeper trouble follow.

Almost two years later, following repeated troubles in the family, a ritual consultation was organized. Libations were poured, eggs broken, fowl sacrificed, money offered, voices emerged through the medium. It was revealed that the twins were requesting acknowledgment that they came from a rock cluster at the Korle Gonno beach, near the edge of the water and not far from Ataa Jata's shrine, two stones prominently situated together but divided by a noticeable gap. It was revealed that the stones saw Otoo when he was singing, drumming, and drinking at the beach with his wife. The stones loved him as he made them laugh and gave them music, and they reciprocated by giving him twins. But somehow, even without knowing that the twins came from the stones, Otoo knew to avoid their proximity. And it was luck that he did, as the consultation also revealed that care must be taken not to step into the passage between the two stones, or a life can be taken back into the waters.

Stories like this one introduced me to the world of water spirits and their meanings in Nii Otoo's community. These spirits always present a dual nature, water, on the one hand, is critically important to sustenance and gift: food, drink, trade, transport, and contact; but, on the other hand, water is equally associated with misfortune: drowning, floods, intrusion, and invasion. This dualism, in all its practical and symbolic senses, has long been intertwined for Ga-speaking fishing people, inhabitants of the coastal area that is now Accra.

Nii Otoo, like his fisherfolk predecessors and contemporaries, knows the powers of Nai, the highest ranking god of seas, just as he knows and drums for rain, which, like water in general, is life-giving, as it nourishes

46. The twin rocks at Korle Gonno beach. *Photograph © 2010 Steven Feld.*

plants, the lowest but still critical member of the hierarchy of life forms: plants, animals, humans, divine, supreme. Water, the sweat of the skies and earth, pours onto the land both ways, in endless libation-like waves, cleansing by giving while taking. This is why Nii Otoo indicates that water as spirit is linked to drumming as spiritual exercise.

Drummers, he told me, know what fishermen know. Give yourself to the water and it will reward you with nourishment and power. But beware, don't fish or drum on the wrong days, or at the wrong times, or in the wrong ways. Regularly give back libation, work, and prayer.

I'm reminded here too of how, talking me through the process of making drums, Nii Otoo verbally paused at least seven times to mention precise moments for pouring libation, from selecting and cutting the tree, to carving the shell, to procuring and affixing the head, to drying and tuning it. Again the parallel to fishing is considerable: one must follow sequences of actions precisely lest wrong signals are made, signals that could bring on material and spiritual difficulty or reprisal. What is acknowledged here is the ever-interconnected spiritual presence of human, ancestral, and environmental forces.

Ethnographic studies of Ga rituals in the 1930s by M. J. Field and in the

1960s by Marion Kilson substantially underscore these matters; as Kilson writes: "An aim of all libations . . . is to invoke the presence of divine beings and ancestral shades."[33] Libation, the pouring of a water-clear alcoholic drink on the ground while reciting a prayer, is widely practiced in Ghana, common to activities as diverse as rites of passage, drum making, preparing land for farming, telling stories, political meetings, and visits to elders. Pouring libation often acknowledges the presence of the dead among the living, announcing and inviting continued participation of the ancestors in critical undertakings by present generations.[34]

Arriving direct from Accra to John F. Kennedy Airport in October 2009 for the New York premiere of his *Bufo Variations* at the Ear to the Earth Festival, it didn't take Nii Otoo but a moment to tell me, with his wink, that he brought "duty free." Playfully waiting just the seconds it took to get the questioning look he wanted from me, he blurted out, "Akpeteshie, man, in the xylophone case!" (Big laughter and finger-pop shake.) I knew

47. Me filming as Nii Otoo pours libation for Rashied Ali at the Village Vanguard, New York. *Photograph © 2009 Michael Motley.*

what was on his mind. We had discussed it the past August when I first called him, just after returning home from Accra, to relay the sad news of Rashied Ali's passing.

By chance we had spent some time during my last Accra weeks that July listening together to John Coltrane's 1966 LP *Live at the Village Vanguard Again*.[35] Otoo liked the LP's original cover image, of John and Alice Coltrane, Pharoah Sanders, Jimmy Garrison, and a very young Rashied Ali standing under the marquee and awning of the famous 7th Avenue South jazz club. Having met both Pharoah Sanders in Accra in 1992 (while playing in Nii Noi's Mau Mau Muziki, which opened for Pharoah's concerts) and then Rashied Ali in Albuquerque in 2007, Nii Otoo was full of the pride of musical connections. "When I come to New York I want to go to the place," he said. "We will," I seconded, as he completed his thought, "And pour."

A few nights after settling into Greenwich Village and rehearsing for his upcoming performance, Nii Otoo and I went to the Village Vanguard and heard a great trio set by the pianist Bill Charlap, bassist Kenny Washington, and the mightily impressive drummer Lewis Nash. We sat right next to the drum kit, Otoo's eyes studying Nash's every move with the deepest concentration and pleasure. The next afternoon we returned to the Vanguard, Nii Otoo carrying a generous portion of his local akpeteshie in a small plastic Evian bottle. And standing in front of the Vanguard's red double doors, under the marquee and awning where Rashied Ali stood in that 1966 photograph, Nii Otoo poured libation and prayed for the continuation of his spiritual journey.

"Rashied Ali, oh, sorry sorry sorry . . . I don't know what to say, man. I'm here pouring for you to drink, here at our ancestor's place, Charlie Parker, John Coltrane, Pharoah Sanders, Elvin Jones. Come and drink from what I'm pouring. Rest in peace man, rest in peace. *Tswa! Tswa! Tswa! Omanye aba!* [Invocation: 'Let the message come'!] *Yao!* [Response: 'It is received!']."

Again and again Nii Otoo's message at the seaside, like his message at the Village Vanguard, was the same: include the ancestors in all your thoughts and acts, that is Mother Water's wish, that you pour; don't cross it or she will take you down under the waves.

These, of course, are the jazzy "on top" waves that have been swirling around the Black Atlantic for centuries, everywhere washing in and out with one of its most enduring figures, "Mami Wata," known through West and Central Africa, and the diaspora in the Caribbean, Brazil, and North America. Followed on her many routes and documented deeply at multiple shrines by the art historian Henry John Drewal, the figure of Mami Wata is typically a long-haired humanoid mermaid, often wrapped with a snake. In all instances beautiful but capricious, Mami is likely to harm believers if taboos are violated, but also likely to help and provide for true followers. One of the most ubiquitous and enduring presences in black diasporic popular culture in all media, with an ever-expanding set of rites and interpretations from mermaid cult parades to cyberspace shrines, Mami Wata can be associated equally with terrifying abduction and with many prosperous returns. A figure that has as many regular detractors as celebrants, Mami Wata's representations have proliferated anew in Ghana, despite the damning condemnation of Pentacostal and evangelical Christianity's everlasting light.[36]

Ghana, of course, is a very potent place to reflect on stories of what the water gives and what it takes. Here, thirteen castles dot the shoreline between Accra and Sekondi, mostly built in the second half of the seventeenth century, by Portuguese, British, Dutch, Danes, and Swedes for sale and transport of Africans. The term "castle," or even "fort," rather too politely inscribes the legacy of regular attacks, fighting, and takeovers at what were more obviously dungeons and factories of the slave trade. Over a four-hundred-plus-year period, on the order of ten million people were forcibly taken from Africa, as many as four million of them in the fifty-year period from 1760 to 1810, by which time most European nations had abolished the trade.[37]

The exhibit *Mami Wata: Arts for Water Spirits in Africa and Its Diasporas*, which toured the United States in 2008–9, traced this dispersal along the tributaries of Mami's fluid routes. The catalogue essay by the exhibit's curator, Henry John Drewal, pinpoints early origin sites and then the centuries-later African dissemination of a nineteenth-century German print depicting a light-skinned, non-European circus snake charmer with a waterfall of densely dark hair draping a long dress and fish tail. Drewal also details the later layers of interwoven South Asian iconic influences introduced by a next wave of merchant immigrants seeking their fortunes in Africa.

By chance, I visited the Mami Wata exhibit, a cumulative Black Atlantic Afro-float, just after it arrived at Washington's National Museum of African Art, and at a propitious time, powerfully attested by the spontaneous on-site shrines that emplaced mini-memorabilia of the recent election of Barack Obama to the presidency under, over, or alongside coins, candles, and cards, shells, soaps, and scents. The suggestion was palpable: just when you think it is almost impossible, something or someone amazing can wash up on your shoreline and renew your sense of struggle and salvation.

Like Mami Wata's followers in Washington, D.C., who got right into the groove, Nii Otoo does not take such ideas lightly. As he tells it, for years he played and he prayed, and for his service and his faith the water brought him a pair of light-skinned dolls who offered work and money. One was me. The other was the artist Virginia Ryan, who over a five-year period in Accra made two thousand nine-by-eleven-inch constructions called *Castaways*, sculptural paintings transformed from washed-up materials collected on Ghana's shorelines in a long-term meditation on the ocean's lost-and-found legacy of desire and displacement, sustenance and slavery. Nii Otoo assisted Ryan by organizing and working with crews of children in his beach community to collect, comb through, and categorize some of her *prima materia*.[38]

In 2007, the year of Ghana's fiftieth anniversary of independence and the two-hundredth anniversary of the abolition of slavery by the British Parliament, an exhibit of seven hundred of Ryan's *Castaways* was mounted at the Whitworth Gallery in Manchester, England. The exhibit was accompanied by my audio installation, the watery sound of a continuous and seamless mix of eight separate spatial stereo sound tracks recorded at the water's edge, in the ocean, in and behind rocks and rock pools at Anomabo beach, one of Ryan's key collecting sites, close to a slaving fort. As viewers move toward the waves of Ryan's *Castaways* mounted in tight rows on the gallery wall, the ocean sounds roll in from behind in surround sound, inviting sensuous engagement with the beach as a contact zone, where what washes out and what washes in can be imagined as the detritus of history in a huge seashell, the Gold Coast becoming the Black Atlantic.

As an additional installation accompaniment to *Castaways*, I produced a DVD, *Where Water Touches Land*. The video consists of time manipulations of multiple visual elements, from still photographs of the shoreline's sand and water formations, to portraits of individual *Castaways*, to video of Ryan at Anomabo beach collecting washed-in objects, and in her Accra studio working on composing and transforming them into *Castaways*. The video uses as key soundtrack material ambiences from

48. Recording at Anomabo beach, where water touches land, for
The Castaways Project. Photograph © *2007 Nana Agazi.*

the *Anomabo Shoreline* recording. But it adds additional ambient sounds
mixed with string, xylophone, and percussion improvisations by Nii
Otoo together with Nii Noi Nortey.

When I returned to Ghana in June 2007 from the installation and
opening in Britain, Nii Otoo, particularly proud of his participation in
this project and its material and musical connections to the water, asked
to see the installation photographs. "I like this one," he said looking at a
picture of some students in the exhibit hall. What is striking in that image
is that the students are not standing at the wall looking at the *Castaways*
but sitting in front of them on the gallery floor, as if relaxing on the beach,
the visual and acoustic waves rolling in. "They are sitting below them and
the ocean is sounding on top everywhere, I hear it, crossing."

Crossing lands and waters himself in the 1990s, Nii Otoo left Ghana
twice, for tours and residencies with sponsored Ghanaian cultural drum
dance ensemble groups in Switzerland and England. Although surrounded by Ghanaian musicians, he found Europe difficult, first because
of social isolation, second because of musical alienation.

"In London we played the same thing every concert, every rehearsal, every time, same thing same thing. Tradition. But me, I always want to learn tradition and then add and change, I always want to make jazz." Here Nii Otoo uses the term "jazz" to refer to the expansion of traditional knowledge and practice, to mean layered addition, modification, creative explorations that move the familiar into the unknown and back. For him "jazz" is something that fits "on top" of tradition, namely embellishments, ornamentations, additive coatings that densify ground with emergent figure. What was striking in Nii Otoo's comment was its experimental and cosmopolitan embrace of expansiveness, and his use of the word "jazz" to announce it. Here's someone who is surely more a master of deep ritual traditions than Ghanaba or Nii Noi, but who, just like them, is very clear about not confusing the concept of "tradition" with mere repetition.

Nii Otoo traveled later as well, to perform with Accra Trane Station in Italy in spring 2007, and then with Nii Noi and me to the States twice, the following summer and fall. While treated with warm respect and admiration by audiences and new acquaintances on each occasion, the fact of good compensation opened up a major contradiction. Again we're back to class issues. Nii Otoo was worried about being perceived at home as having received big money abroad. To protect himself from multiple familial and fraternal claims on his earnings, he told people that he was not paid for the work. Nii Noi caught wind of this and was deeply insulted, feeling the implication to be that it was he, as group leader, who had slighted Otoo, when in fact they were paid equally.

Perhaps I contributed to the miscommunication, too. The U.S. visas I managed to acquire (with all the post-9/11 difficulties) for Nii Noi and Nii Otoo were in the cultural exchange category, and marked "no paid performances." I instructed Otoo to be very careful if questioned at customs and immigration on return, and to tell any inquiring officer that he had not been paid for his work in the States, that he had simply received expenses, with compensation to come later in the form of local resources (instruments, equipment, work) upon my return to Accra.

In any case, the entanglements of these stories contributed to a breakdown of communication that suspended the Accra Trane Station project in 2008. Trying to work these problems out with Nii Otoo brought us back, again and again, to the financial complexities of fitting cosmopolitan musical ideals onto existing class structures.

"You see, Prof, people always ask me same thing, always same thing:

'How much does the white man take?' And I say, 'Listen, the white man takes no money when we play, the money comes to us, to Nii Noi and me, and we split it and give something to Agazi for transport, for equipment we need.' And they say, 'No, you are foolish, the white man is working with you and you get the work because of him so he must be taking the big money like a boss and paying you small. He is tricking you.' And I say, 'Oh, Charlie, you don't understand correct ways. The white man is just musician like us, but because he is professor his school pays good work money, so he takes nothing on top when we make performances. That is how we are working. You foolish people are just sitting and waiting for the boss to chop everything and pay you small-o. That is Ghana way. We are working fine, international way.' "

"And what do they say when you tell them that, Otoo?"

"I tell them like that and they say, 'Oh, Otoo you are the foolish one, it is not like that. You are still poor-o! How do the whites get so rich from us if it is like that?' So me, Prof, I can't explain it, they only know the local way. Everything is chiefs on top and small boys underneath, *eh hehh*, bosses on top and small boys underneath. That's how they chop. They are only thinking one way. That's all they have to think."[39]

On my return to Accra just after Nii Otoo's New York visit to perform *Bufo Variations*, I overheard him recall his travels several times to mutual friends, and the idiom was, as ever, class-laced work pride, coupled with the pleasures and protections of his "working fine, international way."

"Charlie, you see," he told Agazi one day as we set up for a recording session, "even the China restaurant people they know you, when you play they know you, yeah, and so they bring food free, correct. Yeah, they like to hear it, man, so they dash you small [give a little tip], oh nice food Charlie, nice food, plenty. They are shaking my hand, shaking Prof's hand, shaking Jefferson's hand, fine, oh, everything fine. Correct ways."

What Otoo was narrating there to engineer Agazi comes from a dinner scene at Joe's Shanghai Restaurant in New York's Chinatown, where we dined with the drummer Jefferson Voorhees and close friends.

"These are drum sticks! Human beings eat with forks!" Otoo said with his wickedly playful smile as he sat down and unwrapped the chopsticks placed in front of him. I turned to ask the waiter to bring a fork and by the time my neck came back around to the table Otoo had the chopsticks in hand and was drumming away on the tabletop of glasses, cups, and plates, not just tapping, but drumming, really drumming. Feeling somewhat self-conscious about being the only non-Asians in the restaurant, and wishing to avoid any sort of scene, I told the waiters starting to hover and comment that Otoo was a famous drummer visiting from Africa, and before we knew it all the waiters were gravitating to our table, joining the laughter, one even delivering a metal pot from the kitchen to add to Otoo's drum set.

In time the brief drumming scene broke up into rounds of applause, laughs, and many smiles. We enjoyed our dinner, and were then pleasantly surprised by complimentary desserts delivered with many bows to Otoo. And as we left, our thanks were again greeted by much bowing to Otoo from the wait staff, and a departure gift of some dozen sets of chopsticks in Joe's Shanghai wrappers.

"Nice one!" Otoo said as he walked outside and lit a cigarette, satisfied that he could even draw an admiring crowd in a foreign restaurant. "Yeah! Nice one! Correct!"

Just as elated and exuberant as Otoo could be in local or remotely cosmopolitan settings like that, he could equally turn depressive and desperate at home when the topic was money, an emotional register that I came to see regularly each time before departing Accra for a period of months. On one such occasion I added some dash money on top of Otoo's regular salary and asked as I was leaving if I could help out with the cost of some instruments for the drumming school I helped him set up to make some money while I was away. Much as I understood the class-laden rhetoric, I was still shocked by his response:

"Instruments? No. To help me Prof, I prefer a machine for grinding corn, a machine for grinding pepper. If I have no money, if I have no gigs, I can still grind my corn and make *banku*. With one corn grinder, one flour grinder, people can make a house, yeah, I tell you, there are people in the market who got the money to build a house just like that, because you work every day, there is money coming. Music there is no money every day, just money coming few gig days. So one day money, many days no money. Only when you are here I am working working. When you are gone I suffer for work, I tell you, I suffer, with music I only suffer."

So where are we now?

The currents of Guy Warren/Ghanaba's musical cosmopolitanism pulsed over Ghana's shore in overlapping prewar, wartime, and postwar colonial and postcolonial musical waves that washed jazz, calypso, highlife,

Afro-beat, Handel, and European classics into the spiritual flow of African ritual drum languages, Buddhism, Christianity, and Islam, not to mention the ever-present political flow of wartime spying, British-American dialectics, Nkrumaist cold-war social humanism, and Ghanaian anticolonial nationalism.

The currents of Nii Noi Nortey's musical cosmopolitanism washed over Ghana's shores in overlapping Black Atlantic waves that splashed diasporic reggae and black American avant-garde jazz onto postcolonial and Pan-Africanist movements from the United Kingdom, Caribbean, and Africa. That contact made acoustically fluid the intermingled struggles for African and diasporic freedoms, American civil rights, and U.K. black British multiculturalisms. The figures of Bob Marley, Fela Kuti, and John Coltrane swam and surfaced in the same cosmopolitan pools as those of W. E. B. Du Bois, Marcus Garvey, Malcolm X, and Frantz Fanon. Nii Noi not only made a place for them all in sound, sculpture, and speech, but poured their story like libation into the deeper historical ocean that linked the seventeenth- and eighteenth-century Asante empire to the eighteenth- and nineteenth-century European empire, through the figure of a black Beethoven.

Even if Nii Otoo Annan's story has none of this fabulously far-and-wide, intensely intellectualized musical-cultural-political synthesis, it is an equally compelling tale of cosmopolitan transport. Gifted with both natural pitch and ambidexterity, Nii Otoo's spiritual sensitivity, mastery of polyrhythm, and love of improvisational play takes him fluidly from toads, crickets, and water to an uncanny ease in diverse traditional and popular musical styles, on a range of African and Western percussion and melody instruments, into the vanguard of free jazz drumming, and even a little fun with Bach. His drum kit alone, mixing instruments from several coastal, northern, and southern regions of Ghana together with jazz cymbals as well as techniques of stick, brush, mallet, and hand play, speaks volumes about cosmopolitan imagination and practice. Yet this musical expansiveness is always tensely positioned in relation to a powerful countergrip, the ever-reproductive contractions that come with limitations of education, the strictures of class. That's what makes this so different from more privileged cosmopolitanisms, while so resonant to how the desire for expansive agency plays out in musical experiment that, just as for Ghanaba and Nii Noi, sails the spirit sea of emplaced acoustemology.

FOURTH CHORUS, SHOUT TO THE GROOVE

Por Por

From Honk Horns to Jazz Funerals

via New Orleans

49. Vice holding por por horn to tsolorley in La.
Photograph © 2005 Steven Feld.

The story of Nii Otoo Annan's *Bufo Variations* considered musical intersections of working-class and environmental spiritualism. Those issues expand considerably in the story of how a union of Accra lorry and minibus drivers makes ritual funerary music with squeeze-bulb truck horns. Parallel to the way I came to sense Nii Otoo's musical relations with toads and with the ocean, I came to hear these car horns resounding an acoustemological triangle linking place to cosmology through sound. The transit in this case fuses horn honking to the environmental time-space called "the road," and the pervasive spirit world of its past and present passage.

"Por por" is the name of both the honk horn instrument and the music invented for and with it by Accra's La Drivers Union. The story takes us into a world of multiply intertwined materialities, from trucks and mini-buses called trotros, to the work, wealth, and pride of union drivers, and to the ritual symbolism of their now-antique squeeze-bulb horns. It is about how those horns were transformed from signal devices on the trotro vehicles to musical instruments off them, and how drivers employ those instruments to perform memorial music for driver funerals. It is about funerals as the spiritual mega- and meta-genre of Ga life in Accra, a multiple-media layering of speech, song, ritual wailing, instrumental dirges, music, dance, libations, parades, and displays of cloth, documents, uniforms, insignia, paintings, signs, photographs, souvenirs, food, drink, and coffins.[1]

The funeral as the main arena of por por performance is revealed in my film *A Por Por Funeral for Ashirifie*, which follows the events of a band member's funeral with a telling intimacy. From the performance of musical condolences for the immediate family to several days of honking and singing in trucks and hearses, at the mortuary, in street parades, at the wake, at the funeral services, and at the gravesite, the por por band's honk-out as musical undertakers and joyful celebrants works to console and soothe sadness, but equally to energize and animate community participation, in particular drawing out dancers who pump imaginary tires while strutting the streets.

To explore the fusion of por por's acoustic and material culture, I'll start by reprising a stream of conversations I had with the late Annette Weiner, a formidable presence in the anthropology of material culture studies whose feminist reinterpretation of Bronislaw Malinowski's Trobriand Islands ethnography opened up significant new vistas in exchange theory for Papua New Guinea and beyond.[2]

In the 1980s, when we both worked on Papua New Guinea funerary arts, Annette was a generous critic of my work on Bosavi women's funerary wailing, vocal polyphony, and intertextuality. In that context we talked about how New Guinea mortuary rituals perform the public emotional business of dealing with death at the crossroads of enmity and sociality, distress and solidarity. We talked about the varieties of funerary exchange and the ways objects stand in and for persons. We talked about how person-ness and thing-ness are endlessly entangled in the life-

50. *Por Por Funeral,* DVD cover. *Art © 2009 Nicholas Wayo.*

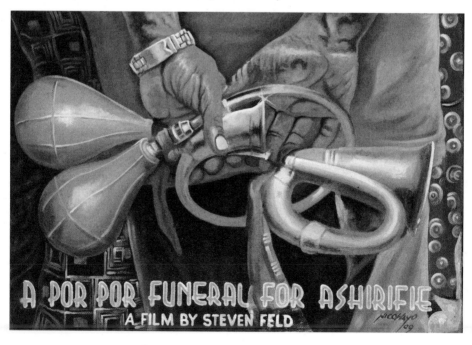

worlds of Papua New Guineans, as she so deeply documented in her Trobriand Islands ethnographic work.

I told Annette that the absence of material object exchanges at Bosavi funerals led me to think about how the use of words, texts, voices, and sounds could constitute a similar network of exchange and social reproduction. I told her that her work on the circulation of Trobriand material bundles had sonic parallels in Bosavi, where ritual wailing at funerals voiced poetic texts that were then recycled in song and speech, acoustically carrying forth the work of remembrance. I told her that while Western epistemology, and anthropology's received divisions, strongly insisted on the difference between the material and the ephemeral, I was more and more convinced that there was little if any difference between them in the production of memory in Papua New Guinea.[3]

Annette took issue with that, arguing that there were real problems amalgamating or collapsing the exchange circulation of vocal practices like names, words, and songs with cloth, carvings, bundles, and baskets. She maintained that it was important to distinguish material from ephemeral, especially as regards circulatory consequence, despite our agreement that all of this business was ultimately about reputation, and how to look after it.

Fast forward now to a later conversation, one Annette had in her last months with two of her closest friends and NYU colleagues, Fred Myers and Barbara Kirschenblatt-Gimblett, reproduced as the final chapter of *The Empire of Things*, Fred's edited collection of material culture essays dedicated to Annette. In that conversation Annette commented on the distinctions between perishable and permanent objects, their durability and temporality, indeed, their material renewability. She said: "I came up with an idea that actually I got from a Nobel prizewinner at the turn of the century. He talked about things that have a permanence having energy, and they continue to have this energy. That's what allows them to circulate and become other things. *Something that is iron can be smelted down, it can have another life, these things continue*" (emphasis added).[4]

Which leads me to ask, again: Is sound really any different? Does it not have this kind of energy to make new lives, new circulations, permanance-through-transience? Can voices and sounds be smelted down like iron? Research on Bosavi women's funerary wailing answered yes; I've now come to the same conclusion for the por por story. Here's why.

Brass-tube squeeze-bulb horns called por por were ubiquitous as signal and warning devices on Ghana's lorries both before and after the arrival of vehicles with electric horns. Drivers of timber trucks working preindependence Gold Coast forest roads in what became Ghana began the process of transforming their por por horns into musical instruments. First the horns were brought together with small percussion as a kind of ensemble noisemaking to ensure protection to the crew of a disabled vehicle after dark in the bush. Punctures were a frequent occurrence on forest roads. As tire innertubes were pumped back to pressure, driving mates surrounded the vehicles and banged wrenches on tire rims while honking the por por horns to scare off dangerous animals and energize the pumping. In time, the noise of warning transformed into a music as the drivers layered short horn phrases over the tire-rim pulse patterns of distinct ethnic and regional rhythms. Simultaneously, the up-and-down motion of pumping the punctured tires was turned into an enthusiastic gesture of accompaniment, leading to the kind of tire-pumping dances seen in *A Por Por Funeral for Ashirifie*.[5]

51. "God Never Sleeps" tsolorley in La. *Photograph © 2006 Steven Feld.*

In the 1960s, the Ghanaian government declared the wooden lorries too vulnerable for inner-city passenger transport. So the vehicles, locally known as tsolorley, "wooden lorry" by Ga-speakers, or "mammy wagon," due to the central role of women in agricultural transport, became restricted to long-distance transport. Today they are a relatively rare sight in Accra, replaced by metal minibuses still generically called trotro. Nonetheless, in La one still sees the wooden vehicles frequently. An important part of the local economy, they are also a link to broad networks of village agricultural business, as well as symbols of La's unique place in Accra's transport history and its acoustic resonance through por por music.

A key reason why La township holds its unique place in Accra's driving history is because the Burma Camp Barracks, a sizeable colonial station, was located on land owned by the people of La. A great number of transport vehicles were in the vicinity during the long colonial period and men from La sought employment at the barracks, many taking up driving as a profession or becoming specialized machinists or car mechanics. As further reference points in the narration of this story of local pride, I was always quickly told that Ataa Awuley, the first Ghanaian to gain an Accra driver's license during the colonial period, was from La, and that Sir Frederick Gordon Guggisberg, commander-in-chief and governor of the Gold Coast in the 1920s, had a personal driver from La, Dzatei Abbey, whom the community proudly renamed Dzatei Guggi.[6]

The theme of community pride is also marked in the use of the name La. To many Accra residents and visitors the township is known as Labadi. But many, maybe even most of La's residents today insist that the name Labadi comes from the colonial designation "La-Bad," the "bad" bit of the name a consequence of an early colonial incident where refusal to pay newly imposed colonial taxes led to incidents of violence. While the idea is deeply held locally, following a directive from the La *mantse* (chief) in 1991, professional historians regularly dismiss it, arguing that the imposition of colonial taxes only dates to the mid-nineteenth century in Accra, while maps and other documents with the name Labadi or Labade can be found going back one hundred years earlier. Despite the contestation, the proud local use of the name La speaks to the ideological power of naming as resistance in postcolonial history.[7]

But back to the central position of vehicles and their local material culture stand-ins: La's driving history is also evoked and memorialized by

52. Modin Sane coffin in La funeral procession.
Photograph © 2002 Nii Yemo Nunu, Kotopon Afrikan Images.

driver coffins modeled on specific trucks and buses. The practice of burying distinguished drivers in replicas of their vehicles parallels the larger practice of burying successful fishermen in fish coffins, mobile phone vendors in phone coffins, bar owners in beer bottle coffins, pilots in an airplane coffins, and so forth. These elaborate sculptural coffins, including tsolorley coffins to honor prominent drivers, are made in neighboring Teshie and Nungua at the workshops of carpentry artists like Paa Joe and Eric Kane, whose grandfather, Kane Kwei, was the first to popularize the colorful art of personalized coffins honoring a life's work. Eric Adotey, once apprenticed to Paa Joe and now proprietor of his own business in La, also carved the first minibus coffin for the well-known driver and unionist Ofolikumah Mensah, whose trotro was named Modin Sane, "The Black Man's Story."[8]

At the January 2008 funeral for a driver from neighboring Teshie, Humphery Ablorh Annang, known as "Humphery Bogerd," the Por Por Group was called on to send up the body with a session of spirited honks. Just outside the funeral chamber stood a coffin modeled on a classic wooden-body Bedford tsolorley. Prepared by one of the local workshops, it waited ready to receive the body for its final journey on the succession of literal and spiritual roads to follow. This one was painted with "Humphery" on its signboard, following the practice of inscribing a vehicle with personal names or distinctive phrases or proverbs associated with a driver, his personality, his road stories. Like the vehicle, the name is memorial testimony to reputation. Indeed, the material history of the vehicle and its driver's work is completely merged with the circulatory history of that driver and vehicle's name, and its repeated verbal citation.

Take the story of Ataa Anangbi Anangfio, a pioneer transport operator. Licensed in 1941, he operated a highly successful fleet of three Austin vehicles inscribed "M.V. Labadi" from the early 1940s to late 1950s, moving passengers and goods on the Accra-Sekondi-Takoradi roads. Anangfio chose the name M.V. Labadi for his fleet to expansively link the La(badi) region to the best-known passenger ship of the day, the M.V. (motor vessel) *Aureol*, an ocean liner that carried more than three hundred passengers and made fortnightly trips from Liverpool to Accra and Lagos in the same decades.[9]

From the later 1950s and early 1960s, Anangfio operated Commer trucks and provided transport and moving services for the Ghana National Construction Company. After the coup in 1966 and until his death in 1973 he worked for the American Embassy in Accra, providing transport for USAID operations, as well as chauffeur services.

Anangfio was the father of my collaborator Nii Yemo Nunu, the La-based photographer who has imaged local history for twenty-five years, and who since 2005, has worked with me to record and document the por por story. On one of the days he came to talk about his father's driving history, Nii Yemo brought a thick packet of documents for me to scan: his father's licenses, union and sports club membership cards, passports and intercountry driving permits, banking and saving account books, all material testimony to a reputation. He explained that these objects and documents memorialized his father's work and wealth as a driver, and that he was proud to have them to show some thirty-five years after his father's death.

While I abstractly understood the Ghana parallel to the Papua New Guinea sentiment here, that photos, licenses, and documents, like a worker's coffin, will stand in for a driver's memory, his reputation of "name," the material significance of work to memory and memory to work was brought home to me more directly one afternoon as I traveled with the La Por Por Group.

"Prof, do you want us to bury you in a camera or microphone?"

53. Ataa Anangbi
Anangfio with
"M.V. Labadi," 1952.
*Photograph © 2010
Nii Yemo Nunu,
Kotopon Afrikan
Images Collection.*

"Uh . . . I don't know, Amarh [dumbfounded pause] . . . I mean, I've never thought about it."

"You see, it's your work, like driving is our work," he offered quickly. "So your coffin will tell the story of your work, that's why you can have a camera or a microphone."

When Nii Amarh Amartey said those words to me I was wearing a stereo microphone on my head and had a video camera in my hands. I was seated next to him in a minibus trotro filled with other Por Por band members and we were returning from the funeral of a prominent driver who was buried in a carved wooden replica of his vehicle.

A few days later, having thought a bit about the nonchalance of Amarh's question to me, I repeated it to Nii Yemo, signaling the awkwardness I felt about choosing my coffin at a time I hoped to be well in advance of its necessity. "Of course!" he responded immediately. "You made Por Por's

CD and you are making Por Por's movie, so it's correct, Prof, Por Por can bury you in a microphone and camera!"

"*Both*!?"

"Of course! You are a man of great wealth! None of us can match you! You can have two coffins! You see! They can even put both in one grave! Two coffins! Correct, heh heh, then Por Por will blow twice as hard to bury you! [much laughter]. And me, I will preserve it in pictures for the *wwhhoollee* world to see!" (More laughter, much more, this time including mine.)

Nii Yemo made that comment as we sorted through his picture collection. He had first shared a large stash of family photographs with me in 2006 when we were working on the Smithsonian Folkways CD *Por Por: Honk Horn Music of Ghana.*[10] So I was surprised when he brought an equal number of completely different images more than three years later. One group of those images, taken during independence activities in March 1957, reveals that Nii Yemo's father was a member of the Ghana government's elite "Drivers Selected Team," drivers who transported foreign dignitaries during independence ceremonies in sharp vehicles like the newly arrived fleet of Chevrolet sedans gifted for the occasion by the U.S. government. In a group of those sepia images, we see Ataa Anangbi with the new vehicles and with other drivers, all wearing a stylish uniform.

"Wow, they really dressed for the occasion," I commented, looking at a photo of Anangbi sharply outfitted and casually leaning up against a shiny new sedan with its special government GV 138 license plate.

"I still have it," he said.

"You have the license plate?" I ask.

"No, man! The uniform!!" he replies, breaking into laughter.

"You still have *this* uniform here?" I asked, pointing, amazed.

"Yes! It's been in the wardrobe all these years. I've never taken it out for daylight once! It stayed with him from that day in 1957 until his death in 1973 and has been with me ever since he died!"

A few days later Nii Yemo brought the outfit, two of them actually, green cotton with yellow pinstripe detail, fresh out of the closet, and perfectly pressed, fifty-two years after his father wore it in the photographs he had brought me to scan.

"You see, it is stylish even today, and can still be worn!" he said, slipping into the outfit as Nii Noi and I watched in complete amazement and broke into applause. "I'm so happy to say that my father was among them on that day. Who knows, he could have driven the queen's representative, or the American representative. I'll never know! But I'm proud that my father was there amongst them because they were all special drivers from their respective quarters. Driving was something very important on that day."

Later that week we made a video with Nii Yemo presenting and discussing his collection of independence-era photographs and his father's uniform. Afterward, as we packed up, he asked me:

"Prof, have you kept something like that?"

"You mean an important family object?"

"Yes, something like that."

"Clothing no, but I have my grandfather's clock, a big one, taller than me. When I was a little boy I loved the sounds and my fascination delighted my grandfather, so he left the clock to me. It stayed in our family house for thirty years after he died, and then it came to live with me. So it has been in the family a long time."

"You see, we all have one custom," he reflected. "Maybe you don't pour libation like we do, but you are including the ancestors in how you live, just as they include you. So when you hear the clock you know your grandfather is around somewhere just as he knows you are aware of him. That is like me having my father's uniforms in the wardrobe. You see, we all have one custom."

The look on my face likely signaled that I wasn't entirely convinced about this, so Nii Yemo continued, developing the thought. "We are keeping the names of the ancestors with us when we keep their things. That is why we inscribe the vehicles. The inscription gives you reputation, because your name then follows to your son, daughter, wife. Even your driving mate can be called by the name of the vehicle. Me, all the time in the streets in La people will call out, 'Hey, M.V. Labadi, where are you going? Hey, M.V. Labadi, how is it?' So the reputation of my father's work is always with me. You don't know how far name goes! Now I walk around town and people call me 'M.V. Labadi' though my father has died more than thirty-five years ago. So when you inscribe something on your vehicle it becomes what I call 'genetic,' it goes through your blood. People call to every family, 'Hey, Sea Never Dry,' 'Hey, Be Sure,' 'Hey, Shark Malo.' They call your children and your children's children, it goes

54. Ataa Anangbi
Anangfio on
Independence
Day, 1957.
*Photograph
© 2010 Nii Yemo
Nunu, Kotopon
Afrikan Images
Collection.*

through the whole family. So you see, these are things that people are very proud of. This is why the inscription will always be remembered. It's the driver's name."

One of the name-as-reputation tokens that Nii Yemo is particularly proud of is the well-remembered song for his father titled "M.V. La-badi."[11] Recorded by the Por Por Group on their Folkways CD, the song begins with the energetic recitation of a local slogan of industrious pride, indicating that La people are working before the cock crows.

LEADER: *Dade kotopon!!*
GROUP RESPONSE: *wɔ gbɛ La gbɛ!!*
LEADER: (Louder) *Dade kotopon!!*
GROUP RESPONSE: (Louder still) *wɔ gbɛ La gbɛ!!*

Olojo ("Hello Joe") Mensah, the song's vocal leader, continues in a spoken voice to reveal the theme to the assembled group:

LEADER: Yes, we will tell the story of the old drivers,
   those who firmly established the La Branch Union.
   Yes, these are the elder lorry owners.
   Our father Anangbi,
   he kept his lorry as shiny and smooth as a porcelain plate.
   Wherever he went, people admired him, both in La and Teshie.
   One says, "I will go with you, Anangbi,"
   another says the same.
   But the most beautiful lady in Teshie,
   when she sees the lorry coming,
   she sings out this one thing:

Then the sung refrain:

LEADER: M.V. Labadi, Anangbi-o, please, I will go with you,
   M.V. Labadi, Anangbi-o, please, I will go with you.

The group repeats the refrain four times with Hello Joe, as the por por horns and small percussion come in to join, leading to the first verse, and repeated refrain.

LEADER: On all the journeys on which Anangbi goes
   he brings cassavas, he brings cocoyams.
   That's why Teshie ladies love him,
   And why La ladies also love him.
   They go on to have children with him—
   Oh drivers! Why do you like making many babies?
   Let us call Nii Yemo to tell us about the messages of drivers!

CHORUS: M.V. Labadi, Anangbi-o, please, I will go with you,
   M.V. Labadi, Anangbi-o, please, I will go with you.

At this point, and over an instrumental interlude Nii Yemo steps up to the microphone to rap the names of some of the classic vehicles from his father's M.V. Labadi era. The names, here translated, are originally in English, Pidgin, Twi, and Ga.

NII YEMO: No Time to Die
   It Pains You, Why?
   Sweet Mother
   Ghana Is Sweet-o, Baby Yaa

Who Be You There?
The Black Man's Story
Look People Like This—They Talk What They Don't Know
Don't Mind Them
No Haste
Don't Be Foolish
If They Hate Us
Super Fine, Fine, Fine, Fine

CHORUS 1: M.V. Labadi, Anangbi-o, please; I will go with you,
M.V. Labadi, Anangbi-o, please, I will go with you.

CHORUS 2: I went to buy cassava, [2x]
Anangbi-o please, I went to buy cassava, [2x]
I went to buy cassava to pound fufu for my love to eat,
So that in the night I will go to him to love me.
They will go, they will come,
We'll go to sleep.

OLOJO: Nii Yemo! Continue with the drivers' messages!

With more instrumental fanfare Nii Yemo again steps up to the microphone to recite more names of classic vehicles. The names, here translated, are originally in a mix of English, pidgin, Twi, Ga, Ewe, and Hausa.

NII YEMO: Who Will Know?
If It Is Full It's Up to You to Carry
Patience
It Is Mighty
Yours Is Yours
Salam Alekum, Alekum Salam
Hallelujah!
Think Through Messages
Spirit and Medicine
It Is Well with Us
Looking at Your Mom? Look at Your Dad!
Allah Satisfies
Look, We Don't Disturb Nature
Poor No Friend-o
We Will Hear Messages

55. "May Be,"
mud flaps.
Photograph
© *2007 Steven*
Feld.

Nii Yemo continues, calling the band back in:

NII YEMO: Por por, Olojo,
 What do you say?
 What do you say?

The band comes back in with instruments and voices to close:

CHORUS: M.V. Labadi, Anangbi-o, please, I will go with you,
 M.V. Labadi, Anangbi-o, please, I will go with you.

As we listened to a playback of the recording in the following week Nii Yemo reflected on its history: "When I was a child they were singing this song in honor of my father, about the goods he was carrying, the people he was taking to their destinations. But I was really surprised that the Por Por Group was able to sing it because many of them were not born at that time, so that means the legend has been living, you know, that they heard the song being sung somewhere. Maybe they were even hearing some of the other trotro names for the first time when I recited them that day."

But the first name Nii Yemo cited is surely one that virtually everyone knew, as it is one of the best-remembered lorry legacies in La. Trucking both people and fish, the well-known driver and spiritualist (twice a pilgrim to Mecca) AlHaj Okantey called his vehicle "No Time To Die." The name came from a 1958 movie starring Victor Mature, about the Nazi capture in North Africa of a British tank corps sergeant who tried to assassinate Josef Goebbels. The signboard inscription "No Time To Die" even inspired a book of lorry poems.[12]

Following Nii Yemo's instruction that I always explore the multiple sources of vehicle names and the ways they come to stand in for drivers and their reputation, I asked "Vice," the Por Por Group leader, and the union vice chairman, Nii Ashai Ollennu, about the signage of his tanker vehicles in his working days.

"Vice, did you inscribe your lorry?"

"Oh yes, Prof, I did," he replied. "I wrote 'May Be.'"

"Why did you call it 'May Be'?"

"You see, Prof, when you are driving, people ask you *sooo* many things and all you can say is 'May be.' When they ask you if something is true or another thing will happen, you can't really say. Either it can happen or not, it can be true or not. So that's why I called my vehicle 'May Be.'"

In January 2006, Nii Yemo and I commissioned the Accra artist Nicholas Wayo to make a cover painting for the forthcoming Por Por Group's CD. We asked Nicholas to paint a classic independence-era Bedford trotro bearing the La Drivers Union logo—hands on a steering wheel topped by a crowing cock symbolizing industriousness, and surrounded by a por por horn and double bell. We also asked him to site the vehicle heading down the La road along the cloudy Accra seacoast, an image from a song. Nico suggested "Sea Never Dry" as the front signboard inscription.

The phrase was inscribed on a 1950s trotro and comes from a well-known song by the trumpeter and highlife king E. T. Mensah. Mensah's portrait hangs at the La Drivers Union office, a unique reminder of connections between Accra's modernist histories of driving and jazz music. Famously associated with Louis Armstrong's much-remembered 1956 visit to Accra and their jam session at Mensah's Paramount Club, "Sea Never Dry" speaks to a central axiom of the fishing business in seacoast Ga townships like La. But among La drivers its double-entendre is particularly at the surface: never a road without women.[13]

In January 2008, two years after that commission for "Sea Never Dry," I brought the union its first royalty check from Smithsonian Folkways Recordings for *Por Por: Honk Horn Music of Ghana*, launched in Accra on the fiftieth anniversary of Ghana's independence, indeed, a U.S. gift to Ghana on that occasion. To accompany the royalty check presentation I asked Nicholas Wayo to repeat the same painting for me to gift to the union office, topping it, in Ga, with "Congratulations and praises to you all." On his own, Nicholas decided to change the signboard inscription from "Sea Never Dry" to "Dromo," meaning "Blessings." As he and his assistant delivered the painting and held it up for a snapshot, I asked: "Nico, why did you change the trotro name?"

He grinned. "Prof, their ship has come in."

Deliverance: once again, the connection of name, of reputation is made, linking the monetary wealth of driving work, the wealth of musical work, and the spiritual force that underlies industriousness.

Indeed, many earlier and most contemporary trotros and taxis also bear some kind of indication of spiritual force, with a Christian or Muslim slogan like "Blessings" on their rear windows, either in English, Ga, Ewe, or Twi. Dozens of names like "By His Grace," "The Lord Is My Shepherd," "Jesus Saves," "Hallelujah," "Blood of the Lamb," "Merciful God," "Pentecost Fire," "The Prophet," "In the Name of Allah," and "Young Hajj" are all indicative of the intertwining of spiritual belief and move-

56. "Sea Never Dry." *Art* © *2006 Nicholas Wayo.*

ment on the road in the conjoined material-acoustic history of vehicles and names.

One day I was listening to tapes with the union chairman, Nii Quarshie Gene.

"Chief, did you inscribe your lorry back in the days when you were a working driver?"

"Oh yes, Prof, of course. In fact, I called it 'Hallowed Be Thy Name.'"

"Why?"

"You see, Prof, because I love the Lord's Prayer. And there was already a trotro signed 'Our Father.' And another signed 'Who Art in Heaven.' So I came behind with 'Hallowed Be Thy Name.' And you know 'Thy Kingdom Come,' he is parking behind the petrol station. We also had 'Thy Will Be Done.' And 'On Earth as It Is in Heaven" still carts goods into town, you can see him at the yard Tuesday afternoons."

"Yes, chief," I say, "just last week I was in a taxi signed 'Our Daily Bread.'" But I stopped short of telling him that on a road called Linguistic Philosophy there was once a driver named Mikhail Bakhtin who inscribed his trotro signboard with a single word: "Polyphony." On the vehicle's rear tailgate he wrote his motto: "Every spoken word is half someone else's."[14]

The use of these religious slogans past and present also relates to how drivers have long acknowledged a spiritual dimension in their work. Drivers believe that spirits of the road will repeatedly test them in encounters that are unpredictable and potentially profound. Many carry talismans or religious paraphernalia and consult spiritualists before particular travels. Since vehicles bring wealth, they must be properly venerated. Drivers perform rituals related to the maintenance of their vehicles, as well as rituals meant to guard against road accidents. Spiritual attention is also required in the course of driving: when a driver comes to a bridge over water, he must blow his horn well in advance to ask the residing spirits for permission to pass.

So to take stock: from the late 1930s, squeeze-bulb horns enter the local driving arena as a commodity, purchased and used on vehicles as a practical signaling device, sounding out place and spiritual warnings, announcements, and requests, marking the everyday life passage of the vehicle, becoming its voice on the road. As such the horn resides acoustically in a figure and ground relationship to the road, to the running engine, and all the other squeaks and hums, the voices and radios, the larger acoustic environment of the vehicle, those who move in, briefly inhabit, and move out of it, and all the sounds that surround its pickups, drops, its movements on the road.

As announcer of passage and presence, the driver attempts to conduct the orchestra called traffic in the symphony hall called the highway. His por por horn becomes his baton, his voice, and that voice, like his signboard inscription, is locally understood to be his "name," in effect, the cumulative material of his reputation.

Off the vehicle, recontextualized as a musical instrument, the por por horn embodies and rematerializes all the sensory dimensions of its prior life. To become a musical instrument, it must be fitted with a new bulb, a larger and more flexible one, capable of faster squeezing, of pushing more air through the brass tubing. "You see, Prof, *alllll* the way from the bee-hind to the mouth," Vice explained as the blacksmith fitted some ultra-flexible number 10 Czech-made enema bulbs to give new voice to the horns. Like the physically forced-air energy of pumping a tire rematerial-

57. La blacksmith fitting new enema bulbs on old por por horns. *Photograph © 2008 Steven Feld.*

izing as the body of dance, the physically forced-air energy of squeezing a bulb brings the honking voice out from the brass horn's body.

All of that indexicality is wrapped in the power of vocal iconicity. *Pɔɔ Pɔɔ*—the reduplicated name is packed thick with the materiality of vocal physics: a pulmonic egressive voiceless bilabial plosive tailing off to double-length nasalized vowels. Roman Jakobson, who urged that the whole of language is a sea of potentially consummated iconicities only a very few of which are ever consummated, delighted in these splish-splash morphophone pileups. The high priest of both linguistic iconicity and poetic parallelism reportedly liked to quip, in his own inimitable English:

"some words

just

TAke the CAke."

Jakobson's famous concept of the "poetry of grammar and grammar of poetry" pointed to the numerous ways that languages aestheticize sonorous sequences and naturalize relationships between the sonic and semantic. In Accra, one encounters many species of this genus of linguistic creativity, but the playfulness surrounding naming is a particular and fundamental way social relations are sounded out.[15]

I recall entering this sensuously sonic empire of names and reputations quite pointedly. "This is my teacher," said Ruti Talmor (then an NYU anthropology graduate student), introducing me to some of her young musician and drum-maker friends at the National Arts Centre during my first week in Accra in 2004.

"Teacher, you are welcome!"

"Hello, thank you, my name is Steve."

"Teacher, you are welcome!"

"Thanks, call me Steve."

"Professor, you are welcome!"

"My friends call me Steve."

"Prof, you are welcome."

"So what do I do to get people to address me by my name?" I ask Ruti later.

"You don't," she said. "You have age and status. They need to show you respect. They can't do that by addressing you by your first name, it would be really uncomfortable. Anyway, nicknames are big here, they're friendly, and important, like respect for seniority."

58. America Man's Boafo at the La Total filling station.
Photograph © 2008 Steven Feld.

Of that I've been endlessly reminded whenever people address me, as they invariably do, with that mixture of polite and playful, formal and informal, distant and close-by, in the name "Prof."

But to understand a little more deeply the materiality of names and naming, take the story of a special vehicle in La, parked at the Total filling station as you enter the town. It is Boafo, "Good Friend," a small wooden truck owned by Frank Annertey Abbey, known to La residents as "America Man." On Boafo's wooden side doors are painted a Ghanaian and American handshake, following the USAID insignia.

In 1988, when President Bill Clinton visited Accra, the American entourage took over the nearby La Palm Royal Beach Hotel. Someone saw Boafo sitting at the La filling station and asked that it be parked in the La Palm's driveway during the official visit. America Man obliged. Rumor has it that Bill Clinton and some ranking Ghanaian politicians were photographed shaking hands up against the vehicle's USAID-inspired signboard. But nobody has ever been able to locate that picture. America Man is still trying. He has begged for my help on every occasion that we have met.

Per chance, Nii Yemo and I walked into a La bar for some refreshment in late February 2008, and there we encountered America Man.

"America Man, how are you? It is good to see you again."

"Oohh, America Prof, you are welcome! Welcome, Prof, oh Welcome!! Fine! Fine! Prof, take a seat with me."

Nii Yemo brought us a round of Guinness malt drinks and as we sat I asked America Man the question of the moment.

"America Man, did the La Palm ask you to bring your Boafo during last week's Accra visit of President Bush?"

Long pause.

"John Kennedy," he answered.

Pause.

"John Kennedy, yes, John F. Kennedy."

An even longer pause as he adjusts his Ray Charles–esque tortoise shell wraparound knockoff Gucci sunglasses.

"Yes, John Kennedy. That's why I painted Boafo with an American handshake. I saw your America for a *loong* time, Prof. Washington, D.C., Maryland. Chevy Chase. Silver Spring. I drove. Once all the way to Florida. Yes, John Kennedy, John F. Kennedy. The man."

Another long pause.

"And Bill Clinton too. Yes, Bill Clinton. I love him too."

Later Nii Yemo tells me that one of the three jumbo airplanes that the Bush party brought to Accra for their twenty-four-hour drop-in was filled with presidential vehicles. This time, when the American entourage took over the La Palm Royal Beach Hotel, the driveway was packed with a fleet of armored Cadillacs.

"All the drivers from La walked over to see them," he said. "But the place was surrounded by rings of soldiers and security. Everyone was chased away. None of us were welcome. That's why America Man didn't speak your president's name."[16]

When he lived in the States, America Man took the name of the boxer turned tough-guy-thug actor Jack Palance (whose own original name was Volodymyr Palahniuk). America Man called himself "Jack," or "Palance," sometimes "Heavy Palance," or "Palance Motherfucker." Sometimes he called himself by names of his favorite Palance films, the 1952

Shane, or the 1953 *I Died a Thousand Times.* He also called himself "The Meanest Guy That Ever Lived," after a country song written and recorded by Palance in the early 1960s. But people in America were, not surprisingly, confused when he introduced himself as "Jack Palance." So he also called himself "Lee Palace of Africa," "Lee" for short.

"Everyone knows Africa has chief's palaces," he told me, "and I loved Jerry Lee Lewis. And Lee Marvin too."

Today on the streets of La he is America Man. Some friends just call him "Lee." More call him "Jack." Many assume the name equally comes from his love of Jack Kennedy, whose image he had painted next to his own on the side of his vehicle. Beneath a U.S. flag on top, and over the windshield signboard, he painted the words "In God We Trust" bordered by the insignia of Lucky Strike cigarettes.

"Why did you sign Boafo 'In God We Trust'?" I ask.

No pause.

"You know why!" he blurted out. Big smile.

In November 1999, Queen Elizabeth visited Ghana to meet with President J. J. Rawlings. The royal entourage took over the La Palm Royal Beach Hotel. America Man went all out and really spiffed up the truck, down to the impeccably shined overlarge whitewall tires, something rarely seen on even the most expensive cars in Accra, and never on trucks. He got his picture into a glossy magazine spread about the visit. He wore his vintage USA T-shirt and bermudas, or donned his Panama hat, carried his classic sixties American transistor radio, decked out the vehicle with U.S., Ghanaian, and British flags, and offered himself as a symbol of intercultural friendship on the road.

He posed together with his wife, Juliana Anyekai Adjei, whose U.S. flag headwraps, Keds, and bermuda shorts took them back to suburban Maryland in the sixties. Juliana too is no stranger to uniforms, to style. She has worked for years as an officer in the Ghana Fire Fighters League. At home she is comfortable in T-shirts and cloth wraps. She never goes to work without a freshly pressed uniform. America Man is the same in his dress habits.

"Why do you wear white gloves when you drive, America Man?"

"Respect, Prof, R-E-S-P-E-C-T, find out what it means to me," he chants, in the Aretha Franklin cadence, switching off seamlessly to "if you don't respect yourself ain't nobody else . . . ," his voice trailing, allowing me to mentally fill in the echo completion of the consequent phrase from "Respect Yourself" by the Staple Singers.[17]

On most days America Man used Boafo to cart cinderblock bricks made in the yard next to his house. He was a working lorry driver, industrious and proud. Then there was an accident in 2004 that left him with a broken leg and other wounds, destroyed the truck's wooden shell, and otherwise severely damaged his vehicle and sent him down the alcohol road. Juliana nursed him back to health.

"Each day," he told me, "I sat outside next to my painting of President Kennedy, and remembered the stories of how his back pained him so. It helped me gain my strength again. By the grace of God I recovered."

America Man eventually rebuilt the wooden shell of his vehicle. In 2005, with his leg somewhat healed and the truck back together, he called on his friend, the photographer Nii Yemo Nunu, to help him celebrate with a triumphant photo. In Nii Yemo's picture, America Man appears on the lorry's roof honking a por-por horn, an image resonant with the La union emblem of the cock on top of the steering wheel.

America Man turned the final page of his picture album. In the last photo he is at Boafo's helm in white gloves and Ghana flag bandana, driving jubilant residents through the La streets, celebrating the Ghana Black Stars soccer triumph over the United States of America.

"World Cup, two-oh-oh-six," he said. "We BEAT you!! *Eh Hehh*! The Lord works in mysterious ways, Prof!" Big laugh.

A month after the Bush visit and those conversations with America Man, a call from Nii Otoo, then one from Vice, woke me earlier than usual. It was March 28, 2008. "Prof, the good Lord has taken our brother Ashirifie, rest his everlasting soul. The Lord works in mysterious ways, Prof. We have lost our brother and we must now prepare to *blooow* to send him on his journey."[18]

Like Vice, Ashirifie had been active since the late sixties in the Por Por Group. By the time I met him in May 2005, he was well in place in his driving retirement job as superintendent of the union office, holding the keys, opening and closing, greeting, keeping the office clean and organized. He was also caretaker of the Por Por Group's instruments and their uniforms, lovingly ironing and folding the yellow, black, or red T-shirts before each performance.

The news of Ashirifie's passing was shocking to me. I had just been

59. America Man and Julianna with their JFK painting, La.
© 2004 Nii Yemo Nunu, Kotopon Afrikan Images.

60. Nelson Ashirifie Mensah. *Photograph © 2008 Steven Feld.*

cataloguing pictures and video that I shot of him leading the band at a funeral in Teshie three months earlier. I saw him regularly after that event, and in the weeks just before his death we visited at the union office. On one of those occasions I brought a visiting Santa Fe colleague, the blacksmith and sculptor Tom Joyce, with me to hear a rehearsal. Ashirifie ushered us in that evening, placed our chairs in the best location, and was very present to us. I recall Tom remarking on Ashirifie's gentle and sweet demeanor as we went home that night. There were no visible signs of any health issues then, or for that matter over the previous three years, though Ashirifie walked with a slight limp.

Ashirifie's vibe was always playful; wherever he was, a deck of cards was always nearby. And among other things it was surely that vibe that invited nicknames. Friends like Nii Noi played on the sound of his name, transforming it to Sheriff, smelting it down to Ricky. Who knows which came first, Ashirifie's cotton plaid shirts or being nicknamed Ricky Nelson. But he was a respected man. Rarely was he just called Ricky. It was always Ricky Nelson, Mister Nelson, Sheriff Ricky, Mister Ricky, Sheriff

Nelson. It turns out that he also had the given name of Nelson. In the mid-1990s that led to another nickname: Mandela.

My personal nickname for Ashirifie was "Lester" because of the way he would swing his por por horn up and off to the side, or in frontal circular motions, recalling the gestural practice and bodily stance of Lester Young, the famous tenor saxophonist of the Count Basie band. And Ashirifie fancied caps and hats. In his collection was a black felt one that also recalled the stylish honkers and shouters and big-band saxophonists of the fifties era, although Lester Young was more famously known for wearing the pork pie hat.

Jazz legend holds that on the night Young died the news was passed to the bassist Charles Mingus while he was playing on the bandstand. A kernel from his improvisation in the moment became the opening melody of his composition "Goodbye Pork Pie Hat," a sensuous jazz lament memorial to Young. The song took on an expanded listening life when Joni Mitchell wrote lyrics to it in 1979, just before Mingus himself died, and recorded it on *Mingus*, her tribute LP to the bassist. The first stanza's lyric evokes Young as "the sweetest, swinging music man" with "a porky pig hat on."[19]

Like the hat that tops the head, reputation here is the accumulation of names one acquires through life, the ways they are stacked up with gigs played, roads driven, flat tires pumped, funerals attended, uniforms ironed, doors locked and unlocked, floors swept, libations poured, drinks drunk, stories told, handshakes snapped.

I had often enough thought about these things while attending funerals with the Por Por Group. But now I found myself having to confront them more viscerally in the shock of Ashirifie's passing. And then, just before I left Accra for a few weeks in the United States and Europe, came the request that I momentarily suspend the more historical por por film project that occupied Nii Yemo and me, and turn my attention, on return to Accra, to making a film document of Ashirifie's por por funeral. When I got back to Accra a few weeks later I found out that the funeral would take place on May 10, a relief, as I held a ticket to depart Accra late that night.

A week before the funeral, I accompanied the band to Ashirifie's family compound. The group wanted to bring musical condolences to the family and to introduce me, and the presence of my video camera, to many who had not previously seen me. I in turn wanted to give some photographic portraits of Ashirifie to his children, meet more of the family, and to make a donation to help defray the funeral expenses.

"Some of us have never seen a white man cry," the union chairman, Nii Quarshie Gene, says (in Ga), on camera, addressing the senior women mourners presiding over the event. To authorize and explain my participation in the hybrid role of mourner and videographer, the chief knew just what to say to both lend prestige to the funeral, and to create an instant trust among people who didn't know me.

What's less audible on the film soundtrack in that moment is the overlapping comment that Ashirifie's brother Odoi, sitting next to the union chief, makes down the line to his nieces Dede and Kai. "Right hand man!" he says, in English, ironically referring to Ashirifie's nickname for me. It's a name that derives from a story Ashirifie liked to laugh over and tell, about the day I showed up early for a meeting at the union office, and did the very unsenior, very un-white-man thing of assisting him to set out the chairs for the event.

Among Odoi's more formal roles that day was to present a gallon of akpeteshie, the local gin, to the band during the event so that libations could be poured and the music continue in Ashirifie's celebration and memory, amidst a great deal of distress, ritual wailing, and heavy talk. The suspicion of foul play, the implication that Ashirifie was taken down by a secret enemy, lingered everywhere around his death. It came to the surface that day and in each public arena where libations were poured throughout the funerary process.

In front of the office, a union elder, Ataa Anum Sowah, poured the libation that rallied the band before they proceeded to the funeral to play. He addressed Ashirifie directly, admonishing him to "look in the mirror" and take the life of the one who had taken his. At the funeral service in front of Ashirifie's coffin, a senior man poured libation and also addressed Ashirifie, telling him to rest in peace if he was going of his own accord. But if someone took him, he should reciprocate and "show signs of it in three days" (following the Ga belief that the soul continues to inhabit the body for three days). And pouring over the coffin as it was placed in the grave, another senior man tells Ashirifie, "This drink we are pouring for you, leave some for the one who destroyed you," adding that he shouldn't wait too long to "take" the responsible one, "whether from your mother's side or your father's side."

As we worked on the editing and subtitle translation of the film's final sequence with that powerful libation speech, I asked Nii Yemo the name of the elder with the astonishingly deep and resonant voice who poured and spoke it. He said he didn't know him by name, he hadn't met him before, but would check up so that I could add the name to the final film credits. A few mornings later, Nii Yemo sent the name, with no other comment, as a text message from his cell phone to mine: "Ashirifie Frank Sinatra." Over and over, again and again, it's name as reputation, resonance as memory, age as authority.

If senior male speeches accompanying libation were delivered with calm yet pointed direct address to Ashirifie, the powerful contrast was the sung-texted crying that women performed through the process, most powerfully throughout the final sequence of overlapping bells, songs, prayers, horn honks, and conch shell and flute laments as the band and closest mourners surrounded the body and sounded their presence to Ashirifie before he was placed in his coffin. "Why leave this beautiful life?" one crying woman asks, her sorrowful rhetorical question overlapped by numerous others telling Ashirifie to wake up and come back, reminding him, and everyone listening, of the pain his passing has produced.

In the final moments of that sequence, just before the coffin is brought into the room to receive the body, the por por players break into "Novi Deke," a song whose simple text laments, "I have no brother, I'm all alone, finished without you." As they sing, Olojo (Hello Joe) Mensah's voice rises above the horns, shells, and wailing. Waving a yellow-and-black Por Por band uniform T-shirt over the body, he addresses Ashirifie a last time: "Ashirifie!! Here! We wore this shirt with you! And you wore it with us! Now we are giving it to you to take on your journey." With that he lays the shirt on Ashirifie's chest, a final act of vocal and material respect to link a past and future of work pride on the por por "road."

Filming that sequence, and thinking throughout the funeral of how themes of work, pride, citation, circulation, and reputation were always at the surface, I felt glad about the intervention I had staged earlier in the week by inciting a unique viewing of *Rejoice When You Die*, the black-and-white photographic record of the classic New Orleans jazz funeral tradition by the distinguished photographer Leo Touchet.[20] Before the funeral events began, I had given the book to Nii Yemo, asking him to look it over, so that in time we could talk both about the ritual and the photographs. But as he was immediately enthusiastic about the book, Nii

Yemo decided to show it to Vice, to energize and encourage him going into the work of retrieving Ashirifie's body from the mortuary and proceeding with the funeral. We had scheduled some time that week with Vice to film him buying new bulbs for some por por horns and taking them to the local blacksmith for fitting. When we all got back to the union office that afternoon, Nii Yemo sat with Vice and spontaneously showed him the book, surprising him with it page by page.

Nii Yemo frames the conversation with Vice by telling him that I brought the book to Accra so that they could compare the por por and New Orleans jazz funerals. Throughout their viewing, which appears as an appendix to the filmic chronicle of Ashirifie's funeral, Nii Yemo creates an interpretive framework to link the two ritual practices, indeed, produces a proud and authenticating origin narrative for Africa and Accra. "It makes you wonder how after five hundred years blacks over there celebrate like us," he begins. And just a few picture pages later, coming to an image of mixed race musical groups: "There are also whites who participate. It's become everyone's custom there."

In one of the conversation's most animated moments, Nii Yemo and Vice look approvingly at pictures of a New Orleans practice thoroughly familiar to them, energetic community participation, dancing in the streets, behind, alongside, and around the musicians. "You see how everyone is wild here!" Nii Yemo says, pointing to a two-page spread of images with dancers taking over public space. "Everyone is inspired! . . . They are moved to join the second line!" And a few images later, referring back just a few days to how young dancers took over the musical condolences as the band played at the family compound: "The musicians inspire the dancers just like you did for Ashirifie's family!"

The New Orleans jazz funeral and Accra's La Por Por Group are products of unique histories; neither originated at the site of the other and neither developed in the light of awareness of the other. But in Accra (and maybe in some quarters of New Orleans too) it would be impossible not to claim the pride of racialized history, the pride of historical relatedness, the pride of cultural connection. The common themes and practices are indeed powerfully present: musical parades with danced community participation, drivers and musicians as wardens of "the road" of work and life passage.[21]

The sense of felt and imagined intimacy becomes more heightened the moment Nii Yemo indicates to Vice that participants in Touchet's New

Orleans images "look like people we know around here!" Without missing a beat, he enthusiastically continues: "They are our kinfolk!" and Vice instantly overlaps, strongly repeating the same exact words.

As they come to the closing images, Nii Yemo sums up the relatedness for Vice, this time adding intentionality: "They do this to remember our common tradition when they were here with us," he says. "All these years they've been gone they've preserved most of the customs. . . . This is just what we do here. . . . We all have one custom, playing and dancing."

While it was that story, in a souvenir book about New Orleans, that I brought back with me to Accra from America in anticipation of Ashirifie's por por funeral, it was the more local story, about the material memory of driving, that I had brought with me a few weeks earlier to the United States in the form of a tsolorley souvenir made by Odoi Perkoh, son of the union counselor Al Haji Perkoh. Odoi had developed a nice business making souvenir miniatures of the wooden tsolorley trucks to sell at gift shops in some of Accra's high-end hotels, Golden Tulip, La Palm, Novotel. My tsolorley was yellow, the inscription on its signboard "In God We Trust."

Visiting with me just before I left Accra for New York, Nii Yemo commented: "It's a special one, Prof, you see, because you Americans trust in God to bring you money. This one is your yellow cab, it brings good money like a trotro, so it can be called 'In God We Trust.' You know, that is why we Ghanaians love your American money, because it says that you trust God. Did America Man tell you that too?"

"Well," I say, "not every American who works for his money believes in that. I mean it's not really a literal expression."

"Oh yes, of course," he continued, "but it is like what we inscribe on a trotro, something that is a good memory to inspire us in our work. 'In God We Trust.' Me, I don't go to church but I like the sound of 'In God We Trust' very much. So I enjoy seeing it on the American money, like I enjoy seeing 'No Time To Die' or 'Ben Hur' on a trotro."

Pause. Then he looks at me quite seriously.

"Prof, you will be receiving money now when you go to America, right?"

"Yes, for my teaching work, for lecturing."

"You see! Your mouth is your lorry. They will pay to listen. Tell them about 'In God We Trust.' These vehicles are wealth to drivers like teaching is wealth to you. You hear! This is why 'In God We Trust' is a good tsolorley for you, Prof! Drive it well! Tell them!"

61. Nii Yemo with souvenir "In God We Trust/Cool Running" trotro. *Photograph © 2008 Steven Feld.*

"What about 'Cool Running'?" I ask, referring to the inscription on the souvenir vehicle's tailgate.

"Oh!! 'Cool Running.' You know, America is *soo* cool, everything is cool from America. Miles Davis! *The Birth of the Cool*! Cool, man, cool!"[22]

He can't stop laughing. Finally he does. "You see, Prof, Dodge introduced 'Cool Running' in the years before independence. That is what they called their special engine, 'Cool Running.' We loved the Dodge, we loved the cool-running motor vehicles. America is well known to us! America is 'Cool Running.'"

Nii Yemo knows about American cool. He is typically dressed in Keds, Levis, a photographer's vest over a T- or tennis shirt, and big aviator sunglasses. Ghanaba gave him the nickname "Flick" and in years past he rode a motorbike, the gas tank inscribed "M.V. Labadi" on one side, and "Shoot Out" on the other. His favorite film and trotro name is *Rebel without a Cause*.[23] But he says he got cool when he started spelling Africa with a "k," as in "Kool" cigarettes.

When we met in May 2005, Nii Yemo told me that he became a photographer in 1986. Before that he had a contract job supervising air conditioning repair for the American Embassy in Accra, from 1970. After technical school in Kumasi to study radio electronics, he started with the U.S. Embassy just about the same time that his father was a chauffeur driver there, the job Anangfio held until his death in 1973.

"Tell me about working for the Americans in those days."

"Prof, you see, that was something else-o. Because in the days of Gerald Ford we had a wonderful surprise. Yes. Shirley Temple Black. She was the embassy boss from America. Shirley Temple Black. Oh, how we loved her! She came from the movies all the way to Accra! We loved the American movies, so of course we knew the little Shirley Temple. And when she came back here her hair and name was Black! Yes! She changed her name to BLACK and returned! [Hilarious laughter . . . then. . . .] We loved her husband Mr. Black too. He was very relaxed, going around town in his shorts!"[24]

"So you got to know the family when they were here?"

"Of course! You see, Shirley Temple Black also had a daughter. Maybe she was twenty. And she had a place of her own at the residence. So my assistant and I we were called one day to go there to fix up her air conditioning. And we had to take up the rug around the air conditioner. And there we found that this daughter had hidden a small packet of wee [marijuana]. As soon as I smelled it I said to my mate, 'Oh, the girl is buying a very bad wee. She will be sick!' And I gave him some coins to go and come with proper ganja. Later I finished the work and put the new packet there in the same place for her. Then I told my mate, 'Heh heh, she will like this more-o!' I didn't want her to think she was being set up. So just as soon as I spotted her around the grounds I went to say, 'Don't worry, it was only me, Nunu, who took care of you.' So we became friends. And from then on she always asked me and my boys to look after her wee. She was a real smoker, Prof, she was one of us. I wonder what has become of her. We never heard from her again after your Henry Kissinger sacked her mother."[25]

"Why did you leave the work, I mean what happened in 1985?"

"Prof, do you know the story of Sharon Scranage and the CIA in Ghana in Ronald Reagan's time, when the U.S. was trying to overthrow Rawlings?"

"A little. Wasn't Scranage the black American CIA agent jailed for passing classified information to her Ghanaian boyfriend, an intelligence officer?"

"Correct. His name was Michael Soussoudis, a cousin of Rawlings. After the Americans trapped and arrested them both in the U.S., they exchanged him back for some CIA agents arrested here, ones exposed by Scranage. It was a real mess. So some months later we still knew that this CIA business was not finished. You were bombing Libya so the ambassador wasn't around. Running the place was a new man named Kile, Robert Kile, Robert Lee Kile. He was the admin officer but he was all CIA. The word was around town. And he was a thief. He thought me and my boys were stupid. In fact, he had a business with a Lebanese man called The Colonel [a pseudonym] who lived here in Nima near your place. He ordered containers of air conditioning and refrigeration equipment, all kinds of things for the embassy. But the containers were never brought to me for inventory. They went to The Colonel, who sold them and split the money with Kile. I hated him. So I organized all my boys to expose him and all his theft and CIA business going on in our area. He was sacked. But at the beginning of 1986 they sacked me too and then eighteen more of us."

"How did all that get you into photography?"

"I'm coming with that. You see, after sixteen years work they gave me a sixty-dollar severance. I borrowed another ten from my brother and bought a Canon T50 off an embassy man who was leaving for a different posting. From there I became a photographer. So Prof, you should bring us some malt, so we can drink to Ronald Reagan and the CIA, because without them we might not be working together as we are today!!" (Uncontrolled laughter, both of us.)

A quick Internet trip to Wikipedia as we spoke in the wired-in-world of my Nima apartment told us that Sharon Scranage remains the only person convicted of breaking the American Intelligence Identities Protection Act. She pleaded guilty to three of eighteen charges, got five years reduced to two, and was incarcerated for eighteen months. In the moment of mind-boggling thoughts that swirled through my head, I stopped short of asking Nii Yemo if he had ever heard the names Valerie Plame and Karl Rove.[26]

But to return to Ghana via "In God We Trust," the miniature, as Susan Stewart reminds us in her book *On Longing*,[27] is a central player in histories of nostalgia. Smallness of scale and representational naiveté often combine for charm and market success. The objects stand in suitably as the child that is the imagined other. Odoi Perkoh's trotros sell for twenty-five dollars, very good money, to Americans and Europeans in Accra's high-end hotels. Their sure-to-please cuteness, smooth and pol-

62. Ako Perkoh bearing the union chief's tsolorley linguist staff.
Photograph © 2006 Steven Feld.

ished for tourist consumers, rests in marked contrast to the roughed
detail of the trotro vehicle perched atop the ceremonial linguist's staff
carried by Odoi's father, the union counselor Ako Perkoh, known to all as
Al Haji.

The drivers union here appropriates both the paraphernalia and pro-
cedural pomp of Ghana's chiefly business. The trotro staff, like the chief's
linguist staff, speaks the authority of office. If a driver is to be called
before union elders to answer to charges of misbehavior, it is Al Haji,
bearing the staff, who tracks down the wrongdoer. The staff re-presents
the body and presence, that is, the voice, of the union chief driver, with
the full bearing of his status and power. Upon seeing it, there is no way
out. The one summoned is swept by fear, and obligated to respond.

As Stewart's book reminds us, miniatures and gigantics dance together
in the material economy of nostalgias; they swirl wondrously on the
dance floor of alterity, turning the long-ago-and-far-away into the I was—
or could have been—just there. And the this was—or could have been—
like that. Just like Vice naming his lorry "May Be."

In the swirl of recent mammy wagon representations we also had a trotro on the cover of the CD remix of seventies oldies for the fiftieth anniversary of independence by the Ghanaian pop star group Wulomei[28] and then fresh-painted, Coca-Cola-logo'd tsolorleys greeting visitors in January 2008 when Ghana hosted the Africa Cup of Nations soccer tournament. Like the miniature, the CD album cover or advertisement vehicle make links between acoustic and iconic nostalgias for a lost past and the exciting pleasures of contemporary consumption.

"Nii Yemo, when I get to America I am speaking at New York University in the memory of a friend named Annette Weiner. Like her I studied in Papua New Guinea. Like her I studied funerals. Like her I saw how the things people give and the things they say carry into the future. Like her I saw how name and reputation live in things like cloth or statues, songs or stories. What do you think: I would like to tell the story of how por por sounds the names and reputations of drivers too and leave this little 'In God We Trust' trotro souvenir there in a study room dedicated to her memory."

"Of course! You see! 'In God We Trust.' 'Cool Running.' America is well known to us, Prof. Leave the trotro with them. We will help honor your friend's memory. This is Por Por's work. We all have one custom. Your people will understand. 'In God We Trust' came from your side to here with the American money; now we are sending it back as a small lorry with Dodge engine."

So is a voice any less material than a lorry, the musical use of an old truck horn any less a smelting down than transforming a tomato tin into a carburetor part? Is the souvenir no less a stand-in for the memory work that connects one moment of materiality to another of ephemerality, the echo of a word, a name, a proverb rematerialized, the dance of pumping a tire?

Annette Weiner was unquestionably right about the dynamic interplay between transience, durability, and permanence. She was also unquestionably right about guardianship often trumping ownership, sentiment distinctively pervading materialities of all kinds. The por por story is layered as sensuously thick with all of this as any tale from the Trobriand Islands or the Papua New Guinea rainforest.

But por por's cosmopolitan sound-ecology-cosmology trinity recasts the complexity of smelting materialities to fuse a horn honking jazz, the motor vehicle, and the movies. All intense markers of American twentieth-century modernity, here they are recycled and newly welded together by Afro-spiritualism to forge a transatlantic working-class jukebox of desire, one whose outpourings are as dense and raucous as a New Orleans second line, an identity party where you chose your names and costumes, your songs and sayings, your horns and moves, pump-dancing them on top of the colonial treasure chest.[29]

All that honking, and all the naming that it does, voices histories of reputation. Whether the name is spoken or sung or signed on a trotro, it is a shout-out into the streets of public culture, the insertion of, indeed, insistence on repetition as resonance, a way to keep the memorial in public presence. That's why sound and voice here have no less profound materiality than a truck's rearview mirror. Like the durability of physical material objects, sound rematerializes in echoic hearings, in repetitions, and in multiple mediations, honking the voice of names on the road of reputation. What makes sound distinctive is the way this materiality breathes in the elegant ephemerality of now it's here, now it's gone, and now it's back.

"You see! Your mouth is your lorry. They will pay to listen. Tell them about 'In God We Trust.' These vehicles are wealth to drivers like teaching is wealth to you. You hear! This is why 'In God We Trust' is a good tsolorley for you, Prof! Drive it well! Tell them!"

The simple matter of that kind of repetition, the echoic return of a quote into focus after a few pages, leads to a closing story about voice and sonic circulations, about what Annette called the "continuing power" of smelted down objects.

After our souvenir trotro encounter, I added "Cool Running" to my many nicknames for Nii Yemo, and he in turn reciprocated the gesture, addressing me by those words, using them to mark enthusiasm or approval, often answering or signing off the phone with them. One of the people who heard this banter was David, my driver, who had also over the years become friendly with Nii Yemo.

When I returned to Accra in December 2009, David picked me up at the airport in a vehicle I was seeing for the first time, a recently purchased taxi, and on its dashboard he had a shiny new stick-on placard with the words "Cool Running" floating over a Nike check-stripe logo. On the way home I commented on the sign and that's when David asked me what "Cool Running" actually meant. So I told him about the Dodge engine, and about the souvenir "In God We Trust" trotro that I had taken to America to leave in the NYU Anthropology lounge named for Annette Weiner.

63. Nii Yemo
Nunu, wearing
his father's 1957
uniform, on
"Cool Running"
trotro mini-coffin.
Photograph © 2010
Steven Feld.

"Oh that is very wonderful," he said. "I only know it from when you and Nii Yemo are talking in the taxi, and I liked it *soo* much. 'Cool Running': I was wondering, is it the name of a Nike shoe? So I asked the men who make the window lettering [decals] for the back of our taxis to make me a sign for the inside."

Now David too is known as "Cool Running," his vehicle, his reputation, his engine as running shoe "name" vocally and materially reciting and recycling the work and stories of others near and far.

HEAD AGAIN,
VAMP OUT

Beyond Diasporic Intimacy

64. "May Be" (again). *Photograph © 2007 Steven Feld.*

It's time for a conclusion. I could approach that requirement in a familiar way, through a jazz-detoured reading and commentary on the deeply historical European cosmopolitanism literature, with its clamor over the meaning of universalism, transcendent translation, rights, and justice. And then through a parallel reading and commentary on the more recent deeply multicultural cosmopolitanism literature, with its clamor about whether and where there is really a place for difference in universalism. That literature is powerful for the way it voices anxiety about who is a cosmopolitan by choice and who is a migrant by necessity, about what a world of unhappily forced movements means to new forms of boundary crossing and citizenship, and what a simultaneous world of more wished-for boundary crossings allows us to understand about migrations. These are important matters; they have been, and are being discussed by people I respect and like to read.[1] But I want to resist the kind of conclusion that replaces the territory with the map. I don't have that kind of conclusion; what I have are four nonconclusions and six more stories.

The Intervocality of "May Be"

What does it mean when a working-class Ghanaian, a man with no passport, someone who has not traveled outside Ghana, and rarely outside of Accra, says, "America is well known to us," and tells U.S. Embassy and CIA stories with deep ethnographic authority? What does it mean that drivers are known as Humphery Bogerd, Jack Palance, Ricky Nelson, Lester Young, Nelson Mandela, or Mama Africa, No Time To Die, Be Sure, No Haste, or The Day? What does it mean when the lyrics to soul-era songs by Aretha Franklin or the Staple Singers are the answer to a question about truck driving? What does it mean that the "Charlie" in

Charlie Chaplin can turn into the "Charlie" in Charlie Parker via the "Charlie" of "Hey, guy"?

The por por story, like the others replayed here, was rendered in juxtapositions of local voices and mine, mimicking the way I have listened in to repetitions and ruptures, reemplacing stories in my voice and thus theorizing their experiential authority through performed intervocality rather than through academic contextualization. That focus on voice insists on how cosmopolitanism is produced and circulated in storied encounters. Repeating, retelling, reciting, reviewing, and reworking their content in multiple forms of dialogic auditing and editing, the work of memoir, of remembered viewings and remembered hearings, takes over my own voice. Like the way I keep hearing Vice say, "May Be," then repeat those words to myself, speak them out loud, and write them down while speaking them again.

Repeating and speaking out loud serves to foreground how key experiential tropes are embodied and emplaced in so many of the locally familiar vocal gestures of Ga or Twi-calqued Ghanaian English, like phrase-initial evidentials *Ona!* "You see!" *Onu!* "You hear!" Or mid-sentence word-lengthened emphatics like *tooo* or *noo* or *soo*. Or phrase-final expressive confirmations like *-o* or *alll* or *Eh hehh!* Or the ubiquitous stand-alones "Of course!," "By all means!," "Correct!," or the indexical marker *nakai*, "Like *that*." Writing these vocal gestures out, including them in remembered voicings, serves to foreground how they take me back to whole scenes and sites and tales of wonder, surprise, con/disjuncture, anxiety, irony.

They foreground the way I can only continue to wonder how the Accra jazz cosmopolitanism of por por honk horn funerals can look and sound like New Orleans jazz funerals without any direct knowledge of or direct historical connection to them. Or the way I can only continue to be surprised that Nii Otoo Annan can speak of toads, polyrhythms, Elvin Jones, and the oceanic powers of Mami Wata in the same phrases. Or the way I can only continue to ponder con/disjuncture in Nii Noi Nortey's intertwined engagement of Osei Tutu, John Coltrane, and Ludwig van Beethoven, analogized by a parallel philosophical pantheon of Kwame Nkrumah, Malcolm X, and Karl Marx, topped for good measure by the duo of Bob Marley and Frantz Fanon. Or the way I can only continue to feel an anxious irony about how Guy Warren, Ghana's most famous jazz musician, comes into the ring swinging that the whole narrative of American jazz as a site of racial pride is a racist insult to Africans because it freezes them in the past and denies them both a real historical and contemporary presence.

What kind of jazz cosmopolitan is an African Buddhist who promotes religious tolerance by performing Handel's "Hallelujah" chorus as a mixed Christian and Islamic ritual that politically swells to the ultimate lines of the Ghana national anthem: "And help us to resist the oppressor's rule / With all our will and might evermore"? What kind of jazz cosmopolitan is a non-Rastafarian Rastaman, a self-pronounced "I'd rather be poor" Afrocentric ideologue despite or because of elevated class and educational background, an astonishingly original artist whose unique but locally marginal afrifones are parked in / as sculptural works and only sound a few times each year, typically (Afrocentrism aside) at European cultural institutes? What kind of jazz cosmopolitan is an at-the-edge eccentric prodigy drummer who struggles at the fulcrum of weekend working-poor church gigs and weekday reentrenchment in the darker drink-and-drug reality of his community? What kind of jazz cosmopolitans are bus and truck drivers whose vocabularies include neither "jazz" nor "cosmopolitan" but whose musical practices synthesize and perform the vastness of both?

For Ghanaba, jazz cosmopolitanism involved a lifelong struggle with identity, race, nation, and spiritual fulfillment. For Nii Noi Nortey, jazz cosmopolitanism is a lifelong struggle with making avant-garde aesthetics resound to Pan-African politics. For Nii Otoo Annan, jazz cosmopolitanism is a lifelong process of working-class empowerment as redemptive spiritualism at the simultaneous sites of charismatic Christian churches, fetish priests, and the many drinking spots that dot Mami Wata's open-air beachfront. For the La Drivers Union Por Por Group, jazz cosmopolitanism is a lifelong process of honking road history to honor the reputations, the "names" of departed drivers.

For me, a visitor, an anthropologist of sound listening to histories of listening, collaborating variously as a musician, a phonographer, a photographer, a filmmaker, a writer, a producer, there are many such sentences, many such summaries. But there is always more "on top," no definitive this is that, this means that, this says that, this answers that. There are only new pileups from X to Y by way of Z, reroutings and meanderings, storied accumulations that negotiate authority by emplacing other voices in my own. Like the way I keep hearing, then repeating, Vice saying "May Be."

What I've described about these performances of connection and these disconnections of performance is their overlays of routes and detours, their production of archival projects, their techniques of remembering and reciting, their modes of declaiming and reclaiming, their myriad ways of inventing and recycling. What I've wandered through is their modes of piling up and reorganizing and rearranging pileups of images and sounds, of creating quasi-utopic wishlists. What I've queried is their simultaneous invention and vulnerability, the way every assertion of desire might rapidly be met by an equal and opposing force that neutralizes, cancels, or mutes its efficacy. What I've visually and acoustically tracked are maneuvers to get from here to there, and there to here, and with those spatial presences and imaginaries, their many temporally shifting counterparts, from then till now, now till then, then till when, when till then.

Each intertwining of embodied historical knowledge and practice is met at twists or turns by doubles, phantom counterparts, shout-outs that echo back, images and signs that other presences, other shadows, other ears and voices and eyes and hands, are around, are aware. Like the repeated invocation "The Lord works in mysterious ways." Or its resonance with the Ga proverb *Onukpai ye mli*, "The elders are in on it." Like the por por horns honking the equivalent of a truck named "May Be" on the road to New Orleans. Like Nii Otoo's sounding the shoreline of wonder about what Mami Wata might wash up next. Like Nii Noi's sense that the way he could "hear our struggles when Coltrane screamed" offered "a whole spiritual alternative." Like Ghanaba's insistence on the call-and-response format that sounds his "Eyi Wala Dong" ("That Happy Feeling") as a profoundly African but Buddhist-centered and Islamic-sensitive echo-embrace of Europe and Christianity via Handel's "Hallelujah" chorus.

Always in the background for me, as I've listened to and revoiced these convergences, these dis/connections, has been the concept of "diasporic intimacy." Some years ago, I was asked to write a piece on voice, vocal knowledge, and intervocality for a *Critical Inquiry* theme issue titled "Intimacy." I did, by imagining Maurice Merleau-Ponty and Walter Benjamin accompanying me on a listening trip into the world of Bosavi storytelling in a Papua New Guinea rainforest. When the "Intimacy" issue was published, I found myself excited with a nearby piece in it titled "On Diasporic Intimacy: Ilya Kabakov's Installations and Immigrant Homes," by the Harvard literary scholar Svetlana Boym.[2]

To venture into the world of installations by the artist Kabakov about the Soviet home in exile, Boym starts out, like Gaston Bachelard, by tracing the idea of intimacy to that of home, to some very innermost or personal place. That sets up her paradox, "a diasporic intimacy that is not opposed to uprootedness and defamiliarization but constituted by it." She develops the paradox like this: "Diasporic intimacy can be approached only through indirection and intimation, through stories and secrets. It is spoken in a foreign language that reveals the inadequacies of translation. Diasporic intimacy does not promise an unmediated emotional fusion but only a precarious affection—no less deep, while aware of its transience. In contrast to the utopian images of intimacy as transparency, authenticity, and ultimate belonging, diasporic intimacy is dystopian by definition; it is rooted in the suspicion of a single home. It thrives on unpredictable chance encounters, on hope for human understanding, but this hope is not utopian. Diasporic intimacy is not limited to the private sphere but reflects collective frameworks of memory that encapsulate even the most personal of dreams."[3]

The paradoxical intimacy that Boym starts with, the idea of "home," and its nonoppositional diasporic uprootings, is the cosmopolitan transit I have repeatedly described in a very local world of very far-reaching works. Her key tropes, operations, and sites—"stories and secrets," "precarious affection," "unpredictable chance encounters," "collective frameworks of memory"—will be familiar, as they are tracks I have been down over and over with Nii Noi, Nii Otoo, Ghanaba, and the La Por Por Group. In Boym's landscapes, like mine, intimacies are poignant pressings-together and they arise and announce multiply in sound and voice, image and sign. Like Boym's dystopia, my resounding of Accra's jazz cosmopolitanism is full of interruptions, relating equally to the mutually "alienating and illuminating experiences of the metropolis." Like the way I keep hearing Vice say, "May Be."

In sound-rich Accra, these experiences are stitched together by the ways voice turns stories and secrets of diasporic intimacy into intervocality. It's where Accra's jazz cosmopolitanism amplifies Boym's "suspicion of a single home" and honks, drums, or afrifones it into echoic multiples that drive through "the road" of local geographies, criss-crossing and multiply fusing legacies European, American, Caribbean, African, and the ways they have washed in and out and lay on top of history's unruly waves.

As a listener, I've been drawn into a complicity in the stories I've heard, diasporic intimacy becoming intervocality. As a reteller, I've reproduced and amplified that complicity and its key discursive effect, performing arguments about uneven, unfinished, unrealized, or unsung modernity, as well as a more general politics of cosmopolitanism, one that congeals in the poetics of irony. Beyond diasporic intimacy, then, is the idea that a lost beyond is closer than you imagine, that shortcuts or leaps from X to Y via Z perform the storied place of connected memory, creating intimacy rather than effacing it. An image, word, sound becomes a preface to the production of stories about connection and the authority of stating, imploring, beseeching. Any key phrase, any punch line, can do the work of bringing out the effects of a much bigger story. Like the way I keep hearing Vice say, "May Be."

Beyond diasporic intimacy is intimacy shaping and reshaping spaces of significant difference. Here I've experienced musical intimacies, intimacies of playing together, and repeatedly, time after time, event after event, year after year, the constancy of being in the music together, establishing closeness through skilled cocreation, the trust and pleasures of being in heightened and almost always nonverbal collaboration felt and experienced as groove.[4] And I've experienced intervocal intimacies, of becoming part of each others tales, memories, of predicting, overtaking, or interlocking each others voices, hearing the echo of the one in the other. This is the intimacy of a particular authority to report the "s/he said" of something held close in memory, the intimacy of "you see!," the intimacy of "I have a story to tell. . . ."

Beyond diasporic intimacy is where local knowledge becomes intervocal knowledge. Beyond diasporic intimacy is where hearing Vice say, "May Be," makes me unable to resist repeating those words again, and again, and again.

Race Washes Out, Race Washes In

While presenting the first version of these chapters as lectures at Berkeley, I received a kind email from a senior audience member. A devoted Shirley Temple fan, she told me of her delight that the por por lecture mentioned the former ambassador in Accra and, in the question-and-answer conversation after, the local shrine to her that I had encountered. But the email asked why I cut the story off abruptly and didn't say more. I wrote back to say that I was not authorized to show photographs of the Shirley Temple shrine that I had visited, that I had been asked not to tell stories about how the shrine came to be, or about the activities that take place there.

What I can say here is that a Shirley Temple shrine that I know about in Accra (and, who knows, there *may be* others) includes, among many small visual objects, a faded postcard-sized image of the 1939 Salvador Dalí painting *Shirley Temple, the Youngest Most Sacred Monster of the Contemporary Cinema*.[5] In that painting the face of the young Shirley (eleven years old in 1939) is from a newspaper photograph. The collaged head is topped with a painted bat, suggesting vampire, and the yellowed photo of her face connects below to the painting of a lion's body, the small breasts understated, the large clawed paws not. A human skull-and-bones in the lion's midst suggests a fresh kill. At the bottom there is a label that reads "Shirley, at last in Technicolor."

That the child-star Shirley Temple is the baby-breasted predator lion of Metro Goldwyn Mayer is surely Dalí's sarcastic comment on Hollywood greed, an anxiously surreal vision of a young, innocent girl corrupted into a sexualized killer. But neither the name Salvador Dalí nor that kind of cynical riff on the Shirley and Hollywood history has ever crossed the lips of my Accra acquaintances associated with the shrine. Not at all. That piece of the story was only acknowledged to me elsewhere, by an elite Ghanaian businesswoman and art connoisseur educated in Europe and living in the United States, someone with extended but now distant family connections to the Accra Shirley shrine I saw.

What Mrs. Kofi (the name she jokingly instructed me to use if I wrote about her) told me, as we sipped tea and talked alternately about banking and art in her elegant Washington, D.C., apartment, was that it was wonderful that the Dalí painting sites the Shirley Sphinx ambiguously in the desert or at the shoreline. "But," she said, "I'm sure any Ghanaian will tell you it is the ocean." And that's when she acknowledged that the suggestion speaks to or implies a "may be," that this painting evokes the presence of Mami Wata, the spirit mermaid of the ocean, who, through the magic of the waves, and after forty years of her followers' devotion, swept back onto Accra's shores none other than West Africa's earliest film heroine, Shirley Temple.

The Accra painter Nicholas Wayo, who has both painted many local movie posters as well as explored surrealist techniques, was thrilled when I commissioned him to do a local Shirley Sphinx. In his version the glowingly blonded corkscrew curls of the child Shirley, printed from a picture downloaded from her official website and then collaged onto the painting to echo Dalí, are turned into the lion's mane. But the lion's body transforms beyond the original painting, to become a mermaid tail. And the bones on the sand in front of the Shirley lion are drenched equally by splash marks and the orange beach sundown over the background ship-wreck's ribbing. This time the inscription says: "Ambassador Shirley Temple Black returns to Ghana gift of Salvador Dalí and Mami Wata."

When she washed ashore in 1974 as the U.S. ambassador to Ghana, Her Excellency Shirley Temple Black (and as Nii Yemo reminded me often in his characteristic wit, "I'm telling you, we were *soo* happy that she came back *Black*"), Ghanaians were moved by the stories she told in private and public about her equally very much locally loved "Uncle Billy," namely, Bill "Bojangles" Robinson, her childhood dance partner (and Ghanaba's childhood dancing inspiration). The story that some senior retired Accra diplomats repeated to me is that Ambassador Temple Black acknowledged that Bojangles not only taught her how to dance, but also taught her the meaning of racism. She would recount how Uncle Billy never answered when she asked for his hotel room number to visit for dance practice. He left it to her alone to learn that he was not housed in the same hotels, or if he was, it was in a segregated annex or in the drivers' quarters.[6]

One Accra contact, a family member of the ambassador's former driver, told me that Shirley Temple Black often let it be known that she hated Jerry Jeff Walker's 1968 song "Mr. Bojangles" and did not want it ever played in her car or at embassy functions or in her presence. Pre-sumably this was because she thought the song made a bum out of her

AMBASSADOR SHIRLEY TEMPLE BLACK
RETURNS TO GHANA GIFT OF
SALVADOR DALI & MAMI WATA

65. Ambassador Shirley Temple Black returns to Ghana. *Art © 2010 Nicholas Wayo.*

beloved Uncle Billy, despite Jerry Jeff Walker's statement that the song was about someone else.

"Yes, I heard that one," Kweku Asiedu told me and Nii Yemo as we looked through a file of his photographic negatives from the ambassador's Accra years. Once chief of photography for the U.S. Information Services, and a colleague of Nii Yemo's in the 1970s at the U.S. Embassy, Asiedu photographed prominent visitors and distributed pictures to the press. When the USIS closed down and shut the photographic lab he found piles of his work in a trash bin and managed to rescue many sheets of negatives. He showed us a book of them, from the mid-seventies, recalling with Nii Yemo how the most important popular perception of Shirley Temple Black was of a woman who was doing the work of a man. "As soon as she was announced they started showing her old movies to introduce her to younger people in Ghana here. Everyone had to be impressed, you know, with how a movie star, especially a woman, could rise to become ambassador of the richest nation in the world."[7]

That the Accra memory of the child actress is inextricably bound up with the memory of the dancer Bill "Bojangles" Robinson takes us to the locally best-remembered Shirley Temple movie, a racist 1935 plantation film called *The Little Colonel*. The mesmerizing image from that film is of a little white girl taking the big black hand of her butler. This white and black hand-holding moment, and in the 1930s–40s–50s Gold Coast there was nothing common about that, not at *allll*, comes when Bojangles responds to Shirley's moody pouting and resistance to heading upstairs to go to sleep. He gifts her a delightfully virtuosic tap dance up and down and up and down and up and down the stairs. Overwhelmed by pleasure, her mood lifts and she reaches out, takes his hand in hers, and joins him in a toe-tapping magical ascent of the staircase.[8]

The footwork fixation on Shirley Temple as a dancing figure of return, a wondrous childhood presence that tapped back in as an American ambassador, *may be* with a little help from Mami Wata, runs parallel to two other stories I've recounted. One was of the amazing return of Beethoven, believed by Nii Noi Nortey and many others to be of black ancestry, back to Mama Africa, in the form of a gift performance of the Ninth Symphony for Ghana's fiftieth anniversary, *may be* a Mami Wata wash-in along with help from La Scala, the Italian Embassy, and the over-the-rainbow and outside-politics-as-usual cosmopolitan embrace of Daniel Barenboim and Kofi Annan. The other story was about the percussionist Nii Otoo Annan analogizing my appearance, the appearance of a white man paying a regular salary for work, as something like a light-skinned doll washing up to shore, *may be* a Mami Wata ocean spirit gift of return for his years of sweat, pouring his body like libation onto his drums in front of numerous audiences of dancers, congregants, and listeners.

In these Accra stories, cosmopolitanism is a performance of sociality routed through the vehicle of place and fracture of race, *may be* with a little help of the Lord working "mysterious ways," of the elders and ancestors being "in on it." Among intellectuals focused on the historical and sociological complexity of such issues, it is Paul Gilroy who most powerfully theorizes the centrality of music to the kind of performance of cosmopolitan social connection I've been consumed by in Accra.

In *The Black Atlantic*, Gilroy reaches beyond diaspora, beyond both the emphasis on a separation from source, and the possibility for any essentialized reconnection. This leads to one of the most critical features of his vision: a constant acknowledgment of the interplay of transnational and intercultural forces over and beyond origins or originary models of culture and consciousness. Instead he reconnects with W. E. B. Du Bois's double consciousness to explore the making of multiply enmeshed hybrid identities, black, European, American, Caribbean.

And he assumes those identity formations always to be replete with ongoing interchanges, routed through travels real and imaginary, staking out a blackness dialectically formed in, through, and around multiple modernities. Gilroy reminds us of his "preoccupation" again and again: "A preoccupation with the striking doubleness that results from this unique position—in an expanded West but not completely of it—is a definitive characteristic of the intellectual history of the Black Atlantic."[9]

Generously yet critically offering alternatives to any number of nationalist, ethnicist, absolutist, separatist, universalist, or assimilationist analyses, and refusing totalized identity to insist on modernity as hybridity, *The Black Atlantic* paves the road for Gilroy's later work like *Against Race* and *Postcolonial Melancholia*, both of which focus on the demeaning effects of hyperracialized discourse, and the particularly pernicious quality of the polarized thinking that often goes with it in Britain's postmulticulturalism struggles. Espousing a planetary humanist cosmopolitanism inspired by Du Bois's grand vision and Fanon's focus on the social and historical in race, Gilroy's hoped-for politics of postcolony/postempire conviviality resonates with the call for an ethical politics of acknowledged coexistence in Kwame Anthony Appiah's *Cosmopolitanism*.[10]

Another of Gilroy's preoccupations, with the sailing ship as Bakhtinian chronotope, parallels the ways an emphasis on movement—on the water, on the road, on the march, on the lorry, on the train—pervades these Accra stories. Parallel to tales here of Ghanaba, Nii Noi, Nii Otoo, por por, Gilroy shows how music performs debates about modernity through the time-space fusion of lives on the move, debates that are revelatory because they are so often both populist and nontextual. His embrace of music as a nonlinguacentric arena of Black Atlantic intellectualization is thus powerfully recalled in Nii Noi Nortey's summary comment in the Trane Station video that "music's strength . . . [is] the way everything can come together politically and spiritually, without reading books."[11]

Just replay Nii Noi's comment for a DJ moment and travel back to 1956, the moment when songs of freedom and independence paved the radio road for the colonial Gold Coast to become independent Ghana on March 6, 1957. The song "Ghana Freedom" by the highlife king E. T. Mensah was the key local hit in Accra.[12] And had Guy Warren not been in America at that moment *maybe* he would be on this recording date, as he was the original drummer and coleader with E. T. Mensah of the Tempos Band.

That connection was resonant when I listened to "Ghana Freedom" with Ghanaba in the weeks around the fiftieth anniversary of Ghana's independence, in March 2007. Singing along with the opening call and response, "Ghana, we now have freedom . . . FREEDOM! Ghana, land of freedom . . . FREEDOM!," he highlighted the presence of the maracas and bongos, for which he took full credit. He also pointed out the horn-lipping vibrato characteristic of the indigenization of brass band music in Ghana, mentioning what he heard as a generous overlay from the Duke Ellington saxophone section sound. To hear Ghanaba tell it, Mensah's highlife sounded the independence moment in the deep cosmopolitan jazz transit of Ghana highlife meeting Trinidad calypso via Caribbean London and African American New York.

Simultaneously, Mensah's African coastal beacon of diasporic intimacy was mirrored by Trinidadian calypso equally meeting Ghana highlife via London and New York. Listen to that in "Birth of Ghana," recorded a month later in London by the calypsonian Lord Kitchener. Notice that there are no bongos or maracas but a clear foregrounding of African-style hand drumming, call-and-response phrase structures, and small-combo African American swing jazz.[13]

Kitchener took the voice of broadcaster and chronicler in this newsy calypso. But in Ghana today this song is not called "Birth of Ghana"; it is remembered by its key line, "Ghana is the name." And as pointed out with regard to por por music, among Ghanaians and particularly working-class Ghanaians, the English word "name" stands out to signify cumulative reputation and achievement, something worth remembering. Like the public face of a trotro lorry signed by its mantle inscription, or ornamental horn honks associated with its driver, the call "Ghana" and response "Ghana is the name" sounds the sign of independence as diasporic reputation and achievement.

So, the jazzy diasporic intimacy of highlife-cum-calypso "Ghana Freedom" sounding in Accra overlap-echoes the calypso-cum-highlife "Birth of Ghana" sounding Trinidad back to black London. Interestingly, it was Kitchener's "Birth of Ghana" rather than Mensah's "Ghana Freedom" that was playing on Nii Noi Nortey's sound system during the fiftieth-anniversary celebrations in March 2007. Nii Noi's understanding of African independence movements was routed through his 1970s and 1980s U.K. residencies and engagements there with Pan-African, Caribbean, and black British lives. Hence his musical association with the moment of Ghana's freedom also resounded through the diasporic intimacy of black London. Nii Noi was quick to point out that the drums on Kitchener's "Birth of Ghana" calypso were more African-sounding than the drums on Mensah's "Ghana Freedom" highlife. He took this to mean that calypso, as diasporic modernism, could perform Afrocentrism just as easily as highlife, as Afromodernism, could perform its Caribbean embrace.

Now put the United States into the picture. That's where Guy Warren was located in 1956, teaching the "talking drum" to America's number one bebop drummer, Max Roach, and working on his own *Africa Speaks, America Answers* LP. Warren met Louis Armstrong in Accra in 1960, but had he been in Accra in 1956 he would have met him then, on the trip that brought Satchmo with Edward R. Murrow and a CBS film crew. In Accra, Armstrong jammed with the Tempos and E. T. Mensah at the latter's Paramount Club, and played where Warren had dropped out, Achimota College, famously performing Fats Waller's "What Did I Do to Be So Black and Blue?" there in direct dedication to the leader of the independence movement, Kwame Nkrumah.

Among E. T. Mensah's best-known highlife songs at that moment (first recorded in 1952) was "All for You." On the occasion of Armstrong's visit the band changed the lead line lyric from "All for You, E.T." to "All for You, Louis." Indeed, on the airport tarmac, greeting Armstrong's arrival from London, were seven brass bands, according to plan, each perched on the back of a flatbed wooden lorry. As Armstrong came out from the plane the bands sounded a simultaneous rendition of "All for You" and Armstrong lifted his trumpet and together with his trombonist Trummy

66. From left,
Guy Warren
and Louis
Armstrong in
Accra, 1960.
Photograph
© *2010 Afrikan*
Heritage Library
Collection.

Young joined in a joyful jam with the blaring brass bands as he strutted
down the airplane stairs.

I've long appreciated the story of the "All for You" arrival and of Armstrong in Accra from two close-up accounts. John Collins's book *E. T.
Mensah, King of Highlife* tells the tale from firsthand recollections gathered
in conversation with James Moxon, then head of the U.S. Department of
Information and the man responsible for organizing the Murrow and
Armstrong visit. Moxon was assisted on the job by Robert Raymond, who
also chronicled the tour in exceptional detail in his *Black Star in the Wind.*[14]

But the story was also told to me simply, humbly, and with endless
smiles of joy by a local trumpeter who was there to play on that day.
Benjamin Odoi, a neighbor of Nii Otoo's in Korle Gonno, was a trumpeter so Armstrongesque in his own sound that colleagues nicknamed him
"Satchmo" by the 1960s, a name and trumpeting reputation he took to his
grave just a few months after we met in early 2010.[15] And of course the
story of that day was well remembered by drivers who drove Odoi and

67. Trumpeters Louis Armstrong, center, and E. T. Mensah, right, Paramount Club, Accra, 1956.

other musicians to the airport. I was also able to speak to one of the last of them, Mensah Johnny, in the months before his passing in late 2009.

Guy Warren also remembered this event very well, if from afar. While in America, Warren regularly listened to Voice of America for news of Africa and Ghana. But the news of Armstrong and Mensah's encounter on the tarmac and after got to Warren from CBS radio. And those broadcasts were so memorable that Columbia released them on LP, an America-purchased copy of which Ghanaba proudly held in his collection. The sound of the bands playing "All for You," together with the sound of Armstrong's voice and horn joining in, are heard there, framed beforehand by the almost unbearable commentary of the broadcaster Edward R. Murrow. Ghanaba just shook his head and stuck his tongue out when we listened to it together in 2007: "In May of 1956, on the eve of the Gold Coast independence, Louis Armstrong, who is convinced that his great-grandparents came from here, went back, at the invitation of the prime

68. Lord Kitchener, *Birth of Ghana*, in commemorative
jacket, 1956.

minister, and as representative of the great free nation across the sea
where both the blues and the colored people had their first awakening.
Satchmo returned to Africa an international figure, as the crowd roared,
and the bands, seven of them, played an old Gold Coast favorite, now
renamed 'All for You, Louis.' "[16]

The story of Armstrong's Accra arrival and greeting, minus the flatbed
trotro bit, is also told in Penny von Eschen's wonderful *Satchmo Blows Up
the World*, which takes us to the end of any and all innocence about jazz
as soft diplomacy and into the get-real 1950s cold war world of jazz
ambassadorship as ideological business. Satchmo was imagined to be
both a beacon of influence and a source of information. But in fact he
didn't do State Department tours until 1960 even though he was named a
jazz ambassador in 1955. For five years he protested the contradiction in
that designation. As von Eschen puts it: "Armstrong was acutely conscious of the irony inherent in a black man's representing a still-segre-
gated America."[17]

But Eisenhower wanted him. Kwame Nkrumah was a worry in 1956.
The U.S. government suspiciously analyzed his writings and speeches,
collaborated with the British to spy on him, and was more than a little

worried that he had deep socialist tendencies and communist sympathies. And that takes us back to Guy Warren's cosmopolitan career as an OSS-trained American spy, beginning with his return to Accra from a first training visit to the States in 1943. Working as a journalist in Accra in the war years, Warren passed numerous British documents to U.S. wartime intelligence. It is unclear what happened to Warren's spying network after the war. It is also unclear if U.S. intelligence had anything to do with Warren's relocation in 1950 to work in radio in Liberia, or if it had anything to do with the timing of his coming to the United States in 1953, or if it had anything to do with the fact that he remained in the States after Ghana's independence in 1957.

Ghanaba/Warren told me that meeting Armstrong in 1960 was deeply memorable to him. He told me that he was impressed by Armstrong's awareness of race and that Armstrong recounted to him that he deliberately traveled to Ghana with an integrated band so that people would know he didn't think jazz was "a ghetto." He told me that Armstrong's refusal to be a jazz ambassador related to anger over President Eisenhower's refusal to deal seriously with the crisis in Arkansas when Governor Orval Faubus sent the National Guard to block black students from integrating Little Rock's Central High School.

Ghanaba/Warren also told me that Armstrong loved to tell the story of Vice President Richard Nixon's presence as a U.S. representative at Kwame Nkrumah's 1957 inauguration. At a state dinner, the story goes, Nixon leaned over to a man sitting next to him, and patronizingly asked, "How does it feel to be free?" The man replied, "I wouldn't know, I'm from Alabama." Nixon was apparently unaware that African Americans and diasporans were mixed in at his table with Ghanaian politicians.[18]

Telling me that story, Ghanaba laughed heartily and recalled the verve of Armstrong delivering its punch line with hilarity. Imitating Satchmo's gravelly growl voice and gleefully underscoring his double-entendre, Warren slowly and precisely put it this way: "Pops said, 'the cat was stoned, Nixon was stoned!'"

As for E. T. Mensah's song dedication, Armstrong told Murrow and others that he was moved by hearing "All for You" in Accra, particularly its local hymn-like vernacular harmonization, because he knew the melody as a creole song from New Orleans. Well, no variants of it are to be found in key collections of New Orleans songs from Armstrong's time. But more important, there is a long genealogy of this song, and it takes us to the eastern Caribbean, where it is called "Sly Mongoose," and is well attested in Jamaican folklore and 1920s mento lyrics.

The song was documented in Trinidad carnival in 1923, the year it was recorded by the entertainer Phil Madison on Victor. But it is more famously associated with two slightly later recordings, by Lionel Belasco (who holds copyright) in 1924, and Sam Manning in 1925, both Trinidadians who recorded some of the earliest versions of Jamaican mento songs in New York. And while the text of "Sly Mongoose" moves through many variations, virtually all renditions share a common refrain that refers to a trickster with large sexual appetites who goes into a white man's kitchen and steals one of his fattest chickens.[19]

When E. T. Mensah passed away in 1996 the *Ghanaian Times* presented an extensive and appreciative piece about his innovations and accomplishments, including a list of his song compositions. A stickler for journalistic accuracy, Ghanaba immediately wrote a detailed response, beginning, "I read the warm editorial of the 'Times' of September 16, 1996, PASSING OF A 'KING' and decided I should write in to SET THE RECORD STRAIGHT."

Among other items of fact-checking clarification about Mensah's career and works, including a number of song adaptations, Ghanaba offered this one: " 'All for You' was also adopted by E.T. He did not compose it. The tune was brought into the Gold Coast from the West Indies by Liberian and Sierra Leonian seamen. The original title was 'Mongoose' in the West Indies, but the seamen named it 'All for You, Titi' ['titi' is seaman slang for a pretty girl]."[20]

Before hearing "All for You" in Accra, Louis Armstrong likely didn't hear "Sly Mongoose" from the Manning or Belasco recordings from the 1920s. What's more likely is that he heard a swing jazz version of the song, either the one recorded in 1938 by Jack Sneed, or the one recorded in 1939 by Ella Fitzgerald, or the one recorded in 1941 by Benny Goodman. He also could have heard the version recorded in New York in 1946 by Rupert Westmore Grant, the calypsonian known as Lord Invader. In the mid-1940s and early 1950s the song was also in the performing repertoire of, and recorded twice, by Charlie Parker, a musician Louis Armstrong didn't much appreciate.[21]

But the most temporally immediate and likely source for Armstrong's familiarity with the song's melody framework was both more indirect and circuitous. Earlier in the year 1956, before his tour, Armstrong and the same band that went with him to Ghana recorded the song "High Society Calypso" with lyrics and melody by Cole Porter. Their performance of that song opens the very popular Hollywood film *High Society*, in which Armstrong stars with Bing Crosby, Grace Kelly, and Frank Sinatra. Even if Armstrong hadn't heard "Sly Mongoose" before that moment, "High Society Calypso" makes clear that the melody was very familiar to Cole Porter, whose lightly scrambled rearrangement of its melodic motifs flips phrases from the original song's A and B sections.[22]

As for the route that brought the song from Trinidad/Jamaica to Gold Coast, we have to complicate Ghanaba's citation of a direct transmission from Liberian and Sierra Leonian sailors. The layered detour comes via London, where the song was recorded in 1929 in two versions as "Almer Bou" and "Tin Ka Tin Ka" on the Zoophone label by the old-timey-sounding banjo-picking and Fanti-singing of the West African Instrumental Quintet from the Gold Coast. Presumably their recording was made after hearing one of the carnival calypsonian versions recorded just a few years earlier. Despite the presence of this recording by Gold Coast musicians in London, the earliest commercial recording we have from West Africa itself comes twenty years later, the 1949 humorous variant "All for You, Baby," sung by Euphenia Cooper, a Liberian singer, but recorded in Gold Coast by Arthur Alberts.[23]

The point of this fast DJ-ing of the two best-known 1956 Ghana independence songs, back to back with one of the moment's otherwise best-known highlife tunes, a song that is equally a mento, calypso, swing, and jazz tune, is to stress again how the movements of Guy Warren/Ghanaba and Nii Noi Nortey positioned their listening biographies in the larger Black Atlantic cosmopolitan transit that joins Ghana and the Caribbean with the ever-present diasporic figure of American jazz, remembered in Accra most powerfully by the presence of Louis Armstrong. To understand Accra's jazz cosmopolitanism then returns us again and again to the acoustic motions of the Black Atlantic sound, to sonic shimmerings, the audible diasporic intimacy of place as washings in and out of race, and to the rich archive of transnational historical synthesis we have in these sound recordings charting hybrid modernities African, Caribbean, European, and American.

But coming back to the ground, in Accra, I'm particularly reminded of the span of this history by recent encounters that summarize the diasporic intimacy of their fifty-some years. In January 2010 I traveled with

(a) "Sly Mongoose" A phrase; (b) "All for You" A phrase; (c) "Sly Mongoose" B phrase; (d) "All for You" instrumental introduction from B phrase

69. Nii Otoo under wall paintings of E. T. Mensah and Guy Warren, Demina Hotel, Korle Gonno. *Photograph © 2010 Steven Feld; art © 1962 Y. K. Anang.*

70. Gene Krupa and Louis Armstrong wall paintings, Demina Hotel, Korle Gonno. *Photograph © 2010 Steven Feld; art © 1962 Y. K. Anang.*

Nii Otoo to Korle Gonno, the seashore area of Accra where he lived, to see the house compound that remains of a popular hotel of the 1960s, the Demina, whose owner was from Cape Coast. The hotel was also a jazz music nightclub with brothel undertone, the two activities brought together by a large courtyard square for drinking, dancing, socializing, and music performance. Facing the courtyard is a long and high wall. On its righthand side one sees the now weathered and deeply faded wall-painting portraits of the trumpeter Louis Armstrong and the drummer Gene Krupa in action with their instruments, both of the images renditions of widely circulated photographs. And in parallel position, on the left side, one sees the equally large and fading wall-painted portraits of the trumpeter E. T. Mensah and the drummer Guy Warren, similarly in the groove, the images again echoing well-known photographs.

Nii Otoo's comment, as he positioned himself under the painting of E. T. Mensah to request a photo portrait of himself in his home community, evinced a keen awareness of the call and response that reverberates the "over there" as, and in, the "over here."

"You see!" he said. "Horn and drum, horn and drum, E.T., Ghanaba here, Kluupa Gene, Satcheymo there, Ghana here America there, yes, jazz, we are all together, Prof, I'm telling you, all together, jazz, all together, horn and drum, yeah, correct."

Nii Otoo didn't know it, but his "all together, jazz" invocation more expressively echoed another one, voiced by the American president Barack Obama when he spoke six months earlier to Ghana's Parliament in Accra, in his first major speech in Africa after his election. Not included in the text of that speech circulated by the White House is one of the president's most successful off-script one-liners. In complete awareness of the resonant memory of America's most famous musical visitor to Accra, the president brought great applause with his casually improvised prespeech remark about the sound of the animal horn mmenson ensemble whose interlocked hooting enveloped the entrance hall of Accra's Convention Center: "It sounds like Louis Armstrong is in the house."[24]

Cosmopolitanism Gone Primitive?

In 2007, after a complicated visa acquisition process, the Accra Trane Station duo of Nii Noi Nortey and Nii Otoo Annan traveled from Ghana to the United States, their first time to America. I flew together with them, first overnight from Accra to London, then to Chicago. There we parted at U.S. Customs, with me heading into the no-hassle citizens queue, and the two of them, with some post-9/11 anxiety and lots of documents, hopefully the right ones, to the visitors line. Waiting for some time on the other side of the entry booths, I could see them cracking up exuberantly as they departed their interview station. Moving toward me quickly, Nii Otto reached out with an energetic handshake and finger snap as he and Nii Noi broke up into bubbly interchange and expressive cackles.

"What happened, Otoo?"

"Prof, the woman looked my passport and asked am I related to Kofi Annan."

"What did you say?"

"I said, 'Yeah, he's my cousin!' She stamped me fast!" (Uproar.)

Nii Otoo Annan is not related to the former United Nations secretary general, and Annan is not generally a family surname, although it is used that way in both instances here. It typically signifies a fourth-born male; birth order, like day of the week, is one of many sources of Ghanaian personal names.

But quickly put aside whatever this little tale says to you about name recognition in the era of U.S. homeland security while I play a B side of the disc.

Some time later I traveled back to Accra with Nii Otoo after another trip abroad. This time when we landed at Accra's Kotoka International Airport, I went to the foreigners queue, Nii Otoo to the one for Ghanaian nationals. Although the movement in his line was faster than mine, I got to the luggage pickup area about twenty minutes before him, and couldn't figure out why. I waited with our bags. Then he appeared. His look was downcast.

"Otoo, are you OK?"

No answer.

"Hey, is everything all right?"

"They beat me."

"What!? What happened!?"

Long pause. Too long.

"Otoo, tell me, do you need help, are you hurt?"

Finally. "Prof, they looked the passport and said, 'You traveled three times in six months, what did you do?' I said 'I played my drums and met the white students at their schools.' They asked if I had dollars and I said no. They laughed and said, 'Oh, so the whites don't pay you?' I said, 'They are coming with it.' They took me to another room. Another man asked the same things again. They told me to give one hundred to stamp my passport for return. I told the man I will pay ten. They started pushing me from behind and emptied my pockets on the desk. They took all. With their hands they told me to go."

What kind of cosmopolitan so lightly laughs his way into the most powerful country in the world, only to be ripped off on return to his own for the offense of offering too low a reentry bribe after having made some presumed fortune far away? What Nii Otoo didn't say, because he knew that I knew it, is that the officers at passport control sized up very quickly that he does not read or write, and thus they assumed that he is not locally connected to powerful people, that he could be abused without fear of retribution.

Cosmopolitanism didn't do Nii Otoo much good at his border, even though it worked wonders at mine. The cosmopolitanism that was cruel to him is thus now the cosmopolitanism that creates a new location for me as white witness to the performance of reputation as the mean jealousy of internal class divides. One of the things Nii Otoo did not reveal, until considerably later, and over a beer, was that he had cleverly lost only ten Ghana cedis in the deal. Very streetwise to hustling and wary of the vulnerabilities that come with having money in his pocket, especially foreign cash, he carefully hid his dollars in a secret compartment of his drumsticks carry-case.

Nii Otoo's tale is dramatic but not uncommon. Working-class Ghanaians who have overseas visas and go for any kind of work, short- or long-term, tell similar stories, and this even happens in cases where the individuals are not only literate but also well-connected, for example, with diplomats. I recall the account of a man who left Ghana with his embassy employers when they finished their Accra posting and returned to Europe. Six months later, on return, it cost him a fifty-euro bribe to get back in through passport control. Was the high cost of the return calibrated to the imagined fortune he was assumed to acquire working abroad for diplomats?

Another kind of cosmopolitan contradiction was presented to me in conversation with Nii Noi on another return to Ghana some months later. Before he went to London I gave Nii Noi copies of Accra Trane Station's *Meditations* CD to sell there, and he was enthusiastic about placing them in some book and record shops frequented by Ghanaians and Afrocentric diasporans. Later he told me that one of his first stops was a store run by an old friend from the seventies and eighties, a place frequented by Londoners of African and Caribbean descent, a place where he used to regularly hang out with pals from his Misty In Roots days. He asked his old friend, the storekeeper, to play the CD on the shop's sound system. But looking at it, then turning it over and seeing the back cover—a picture of me standing between Nii Noi and Nii Otoo— his friend laid into him with heavy words about working with the white devil, diluting his music, and prostituting Coltrane in the man's market- place. Telling me about this, Nii Noi could barely contain his confusion, and the conversation ended there, with me sensing that any questioning of his friend's separatist sentiments would likely only make things worse.

71. From left, Nii Noi, me, and Nii Otoo with *Meditations for John Coltrane*.
Photograph © 2006 Nana Agazi; art © 2006 Nicholas Wayo.

But the overall issue stayed with me. What kind of cosmopolitan works at home to cross borders and perform a jazz politics of inclusion only to get slammed in the Afrocentric diaspora for selling out?

Whatever else they say about internal class jealousies and external racial sensitivities, Nii Otoo and Nii Noi's tales here speak equally to another cosmopolitan contradiction, the price they pay for working with me. At home they are potentially or actually taxed by petty jealousies or serious animosities, perceived as privileged because a white man provides some paid local work and opportunity. With an overseas component the costs can be higher, including being completely misunderstood for their desire to cultivate foreign connections. Spinning down, Nii Noi put it quite bluntly: "The more work we do with you, the more we will have to seriously deal with detractors."

Some stories about the La Drivers Union Por Por Group add an even deeper layer to these cosmopolitan complexities. In July 2009, when President Barack Obama and his family visited Accra, their itinerary included a brief visit to La Community Hospital. The Por Por Group's members were certainly familiar with the venue. *A Por Por Funeral for Ashirifie* shows the band traveling there from the union office to play at the mortuary as the family retrieved Ashirifie's body, then playing in their vehicle to accompany the body to the funeral home.

The band wanted to honk President Obama and their community on the morning of his visit to the La hospital, and for the occasion wore the new red T-shirts that I had recently brought from the United States. I met them at the Otswe intersection of the Osu to La and La to Castle highways, just across from the hospital, as police and U.S. and Ghana security teams took over the streets, put up barriers, made their presence felt along the roads and in the air and on surrounding rooftops, locking off the whole area. The band started up to energize the gathering crowd, many with American flags, newly printed T-shirts or tailored Obama cloth, and the day's newspapers with large color pictures of the American first family's arrival.

As the group played and Nii Yemo and I took photographs, I spotted a colleague in the crowd, a professor from the States who has taught in Ghana on occasion. I called him over, introduced him to the band, and he stayed among us through the few hours of waiting for the president's motorcade to come and go, the band honking all the while for the street-side crowds and the security and police who swelled around and passed in the endless rounds of checks before and during the presidential visit.

At the end of the event, as the barriers started to come down and the crowds dispersed, I thanked and praised the band the customary way, and in view of all, gave money to Vice, the group leader, asking him to buy and share out refreshment for the group when they returned to the union office. Unbeknownst to me, my friend, before leaving, had also given some money, but privately and exclusively, to a junior member of the group. The money was personally pocketed by that band member, although with a wink to the one other member who saw it happen, a sign that only the two of them would share it.

Meanwhile, out of their awareness, another man, someone who works at the union office but doesn't play in the band, saw the transaction, and concerned about its implications informed Vice that money for the band was in this young man's pocket. A loud altercation followed when the band got to the office, accusations quickly flying everywhere, the offender and the one in his confidence denying receipt of funds. The scene broke up into shouting matches with angry and fractious words leading to near blows until Vice finally leveled the multilayered animosity with "Enough, let's leave it," aware that there was a higher cost to sustained argument than moving on.

Cosmopolitanism gone primitive? Not at *allll*. The story points to something familiar on Accra's streets and in everyday experience. People are used to regularly taking from each other and being taken from by others in their immediate midst, at home, at work, in the community. In fact it is often imagined quite directly as a matter of skillful maneuver, like excellent footwork or tackling in a soccer match to control the movement of the ball, or overtaking another driver on the road with that same verve, sidelining a close competitor.

Such practices are generally called "cutting," and they are part of the ethos of everyday hustling, a concept immortalized for Ghana by the words "Hustling Is Not Stealing," the title of John Miller Chernoff's powerful book of narratives by a Ghana bar girl.[25] While those stories are more about dignities and indignities of a young woman's survival skills in 1970s West Africa, the phrase does define a larger layer of everyday habitus. And part of the hustling idea is that whoever gets it keeps it, and that once the deed is done it is likely not to be undone, whether or not wrongdoing is admitted. What goes along with that is the way people are used to responding, loudly and passionately expressing anger, then letting it fester and fizzle, moving on in bitterness or annoyance, all the more aware of the potential for a future moment when one might opportunistically outmaneuver someone who previously outmaneuvered him.

The ironic twist to this particular scene came just a few weeks later, at the end of July 2009, when the Por Por band had finished the final recording session for its *Klebo!* CD. I went to meet with the group a final time before my return back to the States for four months, and after their rehearsal we had some drinks and conversation outside the union office, talking over the plan for editing and publishing the CD during my time away. I told the group that I would front the cost of the studio engineering, design, and manufacturing for one thousand CDs, costs that could be paid back in time by sales of roughly one-third of the copies. I suggested bringing a few hundred to Ghana for the group to sell locally. Before I could finish the thought, the voice of the bandsman who had pocketed my professor friend's dash money interrupted urgently.

"No! We are the ones who suffered with this work and when they get it and cut us we will suffer more and only they will get the profit money."

His voice was overlapped immediately by the group's arranger, Mas T, (short for Master Tetteh): "You see! People will cut us! If we let our work go outside here then we will loose it. Because we are more strong with this work, people in Ghana here will cut us, I'm telling you!"

And then another piled on: "True, Prof, people will cut you, maybe they have already dashed someone inside, yeah, dashed him small, so when the work comes they get it, in front of you, make their own business with it. You don't even hear of it. You see how we suffer!? Ghana is hard-o!"

Then one of the senior men: "So, Prof, just bring enough for us to hold, one for each, the rest you sell in America. That is the only money we will see, the money you bring, we cannot bring any money to ourselves, if we give or sell just one then it will be in the street, we will loose *allll*."

"OK," I interjected, wishing to calm the obvious worries about the rampant piracy well-known to characterize the local scene with recordings: "I will register it for copyright there and here inside too and . . ."

But before I finish my preamble Mas T is back in: "Oh—ho! This is Ghana, nobody cares about the laws for this, everyone is trying to get something small for themselves, so whatever we make they will cut and chop. Prof, just keep it at your side and sell only for us, *eh hehh!*"

A clear part of the hustling landscape is just what can be heard here: layers of protectionism, suspicion, paranoia, jealousy, anger, disappointment. Why trust anyone in the street when one of your own band mates will grab your dash behind you? What was at stake here was loss of control, the moment when other people's hustling really will turn into stealing, the anxiety that the profit and respect the recording could bring on the outside might be vitiated by the humiliation and loss it could bring inside.

This conversation was not unlike many others I had heard at the union office. I recall being present during lengthy conversations in Ga with the English word "unity" spoken over and over. That word, also the name of a trotro vehicle, points to an ever-complex and illusive goal in a cultural space where quibbling and quarreling and endless fractious and suspicious talk acts out the resentments of being outhustled or imagining that it is likely to happen, repeatedly.

There is, of course, a good deal of serious academic attention to the varieties of cosmopolitan contradiction these stories tell. And I feel close kinship with how that work takes on the need to counterbalance the romance of much cosmopolitanism discourse. Pnina Werbner is one of the theorists I most associate with the analysis of diasporic heterogeneity, with the study of gaps between the experiential life-worlds of cosmopolitan intellectuals and their working-class compatriots, or between cosmopolitans of layered class positions. Like Aihwa Ong in her work on wealthy overseas Chinese traders, Werbner goes to great pains to point out how those privileged with wealth or opportunity might profoundly lack the kind of openness or tolerance often associated with cosmopolitanism.

Homi Bhabha coined the phrase "vernacular cosmopolitanism" to make clear that cosmopolitanism and the stakes in it can mean quite different things if one contrasts Thessaloniki and Cairo, Mumbai and London, Paris and Noumea. Werbner gives the idea a deep historical and ethnographic grounding in her richly detailed books about the life-worlds of Manchester Muslims and global Sufi practitioners. Like Bhabha, she indicates how the multicultural cosmopolitan conversation can overamalgamate places and experiences, making them too uniformly radiate from a centerpoint of elite intellectualization.[26]

72. "Unity" trotro on the Osu-La road. *Photograph © 2006 Steven Feld.*

Here's one way she maps the landscape: "Vernacular cosmopolitanism belongs to a family of concepts, all of which combine in similar fashion apparently contradictory opposites: cosmopolitan patriotism, rooted cosmopolitanism, cosmopolitan ethnicity, working-class cosmopolitanism, discrepant cosmopolitanism."

"Contradictory opposites": Werbner makes cosmopolitanism into a series of questions about the ambiguity of that trope, about shifting locations, about reconfigurations. She asks pointed questions about contradiction and ambiguity, like: "Are we talking about non-elite forms of travel and trade in a postcolonial world, as in the case of the Senegalese Mourides . . . or of non-European but nevertheless high cultures produced and consumed by non-Western elites, such as those of the Sanskritic, Urdu, Persian, or Ottoman worlds? . . . [And] how are we to place minority elites in new postcolonial nations who struggle to defend their vernacular cultures, and seek justice through multicultural citizenship, while being at the same time liberal, tolerant, and highly educated world travelers?"[27]

These "contradictory opposites" connect Werbner's ethnographic work to James Clifford's early and brilliant development, in his book *Routes*, of the idea of "discrepant cosmopolitanism," a notion that came out of his concern to explore differences between privileged and non-privileged travelers, and his loud insistence that it is as short-sighted to imagine cosmopolitans as necessarily elite as it is to imagine cosmopolitan discourse as necessarily elitist.[28]

I like the concepts of "vernacular cosmopolitanism" or "discrepant cosmopolitanism" here in exactly the same way that I like "diasporic intimacy." All proceed from an embrace of oxymoron and contradiction. All proceed from agitation about over-easy naturalization of categories of social formation. All grapple with what I have been grappling with in Accra's jazz cosmopolitanism: the unsettling ironies of uneven experience.

But in my reading, no academic has quite succeeded in voicing the unsettling ironies of uneven experience for Ghana more powerfully than the writer Caryl Phillips. Born in St. Kitts, brought up in Leeds, educated at Oxford, now a New Yorker and Yale literature professor, Phillips is razor-aware of the word-work people do to pin Africans and diasporans down to one kind of essentializing identity or another. He has explored these matters, with uncommon irony and subtlety, over and over.

His novel *A Distant Shore* takes up the affair of a retired British school-teacher, a divorcee, with an African refugee thirty-three years her junior, who comes from a war-torn country; the story is set in a impossibly racist small English town. His biographical fiction book *Dancing in the Dark* enters the life-world of Burt Williams, the famous African American vaudevillian. His historical novel *Cambridge* overlays the testimony of a slave to the journals of a young nineteenth-century upper-class woman sent from England to inspect her father's sugar plantation in the West Indies. Another historical novel, *The Nature of Blood*, weaves the stories of a Jewish doctor who chooses to fight for Israel over an easier life of privilege and security with a reading of *Othello* and the Jewish history of Venice, and then a narrative of an Ethiopian Jewish woman who returns to Israel. The memoir *The European Tribe* reports on a year of wanderings in Europe's white worlds to chronicle the varieties of racism encountered there.

But Phillips's most powerful book for me, *The Atlantic Sound*, complexly mixes novel, history, memoir, journalism, and literary commentary in layered narratives across the Black Atlantic multisites of Liverpool, Accra, and Charleston, South Carolina. He meets a lot of people and

73. "Who Knows Tomorrow" trotro on the Awoshie road.
Photograph © 2008 Steven Feld.

dispassionately observes things that give him deep pause. In one of the
book's poignant moments of ironic distance, he describes the encounter,
in Ghana, with a man he calls Mansour, a man who has already been
deported back to Ghana from Britain and is now trying to get out again,
to the United States of America.

Mansour is neither sentimental nor nostalgic about his African past,
and has little more than a mocking dismissal for why black British or
African Americans might wish to settle in Ghana to reclaim "home" in
any sense of the word. Mansour is not imagining that the outside world
will be particularly generous. As Phillips points out, he knows that by
traveling abroad he will likely be forced to do unrewarding jobs that he
would find beneath him in Ghana. He tells Phillips: "The only way up in
Ghana is out. And then you come back with money and a degree. That is
how you progress in Ghana. You leave."[29]

Cosmo-Spy In early November 2008 I telephoned greetings to Ghanaba from the States. I could tell from his voice that he had become more frail than when I'd spoken to him a few weeks previously. I told him that I'd come to see him in a month's time when I was due to return, a reunion that never happened. After hearing some of his complaints, I told him that I had just read a pair of interesting books by an anthropologist named David Price, books that opened new questions I wanted to ask him about his oss years and spy experiences. I began by telling him the titles: *Threatening Anthropology: McCarthyism and the FBI's Surveillance of Activist Anthropologists* and *Anthropological Intelligence: The Deployment and Neglect of American Anthropology in the Second World War*.[30] Before I finished the words of the second title he cut in and, in his customary way, took over the course of the conversation until its close.

"You see, you've often asked about my life as a spy, but it is you anthropologists who know more about that business!" (Laughter.)

"Well, yes," I overlap, "the founder of modern American anthropology, Franz Boas, even wrote an article of protest about it, I think about 1919, 'Scientists as Spies.' That debate came back again in a big way during the Vietnam War years; I was a college student then and we were very worked up about anthropologists working for the military."[31]

"Well, let me tell you about it during my time. You see, when I was trained in Chicago and went to work with the oss in 1943 there was already an anthropologist working for them in Nigeria. He spent some time here in Accra too toward the end of the war. I'm told he became famous later; his name was William Bascom. I got one of his books secondhand in America, a general treatise on the Yoruba, I think it is still here in my library. Have you heard of him?"

"Yes. I know some of his work. He was trained at Northwestern University with Herskovits, the founder of African studies in the U.S., and became director of the anthropology museum at Berkeley, the University of California, where they have his Nigerian art collections."

"Well, he was pretty high up, assigned to different things, and even wrote a guide to West Africa in 1943, together with Ralph Bunche. Like me they were part of the secret American effort to look carefully at what the colonial British were doing here. I was impressed that Bunche was part of this effort. "

"Why?"

"Well, the Americans knew they needed Africans and Negroes. They knew we could operate more secretly than whites. They needed us because they completely distrusted the British even though they were war allies."

"Did you follow Bunche's career after?"

"Oh yes, of course. You know he was the first black to win the Nobel Peace Prize, I think in 1950. I have several articles about him here in my collection."

"Right. Well, here's a little story about Bascom. He played clarinet. I have a picture of him playing in a faculty jazz band at Northwestern University; it's published in a book of mine, I'll bring a copy for your library when I come. I'm wondering if Bascom or those Northwestern people knew about you when you came to Chicago later, from 1953. A bunch of those Africanist anthropologists were jazz enthusiasts, like my professor, Alan Merriam, he would have been there at that time as well."[32]

"Well, I heard that there were these scholars of Africa there who were also jazz lovers and maybe I was introduced to a few when I played in Chicago. But I don't recall any of them showing interest in what I was doing. You see, what you need to understand about those days in America is that I was a *freak*. Nobody was interested in an educated African who spied for America and played jazz drums! No! I could have gotten more attention just by taking my shirt off and speaking my African language while sweating over an odonno. That's what was expected, you see, that more primitive thing. When they saw me playing jazz the people thought I was just a Negro. It confused them to find out that I was an African. Anyway Steven, you keep doing your research! I'll tell you some spy stories when you come back to see me! And tell your father I like his CD; it's well done, especially the Ellington songs."

Months later, during a visit back to Accra after Ghanaba's funeral, my architect and art historian friend Nat Nuno Amarteifio took me to see the show he made with the artist Kofi Setordji, *Architectural Heritage of Accra, 1920–1940*, at the Nubuke Foundation.[33] On the way back home in his car we were talking about Ghanaba's funeral and the many stories I'd heard about it since getting back to Accra. Nat told me that he heard the daily blow-by-blow because, at Ghanaba's request, the state funeral was managed by his sister Korkor and his nephew Percy.

I knew from prior conversations with Korkor that she had plenty of tumultuous history with Ghanaba, gained from years of presenting him or managing venues where he performed. I was surprised that she accepted to work on the funeral arrangements and asked Nat why she agreed. "I asked her the same thing," he said, "and she replied, 'He was a genius and our only one.' So that's why. As for Percy, well, he became an advocate early on, saying he went into trance when Ghanaba played. So even with all the predictable hassles, and unpredictable ones, he joined on too."

As we traded stories Nat told me that while sympathetic to his sister's reasoning, he felt that Ghanaba's addiction to shocking people tended to bring out the worst in him, producing a sense that he was less an artist and more a provocateur, and occasionally quite mean-spirited. With a chuckle he asked: "Did Korkor tell you about the funeral for Ghanaba's elder sister?"

"No, I never heard about that."

"Well, let me tell you. After the service we were outside the Holy Trinity Church. I was standing with Korkor. Ghanaba came up and greeted her. She asked him, 'Do you know my brother Nat?'

" 'Of course I do,' he replied, and then he addressed me:

" 'A woman named Victoria lived at your house when you were small and I came there to visit her. She was my girlfriend. She was also Nkrumah's girlfriend. He would have her then I would have her.' "

Nat broke into an amazed laughter. "That was Ghanaba," he said. "The guy was something, the way he could destabilize even the most somber occasion."

"Do you remember this Victoria?" I asked. "I mean, was this in any way factual?"

"Oh, absolutely," he replied. "There was an Auntie Vicky who lived at our house for a time when I was young, maybe eight or nine years old. My mother told me that her family had political connections with the opposing party, but she was all for Nkrumah. So she was in a perfect position to gather and pass certain information to him."[34]

I told Nat about Ghanaba's boasts of his affair with Marie Antoinette Wilson Howells, for whom he wrote "The Lady Marie Drum Suite," and to whom, along with his mother and Kwame Nkrumah, he dedicated his memoir *I Have a Story to Tell.* . . . Howells came from a celebrated Arkansas family and used her personal fortune to endow the University of Arkansas Medical School. But in the 1950s she was a well-known New

York socialite with a great many Washington political connections. On several occasions Warren told me that "she knew people" and "made things happen." He was never any more explicit, typically dodging questions about his 1950s U.S. intelligence connections and about why he didn't return to Ghana in 1957 for independence, nor for two years after it.

"I'm not surprised," Nat said. "You know, there was a lot of that kind of intrigue going on in those days, and like Nkrumah with Auntie Vicky, I'm sure Ghanaba used his amorous relationships to barter secrets. Tell you the truth, Steven, it's completely in character," he mused. "Ghanaba was a total cold war invention, you know; the guy was right out of a spy novel."

Cosmo-Local One of the ways my jazz projects mapped themselves onto the larger local cosmopolitics of Accra concerned the public launches of the recordings, always live performances at international venues for very multicultural and mixed audiences, with local listeners joined by ambassadors, government officials, foreign and local academics, diasporans, students, artists, journalists, and nongovernmental organization workers in each crowd. *The Time of Bells, 3* was launched at the World Bank residence and National Arts Centre; *Meditations for John Coltrane* and *Another Blue Train* at the Goethe Institut; *Castaways* and *Topographies of the Dark* together with art exhibit at the Alliance Française; *Por Por: Honk Horn Music of Ghana* at the American Embassy residence.

The situation was initially similar for the films with screenings at cosmopolitan venues for multicultural audiences. *Hallelujah!* was launched in Ghana twice, the short version at the Alliance Française as part of the Environmental Film Festival of Accra, then the full version at Goethe Institut in Ghanaba's presence for his eighty-fifth birthday. Likewise, the *Accra Trane Station* film was launched at the W. E. B. Du Bois Centre for Pan-African Culture, hosted by the Foundation for Contemporary Art–Ghana in their European Union–funded Meet the Artist Series. Those screenings were opened with greetings and introductions followed by conversations and questions where English was the dominant language.

In contrast, at the request of the La Drivers Union, the film *A Por Por Funeral for Ashirifie* was "out-doored" (the Ghanaian English word for a public launch, extended from the more specific meaning, namely, bringing a baby outdoors for the first time to be seen by the extended family and community) on three evenings during a single week in January 2010, uniquely in La, and really outdoors, for standing-room-only audiences, with no announcements or Q & A sessions, and barely a word of English to be heard. In each case we brought a portable screen and mounted the projection equipment on a truck or makeshift stand and "borrowed" electricity from whatever local source could be tapped.

The first showing was near the union office, at the main La trotro terminal, where buses and passengers were coming and going in the ambience of diesel and dust, headlights and honks. The second was deeper in La, at the community family house where Ashirifie's wake and funeral took place. The third was again in deep La, behind the market, in the courtyard of the house of the former La *mantse* (chief).

These screenings generated local excitement; people spontaneously shed a tear, danced a few steps, sang along, shook heads, and acknowledged the loss and remembrance in myriad personal ways, commenting continuously and publicly on who and what they were seeing. Children were particularly energetic in their response, dancing, hooting, pumping arms and fists, becoming totally engrossed, especially in the opening scenes of young boys skillfully dancing when the Por Por Group went to play musical condolences for Ashirifie's bereft family a week before the funeral.

Just before the last showing, as Agazi and I set up the sound and picture equipment, a young girl came up to our makeshift projection table and asked, timidly, and in halting English:

"White man: . . . Jesus movie?"

"NO!" Vice jumped in; in Ga he told her: "Just wait! This is *our* movie! You will see people from around *here*!"

Then he looked over to me with a smile, and switched to English: "You see, Prof, this is *noo* small thing! No! Not at *allll*, not at *allll*!

Cosmo-Class When he visited New York City to perform in October 2009, Nii Otoo Annan asked me to take him shopping. Happy to have dollars in his pocket, Otoo had no local expenses while in America and was very well paid for his performances, making as much money from one concert as he could make from fifteen of his best-paying local gigs in Accra.

Walking from our Greenwich Village apartment down Canal Street to stop at both regular shops and the stalls of many street vendors, Otoo was upset to hear the cost of even discounted seconds of T-shirts (three to five dollars) and jeans (ten to fifteen dollars), remarking how the price was so much higher than at any local Ghanaian market. And to make it worse, there wasn't much verbal bargaining to be done. I told him that this was likely the best we could do on price in the city. He seemed dismayed, and after buying a pair of jeans for himself and some T-shirts for his younger children, said we should head home. As we were walking up Broadway he explained:

"You see, Prof, it's like my father speaks to me, 'Oh, Otoo, you are going foreign so bring me cloth, bring me crocodile' [a Lacoste polo shirt, a classic prestige item of overseas clothing]. And I tell him, 'Listen, the money is only good when I go [to] America and bring *allll* back in my pockets. The money is small if I spend anything inside. Clothes, food, everything high, ten twenty times more high than Ghana here.' So me, I want to go and come, keep the money, finish. That's how they are disturbed with me, yes, my father, mother, childrens, *allll*, they say 'Otoo, you are going coming working fine so why you no bring us something nice-o?' So Prof, I'm explaining you how they are disturbed with me. If I buy for them I come home with little to pay light [electricity bill], feed the childrens, pay school fees, I need plenty for all now, yeah, I need *plenty*."

Cosmo-Name We were on our way to a gig. Agazi was driving and I was seated next to him in the front of his small panel truck, with Nii Noi and Nii Yemo sitting in the rear together with the instruments and equipment. All of a sudden traffic slowed, and we came to a blockade, roadside police stopping vehicles to inspect licenses, insurance validation, and contained goods.

An armed officer walked toward our truck; Agazi and I made the appropriate gestures, and I expected him to wave us on. Instead he came closer, ducking down and peering into the vehicle from my open window. "Ah!" he shouted, straightening up: "Human being in the back! You will go to court!"

As the officer walked away Agazi anticipated my question. "Police no get pay!" he says, overlapped by Nii Noi, instructing me, "It's a regular thing Prof, you know, sometimes their pay is delayed, or they only receive half, and, you know, they have to pay school fees and all that, so any innocent driver will be taxed." I opened my wallet to give Agazi the required "fee" and he held his palm up to flash "stop" when I got to the equivalent of five dollars. As he left the vehicle to take care of business I asked Nii Noi, "Is it really against the law to have people seated in the back of a covered truck?"

"Maybe, but likely the guy was just performing for you, Prof. You don't get a white audience for this every day!" (Laughter.)

Agazi returned to the vehicle and with a smile handed back more than half the money I had given to him. As we took off Nii Noi and Nii Yemo complimented him, repeatedly and vigorously, for his street-smart hustling skills, keeping the cost so low. A few moments later everyone was laughing and mimetically echoing: "Human being in the back! You will go to court!"

And then, in a moment of lull, Nii Yemo said: "So Prof, you see, now you must paint the insignia on Agazi's vehicle. This is how we get our names. It's a story to tell."

Cosmo-Irrelevance Lunching at Kohinoor, a local Indian restaurant, in January 2010, Nat Amarteifio introduced me to one of his friends, a woman about our age, who, like Nat and his sister Korkor, had resided for a long period in Canada. Yemokaa, her name, immediately gave away her La origins. She was amused to hear me, a non-Ga speaker, locate her in the Yemo generational naming sequence Yemo(te)ley, Yemo(tio)kor, Yemo(tio)kaa, Yemo(tio)tsoo, when I told her that my collaborator was a Yemo, the photographer Nii Yemo Nunu, son of a distinguished driver.

"Really?" she said. "My father was a La driver too, Ataa Laryea Kota, ask about him. I didn't really know him, he died when I was very small, but we have drivers in the family to this day. And for some reason, I just love to drive; I could go all the way from Toronto to Detroit without thinking about it!"

Nat asked me to tell Yemokaa a bit about my work with the La Por Por.

"That's really interesting," she responded, after my brief outline, "but tell me, what do younger Ghanaians think about this story, about the drivers and wooden vehicles and por por horns? How do they see this work you have been doing?"

I could only answer awkwardly. "You know, people today might wonder if my interest in this por por music just follows a nostalgia for the colonial days. These vehicles were modern a very long time ago. When people hear I'm making films and CD recordings I'm sure some think I've just come here to profit. Only the La drivers and maybe people our age can imagine the importance of documenting these things. So it's complicated."

"Yes," Nat agreed, "it is indeed complicated. And you're right, Steven. Nobody here would study such a thing; it's just not considered serious as history or art. If they think about it at all, people here will think that the word 'cosmopolitan' refers to elite lifestyles, to the world of bankers and travelers, those who have left to make money or get educated. You'd have a hard time convincing most Ghanaians that driving in La has anything to do with that story, I'm sure of that."

Cosmo-Home On June 1, 2010, five years after starting this project, I returned to Ghana for another two months, excited by my agenda: to work with Nii Noi and Nii Yemo on the book they'd been compiling about Ghanaba, with Nii Otoo on a CD of his guitar compositions, and with the Por Por Group on a historical film drawing from Nii Yemo's extensive interviews with La's pioneer drivers. But what excited me most was returning to Accra with prize money to bring; *A Por Por Funeral for Ashirifie* had recently won the Prix Bartók at the Festival International Jean Rouch in Paris.[35]

Arriving from Albuquerque at the Atlanta airport I was surprised to find that I would be traveling on Delta Airlines' inaugural direct flight from Atlanta to Accra. The red, white, and blue balloons around the Delta counter were soon taken over by a troupe of Ghanaians decked out in colorful kente cloth, joined by an entourage of African Americans, likewise in Ghanaian robes. Of those assembled only Ghana's ambassador to the United States wore a dark business suit similar to those outfitting the Delta VIPs on hand for the ribbon-cutting occasion.

Speeches of goodwill were offered first, a Delta vice president and the ambassador each promoting business and tourism between the United States and Ghana. Then came two Ghanaians performing a welcome dance to a soundtrack played from a small CD boom box. An African American preacher offered prayers in English, and a Ghanaian man introduced as a "traditional priest" poured libation and spoke prayers in Twi.

Finally, there was a brief speech from another man robed in golden kente cloth, gilded armbands, bracelets, crown, and decorative sandals. He introduced himself to the crowd as an "African American chief" and "producer of a black arts festival" sponsored by Delta. He urged the African Americans in the audience to spread the word to "come back home to Ghana," and echoed the message of the Delta VP that with as many as twenty thousand Ghanaians living in the state of Georgia, it was indeed timely to introduce direct flights between Atlanta and Accra.[36]

As the ceremony broke up and the dignitaries mingled with us passengers, I introduced myself to the last speaker, saying that perhaps his black arts festival would be interested to know about some of the artists I had been recording and filming in Accra the last five years. I happened to have a copy of the *Jazz Cosmopolitanism in Accra* DVD trilogy in my briefcase and flashed it before him, mentioning Ghanaba's uniquely Ghanaian "Hallelujah" chorus, Nii Noi and Nii Otoo's Accra Trane Station, and the La Por Por's funeral music for transport workers. I offered to send a sample CD or DVD upon return from Ghana. Taking my business card he was cordial but dismissive. "Thank you, Professor," he said. "But my people only work with *authentic* Ghanaian groups." He walked away to shake other hands.

In the moment it was hard for me not to feel cynical about the way this "chief" so offhandedly judged Ghanaian artists outside some presumably "traditional" paradigm, especially after having just approvingly witnessed what was, by the same policing "authentic" standards, a hokey dance likely choreographed strictly for hotel lobbies. Hmm, I thought, just be glad Ghanaba isn't here to throw the first punch.

The flight boarded, and settling into my seat I couldn't stop thinking about this incident. It wasn't difficult for me to imagine how the historical self-consciousness of black pride lead the "chief" to his rhetorical invocation of Ghana as "home," despite my deep distaste for nationalist homeland rhetorics of all sorts. No, what was difficult was to accept that the "chief" might be caught up in the kind of fence-work politics of "home" that means that his audiences will never hear about a Ghanaba, a Nii Noi, a Nii Otoo, a Nii Yemo, a Vice. That might be cosmopolitanism's cruelest contradiction, I thought, feeling that the best I could do with this experience was just allow it to make personal the kind of hurts or suspicions I'd encountered in Ghanaba's and Nii Noi's riffs about a cosmopolitan Africa getting frozen as a quaint echo rather than real participant in shaping the contemporary expanse of (black) musical history.

When the flight leveled off at 35,000 feet, I jotted a quick note in my diary: "Have I really just been told by an ethno-fako 'chief' that cosmopolitanism isn't culture?" By then it was well-past midnight local time. I set the iPod to continuous play of "Anomabo Shoreline," my Black Atlantic ambient soundtrack of where water touches land at the seacoast of one of Ghana's fort-castles, fixed the noise-canceling headphones over my ears, and drifted to sleep hoping for wonderful times across the ocean.

Thirteen hours later, my Ghana cell phone rang as I stood waiting in the "Other Nationals" arrivals queue at Kotoka International Airport. The screen indicated that the caller was Vice, the Por Por band leader.

"Prof!? Are you in?"

"Yes, Vice, I just landed. I'm inside at the airport."

"We thank God, we thank God! Prof, you are welcome! We are very *very* happy with your news! We are waiting to see you!"

"Thank you, Vice, I'll come to see you soon."

I didn't think to take Vice literally, but the honking started as soon as I walked out the airport door to the sight and sound of eight yellow-T-shirted Por Por band members in full swing. Vice rushed forward to put his arms around me.

"You are welcome, Prof! You are welcome home in Ghana here!"

A few days later I was again thinking about my irritation over the authenticity riff by the "chief." If cosmopolitanism creates space for Paul Gilroy's "multilocal belonging," for the openness that imagines, constructs, and promotes multiple senses of home, what was it that differentiated the "home" that honked me in Vice's por por embrace from the "home" to which the "chief" urged African Americans to return? That took me back to Svetlana Boym's diasporic intimacy, and her book *The Future of Nostalgia*, which powerfully contrasts two species of nostalgia, restorative versus reflective.

"Restorative nostalgia," she writes, "does not think of itself as nostalgia, but rather, as truth and tradition." It emphasizes *nostos* through "emblems and rituals of home and homeland," and the simple and singular narrative of return to a mythic time or place. Reflective nostalgia, by contrast, emphasizes *algia* as social memory, dreams, irony, and the necessary imperfections of remembrance. It avoids the dark side of invented traditions through "meditation on history and the passage of time" and "explores ways of inhabiting many places at once."[37]

Restorative nostalgia is what I know to be so deeply refused by the cosmopolitan home-expanding musical ethics I've encountered in Accra. And reflective nostalgia is what is so deeply embraced t/here in my encounters with being *soo* many places-at-once in the music and its stories. That's where an irony-saturated cosmopolitics meet its poetics, that palpable acoustemological layering of the what is, the what once was, the what *may be*. That's where jazz cosmopolitanism thrives on the riff of diasporic intimacy.

Living and working in Ghana as I write, thinking again about these five years with the people you've now encountered through me, I've come to new ways to know home to be multiple, transportable, detoured, a recycling figure washing in from the waves to honk life and death down life's many roads and across its skies. Listening to Accra's histories of listening, I've come to hear home as a musical lost and found, and one where I am continually gifted by solidarity in difference.

"DEDICATED TO YOU"

Drafted during the jazz hours of spring semester 2009 in Berkeley, and fleshed out over the next year and a half in Accra and Santa Fe, this book occasions many dedications to many you's.[1] At the top of the list comes Nii Noi Nortey, Nii Otoo Annan, Nii Yemo Nunu, Nana Agazi, the late Ghanaba, Nii Ashai "Vice" Ollennu, and the La Drivers Union Por Por Group, all of whom have taken me into sound as a way of knowing the world, a very big world, in a very big way. My deepest hope is that this book and the accompanying recordings and films do justice to their vibrant intelligence, wit, and creative artistry.

Others in the front line of thanks for regular and memorable Accra conversations include Nat Nuno Amarteifio, John Collins, Professor J. H. Kwabena Nketia, the late Joe Nkrumah, and Virginia Ryan. Big thanks too to Ruti Talmor for introducing me to Accra; to Tom Joyce for collaboration on bells and blacksmithing there, in Togo, and at home in Santa Fe; to Maxine Gordon for cheering me on with great jazz storytelling; to Abena Keller Agyepong for sharing her stories about being Ghanaian in Europe and America, as well as for introducing Expresso Italia to Ghana; and to my Nima landlord, Frank Kofi Nyame, his delightful daughters Mame and Eno, and my driver David Ajuik and housekeeper Bless Attigah for their years of friendship.

All the musicians join me to praise the Accra artist Nicholas Wayo for his CD and DVD cover paintings and Michael Motley for their design; Jeremiah Ra Richards for his deeply creative dedication to the videos; Jean and Celia Schwarz for a generous week at home in Paris mixing the *Meditations* sessions; Pete Reiniger for his mixing work on the Folkways *Por Por* CD; Bill Boaz for making his Fourth World Studios home for all the other recording projects; and John Vokoun for photographic support. For art and photographic contributions and permissions here I thank Nana Agazi, Dick Blau, Lorenzo Ferrarini, Mawuko Ghanaba,

Michael Motley, Nii Noi Nortey, Nii Yemo Nunu, Virginia Ryan, Sheff, Ruti Talmor, and Nicholas Wayo.

For performance and film screening opportunities in Accra, I thank the British Council and Korkor Amarteifio; Mats Karlsson, Irena Kunovská, and World Bank Ghana; Adwoa Amoah, Ato Annan, and Foundation for Contemporary Art–Ghana; Eleonore Sylla, Kirstie Adu Gyamfi, and Goethe Institut–Accra; New York University in Ghana; Alliance Française; the W. E. B. Du Bois Centre for Pan-African Culture; and Kwesi Owusu and Claudia d'Andrea of the Accra Environmental Film Festival. And for the request that Accra Trane Station perform at the out-dooring of their newborn son, and years of friendship, thanks to Claudia d'Andrea and Ted Lawrence. All Accra performances and screenings also received local press support for which I'm grateful to journalists Nii Laryea Korley and John Owoo.

For performances with Accra Trane Station in Europe, I thank the Universities of Bergen, Oslo, Basilicata, and Milan; TrendExpo Basilicata; and our Norwegian and Italian hosts Hans Weisethaunet, Tom Solomon, Nicola Scaldaferri, Lorenzo Ferrarini, Palmarosa Fulchella, and Dorothy Zinn.

For performances in the United States, I thank Tom Guralnick and Outpost Performance Space; Susan Foote and the School for Advanced Research; Maria Williams and the University of New Mexico College of Fine Arts and Departments of Music, Anthropology, and Native American Studies; Ear to the Earth; Louise Meintjes and Duke University; and our musical collaborators Alex Coke and Jefferson Voorhees.

For enthusiastic support of the initial project with the La Drivers Union Por Por Group, I thank the staff of Smithsonian Folkways Records, and in Accra, the American Embassy for hosting the CD's launch on Ghana's fiftieth anniversary.

All of my time and work in Accra 2004–10 has been funded by Professor II appointments in Norway, first at the Grieg Academy of Music, University of Bergen, and then at the Institute of Music Research, University of Oslo. For this very generous support my deepest thanks to Hans Weisethaunet, and also to my Oslo and Bergen colleagues Odd Are Berkaak, Jan Petter Blom, Vigdis Broch-Due, Bruce and Judith Kapferer, Tellef Kvifte, Marit Lie, Even Ruud, Tom Solomon, and Erik Steinskog.

The first version of these chapters was presented as the 2009 Ernest

Bloch Lectures in the Department of Music at the University of California, Berkeley. I'm grateful beyond sixteenth notes to my Berkeley colleagues Bonnie Wade, Jocelyne Guilbault, Ben Brinner, and Charles Briggs, and with them, to Clara Mantini-Briggs, Lisa Gold, Ann Pescatello, Keila Diehl, Panos Panopoulos, Catherine Cole, Kwame Braun, Don Brenneis, Wynne Furth, Louise Lamphere, Peter Evans, Susan and Jim Matisoff, Chris Brown, Johanna Poethig, Howie Becker, and Paul Rabinow for their friendship during my semester at Berkeley. Thanks, too, to the participants in my "Anthropologies of Sound" seminar, to Berkeley Music Department colleagues and staff, to Tropical Paradise (Berkeley's Ghanaian restaurant) for well-spiced nourishment, to Jefferson Voorhees for editing feedback on the lecture drafts, and to Kwame Assenyoh for translation support. For inspiring conversations about diasporic cosmopolitics, and at just the right times, in the beginning, and at the close, very special thanks to Jim Clifford and to Jocelyne Guilbault.

Outside of the Bloch lectures, I was honored to first present some of the por por story as the Annette Weiner Memorial Lecture, in April 2008, at New York University. I thank my NYU Anthropology colleagues Fred Myers, Faye Ginsburg, and Bambi Schieffelin for that opportunity to connect Melanesian and Ghanaian narratives for our dear friend Annette. I was also honored to present some of the ideas about acoustemology in the Charles Seeger Lecture to the Society for Ethnomusicology in Mexico City in November 2009, and in Keynote Lectures to the British Forum for Ethnomusicology, in Oxford, England, in April 2010, and the World Forum for Acoustic Ecology, in Koli, Finland, in June 2010. I thank Deborah Wong, Martin Stokes, and Helmi Järviluoma-Mäkelä for these generous invitations.

As I wrote these pieces I was reminded often of my good fortune to have studied and collaborated with anthropologists whose engagements with storytelling, filmmaking, politics, aesthetics, and music were powerfully forged by African encounters. For that I sign a note of deep thanks to teacher-ancestors Colin Turnbull, Jean Rouch, Robert Plant Armstrong, and Alan P. Merriam; to senior and soul brother number one Charlie Keil; and to sister Louise Meintjes. And with them, a very special thanks to the two other senior brothers who so thoughtfully read the initial manuscript: Michael Jackson, who for many years has generously colluded with my wandering, "poetical thinking," and inquiry into being at home in the world; and Paul Berliner, who inspired my turn to the interlocking scholarly and performing paths of thinking in jazz improvisation and Afro-lamellophonology.

I dedicate this book to my parents, in fact wrote it winking back at and occasionally wearing the child's airplane pilot cap they gave me for the sixtieth birthday that arrived as I wrote. Anita and Bob, you are my wings and I thank you endlessly for smiling at me so often, and for being wise enough not to smile all the time.

(Deep breath here): I also dedicate this book to the memory of the jazz saxophonist Michael Brecker, who died in January 2007 as this project took off. Mike and I grew up in Melrose Park, just north of Philadelphia, listening to jazz and playing together regularly as schoolmates. From 1963 to 1967 we explored the music of John Coltrane, and most memorably, witnessed it live in concert. That music and the times of being in it together radically transformed us both. Over some forty years and despite his very demanding schedules, Michael always found time for a call or an email to turn me on to something that excited him musically, or to hang out before or after a club date. His capacity for musical wonder inspired my own when we were teenagers, and does to this day. I really miss him.

HORN BACKGROUNDS, RIFFS UNDERNEATH

Four-Bar Intro

1. Ruti Talmor, "Crafting Intercultural Desire: Transforming Nation, Art, and Personhood in Ghana," Ph.D. dissertation, New York University, 2008.

2. Steven Feld, *The Time of Bells*, 1–5, CD/DVD, VoxLox, 2004–10.

3. Chartered in 2004, the Foundation for Contemporary Art–Ghana, based in Accra at the W. E. B. Du Bois Centre for Pan-African Culture, supports young artists in a range of community-based projects and artistic exchanges, holds regular "meet-the-artist" gatherings, and originates or curates exhibits at a range of local venues. They maintain a web presence at fcaghana.org.

4. Paul Gilroy, *The Black Atlantic: Modernity and Double Consciousness* (Cambridge: Harvard University Press, 1993); Caryl Phillips, *The Atlantic Sound* (New York: Vintage, 2000).

5. Ornette Coleman, *The Shape of Jazz to Come*, LP, Atlantic Records, 1959.

6. Accra Trane Station, *Tribute to A Love Supreme*, CD, VoxLox, 2005; John Coltrane, *A Love Supreme*, LP, Impulse, 1965.

7. This sonic stratigraphy is the topic of my ambient soundscape composition of dawn in this community, *Waking in Nima*, CD, VoxLox, 2010. There you hear a multiplicity of acoustic coexistences, intentionally or unintentionally layered interactions, in figure and ground, variously cooperative, competitive, planned or unplanned, related or unrelated, opportunistic or idiosyncratic. The sound sources, recorded from roofs and treetops from five to seven in the morning where I wake in Nima, include a close and distant mosque, a close and distant evangelical Pentecostal church, song birds, roosters, car alarms, trains, and instrumental and vocal sounds of men and women waking and working.

8. Accra Trane Station, *Meditations for John Coltrane*, CD, VoxLox, 2006; Accra Trane Station, *Another Blue Train*, CD, VoxLox, 2007; Nii Otoo Annan and Steven Feld, *Bufo Variations*, CD, VoxLox, 2008; Nii Noi Nortey, Nii Otoo Annan, Steven Feld, Alex Coke, and Jefferson Voorhees, *Topographies of the Dark*, CD, VoxLox, 2008.

9. *Musical Bells of Accra*, CD, VoxLox, 2006; also *Por Por: Honk Horn Music of Ghana*, CD, Smithsonian Folkways, 2007; and *Klebo! Honk Horn Music from Ghana*, CD, VoxLox, 2009.

10. *Jazz Cosmopolitanism in Accra*, DVD trilogy, VoxLox, 2009.

11. James Clifford, *Routes: Travel and Translation in the Late Twentieth Century* (Cambridge: Harvard University Press, 1997).

12. I'm thinking of Michael Jackson, for example, in *At Home in the World* (Durham: Duke University Press, 1995); *In Sierra Leone* (Durham: Duke University Press, 2004); and *Excursions* (Durham: Duke University Press, 2007). Also, of Kathleen Stewart, *A Space on the Side of the Road* (Princeton: Princeton University Press, 1996), and *Ordinary Affects* (Durham: Duke University Press, 2007); and Keith Basso, *Wisdom Sits in Places: Language and Landscape among the Western Apache* (Albuquerque: University of New Mexico Press, 1996). On recent claims by literary anthropologists for storying as analysis, see Kirin Narayan, *My Family and Other Saints* (Chicago: University of Chicago Press, 2008); Paul Stoller, *The Power of the Between: An Anthropological Odyssey* (Chicago: University of Chicago Press, 2009), particularly 171–73; and Michael Taussig, *Walter Benjamin's Grave* (Chicago: University of Chicago Press, 2006), which professes "a love of muted and even defective storytelling as a form of analysis" (vii).

13. Alfred Shutz, *The Phenomenology of the Social World* (1932; Evanston: Northwestern University Press, 1980); the full quote is: "It is the remembering which lifts the experience out of the irreversible stream of duration and thus modifies the awareness, making it remembrance" (47).

14. Guy Warren, *I Have a Story to Tell . . .* (Accra: Guinea Press, 1966).

15. I thank Ruti Talmor for alerting me to Sebald's *Austerlitz* (New York: Modern Library, 2002), and Michael Jackson for later conversation about it; see his *In Sierra Leone* (Durham: Duke University Press, 2004) for the book's West African resonances. Sebald's deep exploration of relations between voice, memory, narrative form, and verbal-visual interplays is also powerful in *The Emigrants* (New York: New Directions, 1997); *The Rings of Saturn* (New York: New Directions, 1999); *Vertigo* (New York: New Directions, 1999); and *On the Natural History of Destruction* (New York: Random House, 2002). On Sebald's verbal-visual narrativity and the impact of his image practices on photographers and theorists of visual memory, see Lisa Pratt, ed., *Searching for Sebald: Photography after W. G. Sebald* (London: Institute for Cultural Inquiry, 2007), and also J. J. Long, *W. G. Sebald: Image, Archive, Modernity* (New York: Columbia University Press, 2008).

16. Virginia Ryan, *Strangers in Accra* (Accra: Afram, 2004); Virginia Ryan (photographs) and Steven Feld (text), *Exposures: A White Woman in West Africa* (Santa Fe: VoxLox, 2007).

1. Ornette Coleman, *Live at the Golden Circle, Stockholm*, vols. 1 and 2, LP, Blue Note, 1965.

2. John Coltrane, *Kulu Sé Mama*, LP, Impulse, 1966; *Africa Brass*, LP, Impulse, 1961; *Transition*, LP, Impulse, 1970 (recorded 1965).

3. John Coltrane, *A Love Supreme*, LP, Impulse, 1965; *Live at the Village Vanguard*, LP, Impulse 1962; *Expression*, LP, Impulse, 1967.

4. John Coltrane, *Impressions*, LP, Impulse, 1963; *Crescent*, LP, Impulse, 1964.

5. John Coltrane and Rashied Ali, *Interstellar Space*, LP, Impulse, 1974 (recorded 1967).

6. Nii Otoo Annan and Steven Feld, *Bufo Variations*, CD, VoxLox, 2008.

7. A. M. Jones, *Studies in African Music*, 2 vols. (London: Oxford University Press, 1959); Kofi Agawu, "Structural Analysis or Cultural Analysis? Competing Perspectives on the 'Standard Pattern' of West African Rhythm," *Journal of the American Musicological Society* 59, no. 1 (2006): 1–46. On Agawu's critique of Africanist musicologies, see his *Representing African Music: Postcolonial Notes, Queries, Positions* (New York: Routledge, 2003). Veit Erlmann's response to Agawu lays out the stakes for an ethnomusicological politics of difference: "Resisting Sameness: À Propos Kofi Agawu's *Representing African Music*," *Music Theory Spectrum*, 26, no. 2 (2004): 291–304. On broader locations of Western and African positionalities in African music studies, see the distinguished works by J. H. Kwabena Nketia, particularly "African Music and Western Praxis: A Review of Western Perspectives on African Musicology," *Canadian Journal of African Studies* 20, no. 1 (1986): 36–56; "Perspectives on African Musicology," in *Africa and the West: The Legacies of an Empire*, ed. Isaac James Mowoe and Richard Bjornson (Westport: Greenwood Press, 1986), 215–53; and "The Scholarly Study of African Music: A Historical Review," in *Garland Encyclopedia of World Music*, vol. 1, *Africa*, ed. Ruth Stone (New York: Garland Publishing, 1999), 13–73. See too vol. 1 of Nketia's collected papers, *Ethnomusicology and African Music: Modes of Inquiry and Interpretation* (Accra: Afram Publications, 2005).

8. John Coltrane, *Olé Coltrane*, LP, Atlantic, 1961; *John Coltrane and Johnny Hartman*, LP, Impulse, 1963.

9. See, in particular, the summaries by Donald Thompson, "The Marimbula, an Afro-Caribbean Sanza," *Annuario Interamericano de Investigacion Musical* 7 (1971): 103–16; and Michael Sisson, "The Marimbula" (2000), at the website of Cloud Nine Musical Instruments, www.cloudninemusical.com. I thank Dan Neely for sharing his expertise on the bass lamellophone in the Caribbean and particularly in the history of *mento* music; see his "*Mento*, Jamaica's Original Music: Development, Tourism, and the Nationalist Frame," Ph.D. dissertation, New York University, 2007.

10. John Coltrane, *Meditations*, LP, Impulse, 1966; "Love" is the first track on

the B side of the original LP; Accra Trane Station, *Meditations for John Coltrane*, CD, VoxLox 2006.

11. Le Groupe de Recherches Musicales (GRM) was established in 1958 by Pierre Schaeffer, integrated into the Institut National de l'Audiovisuel (INA) in 1975, and has been, throughout this time, associated with the lineage of antiformalist electroacoustic music. Schwarz was a member of the group from 1969 to 1999, working with other *musique concrète* composers such as Bernard Parmegiani, Michel Chion, Luc Ferrari, François-Bernard Mâche, Guy Riebel, François Bayle, and Jacques Lejeune. Simultaneously he held a position as engineer for the Music Department at the Musée de l'Homme and prepared analytic documents and master tapes for their LP then CD series as well as their archive. His many LPs and CDs as a composer are principally published on his own Celia Records label: *Erda/Symphonie*, LP, GRM-INA, 1974.

12. Accra Trane Station, *Another Blue Train*, CD, 2007; John Coltrane, *Blue Train*, LP, Blue Note, 1957.

13. Nii Noi Nortey, Nii Otoo Annan, Steven Feld, Alex Coke, and Jefferson Voorhees, *Topographies of the Dark*, CD, VoxLox, 2008.

14. Guy Warren, *Africa Speaks, America Answers*, LP, Decca, 1957.

15. Gunther Schuller coined the term "third stream music" in 1957. The term was widely discussed in the early 1960s and applied to approaches and practices of John Lewis, Bill Russo, George Russell, Don Ellis, Gil Evans, and David Baker. Schuller acknowledged the influence of Duke Ellington, Charles Mingus, Claude Debussy, and Béla Bartók in his ideas about merging composed and improvised musics into a third stream; see his *Musings* (New York: Oxford University Press, 1986).

16. For discussion of the evolution of the *plan séquence* approach to direct cinema in the context of West African rituals, see Jean Rouch's essays and interviews in his *Ciné-Ethnography* (Minneapolis: University of Minnesota Press, 2004). I learned the techniques of plan séquence filming from Jean Rouch as an inspired student in his Paris classes in 1974. *Hallelujah!* was the first feature-length documentary I made after Rouch's death in 2004 and I dedicated it to him. Coincidentally, I later learned that Rouch himself photographed Ghanaba, then Guy Warren, in 1954 in Accra. A few of these images of Warren and the Red Spots Band at his Soundz Club were featured in *Récits Photographiques*, a major retrospective of Rouch's still photography at the Musée de l'Homme in 2000. The last image in the show's catalogue is of Warren at the drums.

17. Accurate biographical sources for Guy Warren/Ghanaba include Ian Carr, Digby Fairweather, and Brian Priestley, "Ghanaba," in *Jazz: The Rough Guide*, 3rd rev. expanded ed. (London: Rough Guides, 2004), 276; Royal Hartigan, "Ghanaba and the Heritage of African Jazz," *Annual Review of Jazz Studies* 9 (1997–98): 145–64; Ghanaba, *Hey Baby! Dig Dat Happy Feelin'* (Accra: Afrikan Heritage Library, 2002); Benson Idonije, "Kofi Ghanaba: Exit of the Spiritual Drum-

mer," *Guardian* (Nigeria), January 2, 2009; Val Wilmer, "Kofi Ghanaba: Influential Ghanaian Drummer Who Emphasized the African Origins of Jazz," *Guardian*, February 7, 2009; Ghanaba, "The Guy Warren/Ghanaba Saga," autobiographical statement, typescript, May 2007. Also see the memorial booklet for Ghanaba's funeral in Accra, *Celebrating the Life of Ghanaba, the Divine Drummer, a.k.a. Guy Warren of Ghana (1923–2008)*, comp. Nii Anum Telfer, photographs by Nii Yemo Nunu.

18. Guy Warren, *Themes for African Drums*, LP, RCA-Victor, 1958.

19. Olatunji, *Drums of Passion*, LP, Columbia, 1959.

20. Guy Warren, *I Have a Story to Tell . . .* (Accra: Guinea Press, 1966).

21. The La Drivers Union Por Por Group, *Por Por: Honk Horn Music of Ghana*, CD, Smithsonian Folkways, 2007; *Klebo!*, CD, VoxLox, 2009.

22. *Mmenson*, an Akan musical genre using hocketing elephant horns, is traditionally played in Ghana for Ashanti royal processions, typically of chiefs, the paramount leader Asantehene, and stool elders, who come out amid dancers and drummers to receive public praises during major celebrations and festivals. An example can be heard on the track "Mmensoun" (with that alternate spelling) recorded by Roger Vetter in 1979 and published on the Central Ghana compilation *Rhythms of Life, Songs of Wisdom*, CD, Smithsonian Folkways, 1996.

23. The popular song "There's No Business Like Show Business," by Irving Berlin, originally written for the musical *Annie Get Your Gun* in 1946, is also the title of a 1954 movie starring Ethel Merman. The song (and Merman version) had a revival in the 1980s after being featured in the 1979 Bob Fosse film *All That Jazz*. Dizzy Gillespie's composition "Night in Tunisia," became a well-established jazz standard by the mid-1950s. It has been recorded by dozens of artists and is arguably among the best known and most quoted jazz melodies of all time. Although not part of the song's published lead sheet, many small or large group arrangements of the piece use a common sax or sax section vamp. It's this second vamp (rather than the primary bass vamp, part of the song's published sheet music, © 1944 Universal Music Corporation, copyright renewed) that is echoed in por por rhythm.

24. Leo Touchet, *Rejoice When You Die: The New Orleans Jazz Funerals* (Baton Rouge: Louisiana State University Press, 1998).

25. On cosmopolitan philosophy and ethics from the Greeks to Enlightenment, some references that I've found most helpful include H. C. Baldry, *The Unity of Mankind in Greek Thought* (Cambridge: Cambridge University Press, 1965); Pauline Kleingeld, "Kant's Cosmopolitan Law: World Citizenship for a Global Order," *Kantian Review* 2 (1998): 72–90; Martha Nussbaum, "Kant and Cosmopolitanism," in *Perpetual Peace: Essays on Kant's Cosmopolitan Ideal*, ed. James Bohman and Matthias Lutz-Bachmann (Cambridge: MIT Press, 1997), 25–57; Samuel Scheffler, "Conceptions of Cosmopolitanism," in *Boundaries and Allegiances: Problems of Justice and Responsibility in Liberal Thought* (Oxford:

Oxford University Press, 2001), 111–30. Also see the "On Cosmopolitanism" special issue of *Daedalus* 137, no. 3 (2008).

26. Seyla Benhabib, *The Rights of Others: Aliens, Residents and Citizens* (Cambridge: Cambridge University Press, 2004), and *Another Cosmopolitanism* (New York: Oxford University Press, 2008); Hannah Arendt, *Responsibility and Judgment*, ed. with intro. by Jerome Kohn (New York: Schocken, 2003). On cosmopolitanism, justice, and human rights, also see Robert Fine, *Cosmopolitanism* (New York: Routledge, 2007); Gillian Brock and Harry Brighouse, *The Political Philosophy of Cosmopolitanism* (New York: Cambridge University Press, 2005); Pheng Cheah and Bruce Robbins, eds., *Cosmopolitics: Thinking and Feeling beyond the Nation* (Minneapolis: University of Minnesota Press, 1998); David Held, *Cosmopolitanism: A Defense* (Cambridge: Polity Press, 2003); Charles Jones, *Global Justice: Defending Cosmopolitanism* (Oxford: Oxford University Press, 1999); Martha Nussbaum, *Frontiers of Justice: Disability, Nationality, Species Membership* (Cambridge: Belknap Press of Harvard University Press, 2006); Pheng Cheah, *Inhuman Conditions: Cosmopolitanism and Human Rights in the Current Conjuncture* (Cambridge: Harvard University Press, 2006); Jacques Derrida, *On Cosmopolitanism and Forgiveness* (London: Routledge, 2001); Ulrich Beck, *Cosmopolitan Vision* (Malden, Mass.: Polity Press, 2006).

27. Kwame Anthony Appiah, "Cosmopolitan Reading," in *Cosmopolitan Geographies*, ed. Vinay Dharwad Ker (New York: Routledge, 2001), 197–227; quotation at 202.

28. Martin Stokes, "On Musical Cosmopolitanism," paper 3 for the Macalester International Roundtable, Institute for Global Citizenship, Macalester College, 2007, at digitalcommons.macalester.edu. While Stokes's work on Turkish arabesque has long shown a sensitivity to issues of cosmopolitanism, several Africanist anthromusicologists have also contributed to understanding cosmopolitan dimensions of musical formations, whether or not the notion of cosmopolitanism is directly theorized in the foreground. On how cosmopolitanism can profoundly underlie nationalist movements, see Thomas Turino, *Nationalists, Cosmopolitans, and Popular Music in Zimbabwe* (Chicago: University of Chicago Press, 2000). On how cosmopolitanism is reflexively produced by/in globalization and vernacular modernity, see Veit Erlmann, *Music, Modernity, and the Global Imagination: South Africa and the West* (New York: Oxford University Press, 1999). On how cosmopolitanism shapes the gendered politics of mediation in such a vernacular modernity, see Louise Meintjes, *Sound of Africa: Making Music Zulu in a South African Studio* (Durham: Duke University Press, 2003). On how cosmopolitanism underlies historical formation of a modern urban popular music genre, see Christopher Waterman, *Jùjú: A Social History and Ethnography of an African Popular Music* (Chicago: University of Chicago Press, 1990). On how cosmopolitanism underlies the messiest connections between mass-mediated popular music, political culture, and dictatorship, see Bob White, *Rumba Rules:*

The Politics of Dance Music in Mobutu's Zaire (Durham: Duke University Press, 2008).

29. Svetlana Boym, "On Diasporic Intimacy: Ilya Kabakov's Installations and Immigrant Homes," in "Intimacy," special issue, *Critical Inquiry* 24, no. 2 (1998): 498–524, reprinted in *Intimacy,* ed. Lauren Berlant (Chicago: University of Chicago Press, 2000), 226–52, and in Boym's collection, *The Future of Nostalgia* (New York: Basic Books, 2002), 309–26.

30. Whether or not Ghanaba's rejection of jazz mimicry was fully understood in Ghana during his lifetime, a very special appreciation of his radical move was revealed to the Ghanaian public after his death. In the article "Institute Ghanaba Percussion Award," *Graphic Showbiz,* January 22–28, 2009, J. H. Kwabena Nketia promotes the idea that a fitting memorial tribute to Ghanaba in Ghana would be an award for innovation and uniqueness in percussion. Nketia, professor emeritus at the University of Ghana, long the leading scholar of musical traditions in Ghana, and a 2003 cohonoree with Ghanaba at the Ghana National Theatre's Living Legends Concert, is quoted as saying that Ghanaba had "a mind that was not content to be a copycat. And so he was able to bring into the international idiom of jazz a continental African dimension, which others are currently trying to discern, understand and capture."

On expanded and contracted meanings of "experimentalism," see George Lewis, *A Power Stronger Than Itself: The AACM and American Experimental Music* (Chicago: University of Chicago Press, 2008). This is also the place to acknowledge some memorable conversations with Fred Moten about Cecil Taylor and black experimentalisms, and to cite his important book, *In the Break: The Aesthetics of the Black Radical Tradition* (Minneapolis: University of Minnesota Press, 2003). On the broader context of music and racial reading, see the editors' introduction, "Music and Race: Their Past, Their Presence," in *Music and the Racial Imagination,* ed. Ronald Radano and Philip Bohlman (Chicago: University of Chicago Press, 2000), 1–56. On post-Katrina New Orleans brass band scholarship, see Matt Sakakeeny, "Resounding Silence in the Streets of a Musical City," *Space and Culture;* 9 (2006): 41–44, and especially "New Orleans Music as a Circulatory System," *Black Music Research Journal* 31, no. 2 (2011): 291–325.

First Chorus, with Transposition

1. *The Prophet,* by the Lebanese-American philosopher and writer Khalil Gibran (1923; New York: Knopf, 1973) was among the most popular titles of 1960s–1970s world counterculture movements and remains a popular work in the inspirational and new age genres. When I told Ghanaba that second-hand copies of *The Prophet* were available on Amazon.com or in the bookshops of any university town for a dollar, he asked me to bring him ten. As I was jotting a

reminder in my notebook, he said, with a wink, "No, make it nine, I've already given you one, haven't I?"

2. *Jazz*, Ken Burns's mini-series for PBS (2001), remains one of the most successful productions in the public television genre and maintains an active website at pbs.org/jazz/. Burns's coproducer and the series artistic director, Wynton Marsalis, is also director of Jazz at Lincoln Center and himself a celebrated jazz trumpeter. Marsalis was the featured commentator throughout the episodes. In that role he repeats, ad infinitum, the word "gumbo" to summarize the melting pot of music in his hometown of New Orleans. This centralizing of New Orleans as a singular origin place for jazz is one of many oversimplifications in Burns's formulaic history of the music, whatever praise one might have for the detailed and loving attention he and Marsalis pay to Louis Armstrong. The shows were criticized in the jazz community for their romantic classicism, cultural elitism, and lack of attention to jazz after 1960, especially the dismissal of experimentalists, fusion proponents, and avant-gardes. On the politics of jazz conservatism, see Herman Gray, *Cultural Mores: African Americans and the Politics of Representation* (Berkeley: University of California Press, 2005).

I tried to tell Ghanaba that contemporary jazz scholarship was not entirely insensitive to his critique. As an example of newer, progressive work, I gave him, in 2007, the large compilation *Uptown Conversation: The New Jazz Studies*, edited by Robert O'Meally, Brent Hayes Edwards, and Farah Jasmine Griffin (New York: Columbia University Press, 2004). About a year later he told me that he had taken a look at it but was disappointed to find that the African presence was limited to a single article about jazz in Senegal. When I pressed him on the matter he asked me to bring him some recordings by David Murray, the tenor saxophonist who is extensively cited in that piece about returning to roots, because, as he said, "I need to hear where he is coming from." See Timothy R. Mangin, "Notes on Jazz in Senegal," in ibid., 224–48.

3. Marshall Sahlins, *Islands of History* (Chicago: University of Chicago Press, 1987), and *Apologies to Thucydides: Understanding History as Culture and Vice Versa* (Chicago: University of Chicago Press, 2004).

4. The "return and get" sankofa is largely interpreted as a symbol of learning from the past. "One must return to the past in order to move forward" is how the phrase is translated for the 1993 Haile Gerima *Sankofa* film poster. See R. S. Rattray, *Religion and Art in Ashanti* (London: Oxford University Press, 1927); Herbert Cole and Doran Ross, *The Arts of Ghana* (Los Angeles: UCLA Museum of Cultural History, 1977); Ablade Glover and Mark Kwami, *Symbolic Language of the Ashanti* (Berlin: Haus der Kulturen der Welt, 1993).

5. John Collins, *Musicmakers of West Africa* (Washington: Three Continents Press, 1985); on Koo Nimo, see 93–100.

6. Critical groundwork for a diasporic understanding of this remarkably dy-

namic music history is found throughout the writings of John Collins, for example: "The Early History of West African Highlife Music," *Popular Music* 8, no. 3 (1989): 221–30; "Jazz Feedback to Africa," *American Music* 5, no. 2 (1987): 176–93; "The Impact of African American Performance on West Africa from 1800," paper for the 2004 Vereinigung für Afrikawissenschaften (VAD) conference, Johannes Gutenberg University, Mainz, online at www.vad-ev.de. For other distillations see his *West African Pop Roots* (Philadelphia: Temple University Press, 1997), and *Highlife Time* (Accra: Anansesem Press, 1994/1996). The popular culture framework developed by Collins is enriched by ethnographic and interpretive insights in Catherine Cole, *Ghana's Concert Party Theatre*, with companion video, *Stageshakers!*, by Kwame Braun (Bloomington: Indiana University Press, 2001); and new archival and historiographic revelations in Nate Plageman, "Everybody Likes Saturday Night: A Social History of Popular Music and Masculinities in Urban Gold Coast/Ghana, c. 1900–1970," Ph.D. dissertation, Indiana University, 2008. Markus Coester's work on highlife transnationalism also extends Collins's synthesis through fieldwork with Ghanaians and Nigerians in the United Kingdom as well as in the archives of the Ghana Broadcasting Corporation; see his "Localising African Popular Music Transnationally: 'Highlife-Travellers' in Britain in the 1950s and 1960s," *Journal of African Cultural Studies* 20, no. 2 (2008): 133–44.

7. Ghanaba, "The Guy Warren/Ghanaba Saga," autobiographical statement, typescript, May 2007. Achimota College, one of Ghana's most distinguished institutions, has played a critical role in the country's history of producing leaders and cosmopolitans. Understanding Achimota's central and elite position in Ghana is important to the significance of Ghanaba's "bad-boy" reputation there and his dropping out to fashion a very different kind of border-crossing future. A recent review of Achimota's place in national history, educational ideology, and the intellectualization of art in Ghana is Ruti Talmor's "The Invention of Art at Achimota College," chap. 2 of her "Crafting Intercultural Desire: Transforming Nation, Art, and Personhood in Ghana," Ph.D. dissertation, New York University, 2008. Also see Cati Coe, "Educating an African Leadership: Achimota and the Teaching of African Culture in the Gold Coast," *Africa Today* 49, no. 3 (2002): 23–44. A colonial classic on the topic is A. W. Pickard-Cambridge, "The Place of Achimota in West African Education," *Journal of the Royal African Society* 39, no. 155 (1940): 143–53. I found a yellowed and marked-up copy of this piece in Ghanaba's archive; that makes me wonder whether copies were actually distributed to Achimotans in the 1940s to remind them of their elite educational, political, and cultural calling.

As Warren notes, the young Billy did indeed bear a physical resemblance to him; both that resemblance and the Eckstine last name, from his Prussian side, spoke to his mixed-race heritage. Eckstine's class background was not dissimilar to Warren's either, and in that context one also sees the parallels between Eckstine dropping out from Howard University, the elite African American institution, and Warren dropping out from Achimota College. The parallels in the modeling of elite African and African American educational and institutional ideologies are detailed in Talmor's chapter, cited above. Eckstine went on to have remarkable careers as a bebop big band leader (he played trumpet, trombone, and guitar) as well as much-recorded romantic balladeer, whose distinct vibrato and public popularity preceded and prefigured that of Nat "King" Cole. Eckstine was equally known as a trendsetter in stylish dressing, with his patented Mister B collar. The stylishness wasn't limited to clothing; as a singer, actor, recording artist, talk-show guest, Mister B's elegantly suave manner was much admired. But after dropping out, any parallels for Warren came to a quick end. In the long run, he opted for a very different public persona, both the ruffian whose black power–era defiance was iconized by the fist-in-your-face cover image of his *Afro-Jazz* LP, and the quick-into-trance spiritualist–holy man painted in white ochre and wrapped in calico, as in the *Hallelujah!* film.

8. Nii Noi Nortey and Nii Yemo Nunu, Ghanaba's closest collaborators in Ghana, both raised an eyebrow when they read this line on Ghanaba's anti-British sentiments, and pointed out a lived contradiction: that Ghanaba loved pomp and was always fascinated by tales of the British royals. In this context they pointed out how pleased Ghanaba was to carry the sankofa staff and present himself as an alternate kind of chief, the "divine drummer" Odomankoma Kyerema. But they also agreed that this posture of the chiefly, the divine, in all its mimetic royalism and verbal arrogance, was played out daily against Ghanaba's tendency toward a very reclusive home life, lived (despite his ability to afford otherwise) without electricity or modern plumbing for many years, until New York University, partnering with his Afrikan Heritage Library, upgraded the physical infrastructure.

9. Collins, *Musicmakers of West Africa*; on Guy Warren, see 65–71. Collins also takes up Warren in his *West African Pop Roots*, 287–94.

10. Radeyah Hack, "African Drum Wars: The Unknown Jazz Musician," *Stony Brook Independent*, February 15, 2006. The article is published online at www.sbindependent.org/node/849. Its first paragraph reads: "Hailed as provocative, eccentric and innovative, Guy Warren, the influential African drummer and lyricist, was labeled as the 'Invisible Man' of jazz last Thursday. Over a hundred students and faculty members listened to Robin D. G. Kelley present on the topic 'Africa Speaks, America Answers—The Drum Wars of Guy Warren' in the recently renovated Humanities Building." The quotation refers to Ralph Ellison's *Invisible Man* (New York: Random House, 1952).

11. Robin D. G. Kelley recounts the encounters between Guy Warren and Thelonious Monk in his remarkably detailed biography, *Thelonious Monk: The Life and Times of an American Original* (New York: Free Press, 2009); see 243–45. Ghanaba had a habit of letting the Accra press know about anything that made

him feel important. When Kelley initially wrote to request an interview about Thelonious Monk, Ghanaba forwarded the letter to the *Daily Graphic* newspaper, which published it in its entirety on March 26, 2004, headlined "Prof. D. G. Kelley of Columbia University Writes to Kofi Ghanaba."

12. Nii Noi Nortey, "Conversations with Ghanaba," recorded May 1994; typescript in preparation for publication, in Noi Nortey, Nii Yemo Nunu, and Steven Feld, *The Life and Times of Ghanaba, Odomankoma Kyerma, the Divine Drummer* (Accra: Afram Publications). Nortey's conversations with Ghanaba about Thelonious Monk in fact only minimally overlap the many details reported in Kelley's book. But Nii Noi also kept a notebook, about fifty pages handwritten, compiling all of the notes of response that Ghanaba wrote in the margins of jazz books and magazines in his library. A reading of Nii Noi's notebook indicates that Monk was the most frequently annotated and commented-on musician in Ghanaba's responses.

13. Ghanaba (then Guy Warren) lashed out at Olantunji in several places in the early 1960s; the harsh language of being an "exploited fake" comes from his book, *I Have a Story to Tell . . .* (Accra: Guinea Press, 1966).

14. After reading these paragraphs, Nii Noi Nortey pointed out that another possible reason for Olatunji's broad popularity might have been the privileging of Yoruba culture in Afrocentric discourses. He recalled that in the 1970s, Yoruba origins were disproportionately celebrated among the black British of London and Birmingham as an authentic African heritage. He also pointed out the central role, in academic African studies, of many distinguished scholars of Yoruba culture at that time. "You know, man, in those days, there was a whole lot of that 'among the Yoruba . . . ' thing going on."

15. See Nortey, "Conversations with Ghanaba." The theme of collaboration across lines of race, class, and ethnicity in jazz history (specifically in the Jim Crow era of the 1950s) surfaces in numerous jazz writings alongside all of the ways race was inextricably tied to issues of power and control in the music's history. Pluralism clearly meant very different things to different people; it was equally construed as a hopeful sign or a cynical whitewash, an ideal or a façade. Eric Porter's *What Is This Thing Called Jazz?* (Berkeley: University of California Press, 2002) opens up new lines of understanding about how jazz musicians addressed such concerns. Ghanaba's pragmatic take on this echoes one that was voiced by many black artists as well, but, of course, with a sense of African difference. When I read back and reviewed these paragraphs with him he responded tersely: "Correct. I did what I had to do to get my music heard, that's all." One of the places where Ghanaba sounded off in print on this matter was a letter to *Time* magazine in response to an editorial essay of October 19, 1962, titled "Crow Jim," on the subject of reverse discrimination and racial protest jazz. The piece is a treasure trove of the race-baiting reactionary rhetoric that often greeted the late 1950s and early 1960s jazz that embraced civil rights and black

pride. *Africa Speaks, America Answers* is cited in the essay's list of examples of "Negro nationalism," along with titles by Art Blakey, Randy Weston, Oliver Nelson, Max Roach, and Abbey Lincoln. This citation and the essay in general angered Warren deeply. When I talked with him about the *Time* piece, he said: "You see! I told you they were racists! They didn't even look at *Africa Speaks*! They had no idea that I made that record with whites. The whole thing was a setup to incite . . . what would you call it . . . divide and rule . . . it was a setup." Warren's open letter to the editor of *Time* was published in his *I Have a Story to Tell . . .* (168–70).

16. Text transcription and translation from Ga by Kwame Assenyoh and Nii Yemo Nunu, reviewed and approved by Ghanaba.

17. "That Happy Feeling," © Northern Music, 1961. A facsimile reduction of the original four-page instrumental sheet music as published is found on page 30 of Ghanaba's book, *Hey Baby! Dig Dat Happy Feelin'* (Accra: Afrikan Heritage Library, 2002). But no sheet music version of the song was ever published with these lyrics as improvised by Warren on the original recording, and the lyrics were never copyrighted.

18. Bert Kaempfert, *That Happy Feeling*, LP, Decca, 1962; *A Swinging Safari*, LP, Decca, 1962.

19. Bruno Bertone Ballroom Orchestra, *Fox Trot*, for the Strictly Dancing Laserlight Series, includes the Kaempfert arrangement of "Eyi Wala Dong / That Happy Feeling," CD, Delta, 1991.

20. Popular summaries of the Edward R. Murrow and Louis Armstrong visit to Accra can be found in Gary Giddins, *Satchmo* (New York: Doubleday, 1988), and Nat Hentoff, liner notes, *Satchmo The Great*, LP, Columbia, 1957.

21. Quote from page 166 of Henry Louis Gates Jr., "Belafonte's Balancing Act," in his *Thirteen Ways of Looking at a Black Man* (New York: Random House, 1997), 155–79. The essay was originally published in *The New Yorker*, August 26, 1996.

22. Jason John Squinobal's master's thesis, "The Use of African Music in Jazz from 1926–1964: An Investigation of the Life, Influences, and Music of Randy Weston" (University of Pittsburgh, 2007), analyzes one of Weston's recorded versions of "Love, the Mystery of. . . ." Squinobal's analysis (66–71) notes Ghanaian elements of the common timeline bell pattern, *adowa* rhythm, and pitch selection. I never had the opportunity to discuss this analysis with Ghanaba, or for that matter any other aspects of Weston's creation of the bass line he denounced as "wrong"; he was never willing to pursue these conversations. Squinobal extends his analysis to include Art Blakey's version of this song in his Ph.D. dissertation. This work includes a number of historically inaccurate statements about Warren from tertiary sources, and the presentation makes clear that the author has not heard Warren's original recording of "Love, the Mystery of. . . ." However, Squinobal's transcriptions of the Blakey version here, and the early

Weston version in his master's thesis, are precise, as is his notation of the inverse way Blakey and Weston play the timeline. See Jason John Squinobal, "West African Music in the Music of Art Blakey, Yusef Lateef, and Randy Weston," Ph.D. dissertation, University of Pittsburgh, 2008, especially 307–10 and 391–96.

On a number of occasions Ghanaba either asked me about Yusef Lateef or reminded me that he held the man in very high musical and spiritual estimation. Ghanaba was aware that Lateef had converted to Islam in 1950, that he was deeply focused on spirituality in his music, that his studies of oboe and bassoon extended into Indian and Chinese double-reed instruments early in his career, and that this knowledge was, in turn, an inspiration to John Coltrane in his own explorations of the sound of Indian double-reed instruments. Ghanaba also approvingly cited Lateef's performances on *sarewa*, the Fulani flute, learned during a four-year residency in northern Nigeria in the 1980s as a fellow at Ahmadu Bello University, Zaria. On one occasion Ghanaba gladly listened with me to a few tracks from Lateef's 1961 Prestige LP *Eastern Sounds*. One of the last books that I gave to Ghanaba was Lateef's autobiography, *The Gentle Giant*, written with Herb Boyd (New York: Morton, 2006). I don't know if he got around to reading it, but he told me that he was impressed by its list of Lateef's many honors and accomplishments. For a broader contextualization of jazz engagements with African music, see Norman Weinstein, *A Night in Tunisia: Imaginings of Africa in Jazz* (London: Scarecrow, 1992); the Lateef chapter is "Re-visioning the Geography of the Blues" (145–58), and the Weston chapter is "Talking Piano Like a Drum Shouting Freedom" (107–17).

On Art Blakey, see Ingrid Monson, "Art Blakey's African Diaspora," in her edited volume *The African Diaspora: A Musical Perspective*, 2nd ed. (New York: Routledge, 2003), 324–47. On Randy Weston, see his autobiography, with Willard Jenkins, *African Rhythms: The Autobiography of Randy Weston* (Durham: Duke University Press, 2010). The book has a singular and brief mention of Ghanaba, on page 120; there Weston tells the story of hearing and adopting "Love, the Mystery of . . ." as his theme song, typically performed at the end of his concerts. A new Weston CD, whose release coincides with the publication of his autobiography, ends with a brief version of the song; Randy Weston and His African Rhythms Sextet, *The Storyteller* (recorded live at Dizzy's Club Coca-Cola), Motema Music, CD, 2010.

23. Detailed biographical information about Olatunji and his recordings can be found in his *The Beat of My Drum: An Autobiography*, with Robert Atkinson, foreword by Joan Baez, intro. by Eric Charry (Philadelphia: Temple University Press, 2005).

24. John Coltrane, *The Olatunji Concert: The Last Live Recording*, CD, Impulse, 2001, originally recorded April 1967.

25. Quote from page 4 of Eric Charry, "Introduction," in Babatunde Olatunji, *The Beat of My Drum*.

26. Quotes from the April 9, 2003, obituary, "Famous Drummer, Olatunji, Dies in the US," by Jahman Anikulapo for the *Guardian* (Nigeria).

27. The complete June 1962 radio interview with Les Tomkins for *Jazz Weekly News* was published in Guy Warren, *I Have a Story to Tell* . . . (171–89); also see *Down Beat*, April 12, 1962.

28. Max Roach's LP *We Insist! Max Roach's Freedom Now Suite*, was released in late 1960 on the Candid label. With lyrics by Oscar Brown, the LP features singer Abbey Lincoln. Guest percussionists Olatunji, Ray Mantilla, and Taiwo DuVall, are uniquely featured on "Tears for Johannesburg," the ultimate and longest track. For a discussion of this LP's impacts in the larger context of jazz and civil rights struggles of the 1950s and 1960s, see Ingrid Monson, *Freedom Sounds: Civil Rights Call Out to Jazz and Africa* (New York: Oxford University Press, 2007).

29. Max Roach's open letter was first circulated by Ghanaba in Ghana and then beyond. Among the first of friends he sent it to was the British trumpeter and jazz journalist Ian Carr (who passed away just two months after Ghanaba). Warren's *Afro Jazz* LP was recorded in November 1968 with members of the Don Rendell–Ian Carr Quintet plus the Goa Indian guitarist Amancio D'Silva. He also collaborated with Carr on later recordings and performances before the Rendell-Carr quintet broke up. Carr wrote about their collaborations in his *Music Outside: Contemporary Jazz in Britain* (London: Latimer New Directions, 1973), 123–26. Carr circulated the Max Roach letter to the larger European jazz press and quoted these exact lines here in his entry for "Ghanaba," in Ian Carr, Digby Fairweather, and Brian Priestley, *Jazz: The Rough Guide*, 3rd rev. expanded ed. (London: Rough Guides, 2004), 276. On the flip side, see Warren's chapter, "Max Roach and I," in his *I Have a Story to Tell* . . . (54–58). One of the prominent and powerful historian-critics that Warren encountered and most wanted to engage in the United States in the 1950s was Leonard Feather, whose *Encyclopedic Yearbook of Jazz* was published in several editions from 1956 (most recently, in a posthumous revised edition, with Ira Gitler [Oxford University Press, 1999]). Warren lashed out viciously at Feather in his 1966 autobiography. But years later, while visiting Max Roach in New York, he saw an entry that Feather wrote about him in the edition of the *Encyclopedic Yearbook* that Roach had in his library. Once back in Ghana, Warren decided to write to Feather to update him on the local music activities to which he had turned in recent years. The opening salutation of Ghanaba's letter, shown to me years later by Nii Yemo Nunu, who was charged to post it, reads: "Len, you lovable bastard, . . ."

30. *Sankofa* (1993) is the best-known film by Haile Gerima, the Ethiopian-born Howard University film professor. The work is a powerful African-centric portrayal of the brutality and exploitation of the slave trade and of the dungeons that were its staging ground. It is also intensely antiromantic, the obvious oppositional text being Alex Haley's book *Roots* (1976), and derived television miniseries (1979). The experience of living and working at the Cape Coast fort during

the filming formed the background to Ghanaba's engagements, particularly in 1993–94, around the contentious topics of slavery and heritage site tourism. A critical understanding of the unique place of Gerima's *Sankofa* in the history of representations of slavery and the forts in Ghana requires juxtaposition with Werner Herzog's *Cobra Verde*, made six years earlier and filmed in part at neighboring Elmina fort. Adapted from Bruce Chatwin's novel *The Viceroy of Ouidah* (New York: Penguin, 1988), *Cobra Verde* is the last of Herzog's collaborations with the actor Klaus Kinski, a powerful screen personality, to say the least. Herzog exploits Kinski's ability to depict extremes of rage, madness, and lunacy precisely around his intertwined relations with African royalty, slavers, and slaves, set in the ending moment of the slave trade. See too Herzog's 1999 documentary *My Best Fiend*, particularly his comments there on directing Kinski in roles meant to illuminate the far edge of rationality or sanity in the most extreme of out-of-place cultural and environmental conditions.

31. Ghanaba, "The Guy Warren/Ghanaba Saga."

32. Warren's later 1960s engagements in Britain led to two LPs produced (as were his earlier ones from the 1960s) by Denis Preston: *The African Zoundz of Guy Warren of Ghana*, LP, EMI, 1968; *Afro-Jazz*, LP, EMI, 1969.

33. Warren performs on the track "Blood Brothers 69" on the 1972 Ginger Baker LP *Stratavarious* (Polydor), rereleased in 1998 as part of the double album *Do What You Like* (CD, Atco). Baker was also involved as a performer, producer, and studio collaborator with Fela during this period. Basic tracks for the Paul McCartney and Wings 1973 LP *Band on the Run* were recorded at Baker's Lagos Studio. Baker's 1970s studio adventures in Lagos and times with Fela are explored in Tony Palmer's film *Ginger Baker: In Africa* (2006 DVD release). The memoir by the recording engineer Geoff Emerick recalls the making of *Band on the Run* and encounters then with Fela and Baker; Emerick with Howard Massey, *Here, There, and Everywhere: My Life Recording the Music of The Beatles* (New York: Penguin, 2006).

The drummer Tony Allen, born in Lagos of Ghanaian and Nigerian parentage, began mixing jazz and highlife in the early 1960s and was deeply influenced by Guy Warren. He began to work with Fela in 1964, directed Fela's bands from 1968 to 1979, and recorded more than twenty-five albums with him; he is widely credited as cofounder of the music called Afro-beat. Since the mid-1980s Allen has been based in London and Paris. Michael Veal discusses Allen's contributions to Afro-beat in *Fela: The Life and Times of an African Musical Icon* (Philadelphia: Temple University Press, 2000); he is reportedly collaborating on Allen's musical biography; see his website, www.tony-allen.com.

34. The 1971 *Soul to Soul* concert was reissued as a double-disk DVD with soundtrack CD and booklet in 2004 on the Rhino label. I was neither able to verify nor to find a source for Ghanaba's citation of the show's hundred-to-one pay scale. However, the Wikipedia site for the film reports (unattributed):

"While $50,000 was budgeted for paying the American performers, only $1,000 was set aside for the local musicians." That there might be differences in how the event was perceived in Ghana didn't go completely unnoticed in the U.S. music press; see the report by Val Wilmer, "Souled Out in Ghana," *Down Beat*, February 18, 1971, 14–15.

35. Ghanaba's connection to Aklowa developed through a former Achimota College classmate, Felix Cobbson, who was central to its activities. Among many shorter press clips about Aklowa in his library, Ghanaba kept one more detailed article reviewing his anointment there; see Ron Godfrey, "Aklowa—Traditional Africa in an English Village," *Africa Woman* 37 (January–February 1982): 34–35, 62.

36. See Charles Whitaker, "W. E. B. Du Bois: A Final Resting Place for an Afro-American Giant," *Ebony Magazine*, November 1986, 172–78.

37. Ghanaba's comment requires additional contextualization. That he did indeed protest against preservationists and tourist promoters is documented in A. D. C. Hyland and George W. K. Intsiful, "When the Castles Were White, 11," paper presented at the meeting of the International Council on Monuments and Sites, October 27–31, 2003, Victoria Falls, Zimbabwe, at www.international .icomos.org. But it is more accurate to say that Ghanaba was not really anti-preservation but rather deeply suspicious of commercial tourist agendas overtaking historic ones. He often stated that the Ghana Museums and Monuments Board, established in 1969 and meant to look after the legacy of the castle forts, was underfunded, mismanaged, and too easily corrupted by commercial attempts to attract tourism dollars. Those statements were compounded by Ghanaba's tendency toward reactive suspicions about African American business entrepreneurialism in the Ghana tourism sector. Ghanaba's take on castle/fort tourism is best clarified in a pair of editorials he wrote for the *Ghanaian Times*. The first of them, "Stop the Desecration of Cape Coast Castle," September 23, 1993, 4, complains: "You know, there is a drinking bar inside the castle which sells alcohol and plays loud American rock and roll music day in and day out. Shoddily dressed tourists tramp around there taking pictures and laughing at us. Dancing and boisterous cavorting in the castle is allowed freely." The article goes on to call for creation of reverent, respectful, and dignified spaces and more control over them. A second editorial, "Perpetual Flame Proposed for Cape Coast Castle," May 21, 1994, 4, more deeply argued the necessity of preservation. There Ghanaba urges: "The renovation, restoration, and preservation of Cape Coast Castle in particular would try as much as possible to retain all historic events which had taken place within the castle during its occupation by the Portuguese, Dutch, and British so that ITS TRUE HISTORIC IMPORTANCE in this country would be available to our children and generations to come." (In all his writings and letters Ghanaba regularly used uppercase letters for emphasis.) This is also the right place to mention that Ghanaba not infrequently made himself unpopular in front of various diasporan audiences with hostile responses

to conversation about reparations to right the wrongs of the slave trade. He was one of the few people in Ghana, in the context of the making of Haile Gerima's *Sankofa*, in 1991, to state in public that the role of Africans in the trade was considerable, particularly in the interior of Ghana. In 2007 he told me to read Akosua Adoma Perbi's *A History of Indigenous Slavery in Ghana, from the 15th to the 19th Century* (Accra: Sub-Saharan African Publishers, 2004). More recently I was reminded of many sentiments expressed by Ghanaba when I read the op-ed article by Henry Louis Gates Jr., "Ending the Slavery Blame-Game," *New York Times*, April 22, 2010.

On disentangling preservation and tourism agendas in the context of "world heritage" discourses, see Barbara Kirschenblatt-Gimblett, "World Heritage and Cultural Economies," in *Museum Frictions: Public Cultures / Global Transformations*, ed. Ivan Karp, Corrinne Kratz, Lynne Szwaja, and Tomás Ybarra-Frausto (Durham: Duke University Press, 2006), 161–204. Also see Katharina Schramm, *African Homecoming: Pan-African Ideology and Contested Heritage* (Walnut Creek, Calif.: Left Coast Press, 2010).

38. Ghanaba's recitation of his favorite recordings was something of a set piece; he had delivered bits of the recitation to various journalists in the past, and a similar list appears on page 1 of his compilation book *Hey Baby! Dig Dat Happy Feelin'*.

39. After Ghanaba's death, one of these filmmakers, the one with whom he had the longest and most contentious relationship, "borrowed" the copy of *Hallelujah!* that I donated to the Goethe Institut library and incorporated lengthy segments from it into a memorial film he then sold to Ghana Broadcasting Corporation for TV transmission. No permission was requested of me or of the coproducer Nii Yemo Nunu, and no citation of the *Hallelujah!* film as a source documentary appears in his film's end titles. I don't know whether this was an act of deliberate retribution for being dissed in public and in my presence by Ghanaba, or whether it was just part of the often-lamented local practice of ignoring permissions with regard to copyright materials. Local press tributes and stories about the Goethe Institut event for Ghanaba's eighty-fifth birthday include Kouame Koulibaly, "Drums and Choruses at Goethe Institut," *Graphic Showbiz*, April 17–23, 2008, 7; Nii Laryea Korley, " 'Hallelujah' on Screen," *Graphic Showbiz*, April 24–30, 2008, 6.

40. The Associated Press wire service photographic image that repeatedly flashed on TV and appeared in the Ghanaian press during this time shows a young Barack Obama wearing a Hawaiian lei and standing with his white grandparents at his 1979 high school graduation in Honolulu. His grandfather, Stanley Dunham, stands to his right, and his grandmother, Madelyn Dunham, has her eyes closed and head to his chest, hugging him with both arms. At that time the future president wore his hair in a full Afro.

41. Royal Hartigan's article is titled "Ghanaba and the Heritage of African

Jazz," *Annual Review of Jazz Studies* 9 (1997–98): 145–64. Ghanaba was very proud of this piece; he had an extra-large blow-up from it, museum style, mounted on the wall near the doorway to his library. Hartigan is presently on the performing arts faculty of the University of Massachusetts, Dartmouth and continues research and presentation of traditional drumming in Ghana, work he began as a graduate student at Wesleyan in the mid-1980s. An interesting distillation of West Africa and jazz drumset thinking is presented in his book and CD, *West African Rhythms for Drumset*, with the Ghanaian artists Abraham Kobena Adzenyah and Freeman Kwadzo Donkor (New York: Alfred, 2004).

42. "Santa Klaus" was Ghanaba's nickname for Klaus Voswinkel, a German filmmaker with long white hair, with whom he collaborated in 2000 for the film *The Divine Drummer*, together with Robyn Schulkowsky, a Berlin-based contemporary music percussionist who has recorded the work of John Cage, Morton Feldman, Alvin Curran, Luciano Berio, and Christian Wolff. Voswinkel came to Accra in January 2008 to screen, in Ghanaba's presence at the Goethe Institut, a shorter film, *Achimota Concert*. It features a return to the campus of the famous college where Ghanaba dropped out and a performance there, a duo improvisation with Schulkowsky. Voswinkel's memoir about Ghana and his times with Ghanaba is *Die Nacht der Trommeln: Ghana-Notizen* (Weitra: Bibliothek der Provinz, 2009).

43. A public account is Nii Laryea Korley, "Fire Farewell for Ghanaba," *Graphic Showbiz*, April 2–8, 2009, 3, with color photographs spread across 12–13.

44. M. J. Field, *Religion and Medicine of the Ga People* (1937; reprint, London: Oxford University Press, 1961). A few weeks after giving me Ghanaba's copy of the Field book, Nii Yemo put himself in the picture with this text message to my cell phone: "Please see p. 200 of Field's book. My great grandfather i.e., my father's grandpa, sits front in round hat. He was the orchestra's conductor." The image is of an ensemble performing at La, one of Field's key research sites, near Nii Yemo's family homestead.

45. On the historical context of racial perceptions in that moment in Ghana, see Gustav Jahoda, *White Man: A Study of the Attitudes of Africans to Europeans in Ghana before Independence* (London: Oxford University Press, 1961). Regarding this underlining of Field's characterization, and in light of the entire material of this chapter, it is worth pointing out that Ghanaba was sometimes drawn in by stereotype and overstatement. It was well known that when talking to blacks Ghanaba could be terribly dismissive of whites. It was also well known that when talking to whites he could be equally dismissive of blacks. In this chapter I have left the inflections of our three years of conversations just as they were, but want to signpost awareness that they represent just one dimension of Ghanaba's very complexly intertwined registers of talking about race.

1. Accra Trane Station, *Another Blue Train*, CD, VoxLox, 2007; John Coltrane, *Blue Train*, LP, Blue Note, 1957.

2. Key reference works for Fela include Michael Veal, *Fela: Life and Times of an African Musical Icon* (Philadelphia: Temple University Press, 2000); Tejumola Olaniyan, *Arrest the Music! Fela and His Rebel Art and Politics* (Bloomington: Indiana University Press, 2004); Carlos Moore, *Fela: This Bitch of a Life*, 2nd ed. (1982; New York: Lawrence Moore, 2009); John Collins, *Fela: Kalakuta Notes* (London: KIT Publishers, 2009). Key reference works for John Coltrane include Lewis Porter, *John Coltrane: His Life and Music* (Ann Arbor: University of Michigan Press, 2000); Leonard Brown, ed., *John Coltrane and Black America's Quest for Freedom: Spirituality and the Music* (New York: Oxford University Press, 2010); Chris DeVito, ed., *Coltrane on Coltrane: The John Coltrane Interviews* (Chicago: Chicago Review Press, 2010); Ashley Khan, *A Love Supreme: The Story of John Coltrane's Signature Album* (New York: Penguin, 2003). The importance of Alice Coltrane to this musical and spiritual legacy is revealed in Franya Berkman, *Monument Eternal: The Music of Alice Coltrane* (Middletown: Wesleyan University Press, 2010).

After reading this chapter, Nii Noi expressed concern that it perhaps overstated the central position of Coltrane to his listening and practice. He reminded me strongly of how much Coltrane was the "beacon," but of his own simultaneous and deeply parallel engagements with the music of Sun Ra, Rahsaan Roland Kirk, Yusef Lateef, Archie Shepp, Pharoah Sanders, Ornette Coleman, Cecil Taylor, the Art Ensemble of Chicago, and other 1960s–1970s avant-gardists. Listening to Nii Noi talk about Coltrane as the "beacon" reminded me of Amiri Baraka's pithy and perfect summary: "Trane emerged as the process of historical clarification itself." See "John Coltrane, Why His Legacy Continues," in Baraka's collection *Digging: The Afro-American Soul of American Classical Music* (Berkeley: University of California Press, 2009), 192–94.

3. Nii Noi Nortey, Nii Otoo Annan, Steven Feld, Alex Coke, and Jefferson Voorhees, *Topographies of the Dark*, CD, VoxLox, 2008; on the art project, see Virginia Ryan, *Multiple Entries: Africa and Beyond, 2001–2007* (Spoleto: Festival dei Due Mondi/Commune di Spoleto, 2008).

4. Summary narrations of the history of the Asante empire include Robert B. Edgerton, *The Fall of the Asante Empire: The Hundred-Year War for Africa's Gold Coast* (New York: Free Press, 1995); N. Kyeremateng and K. Nkansa, *The Akans of Ghana: Their History and Culture* (Accra: Sebewie Publishers, 1996); J. K. Fynn, *Asante and Its Neighbors* (Evanston: Northwestern University Press, 1993); Ivor Wilks, *Forest of Gold: Essays on the Akan and the Kingdom of Asante* (Athens: Ohio University Press, 1993). The broad West African precolonial and colonial context for this history is summarized in Basil Davidson, *West Africa before the*

Colonial Era: A History to 1850, 4th ed. (London: Longman, 1998); Michael Crowder, *West Africa under Colonial Rule* (London: Hutchinson, 1968); also see Frederick D. Lord Lugard, *The Dual Mandate in British Tropical Africa*, 5th ed. (London: Frank Cass, 1965). A recent general history is Roger Gocking, *The History of Ghana* (Westport: Greenwood Press, 2005).

5. The music and poetry group African Dawn, active in London in the 1980s, was founded by Kwesi Owusu, Sheikh Gueye, and Wanjiku Kiarie, and later included Wala Danga, Vico Mensah, Merle Collins, and Nii Noi Nortey. They released four LPs; the current CD in circulation is the self-produced and self-published *Jali* (1989). The aesthetic ideology of the group, and the larger British black arts context in which its work was placed, has been chronicled by the Ghanaian writer, filmmaker, and media producer Kwesi Owusu in *The Struggle for Black Arts in Britain: What Can We Consider Better Than Freedom* (London: Comedia, 1986), and two edited anthologies, *Storms of the Heart: An Anthology of Black Arts and Culture* (London: Camden Press, 1988), and *Black British Culture and Society: A Text Reader* (London: Routledge, 2000). Owusu's introduction in the last of these books, "Charting the Genealogy of Black British Cultural Studies" (1–18), provides a good historical introduction to the intellectual and artistic world in which Nii Noi participated during his years in Britain in the 1970s and 1980s. A visual companion to that story is Paul Gilroy's *Black Britain: A Photographic History* (London: Saqi, 2008).

Yusuf Hassan, "What Is Ours? Black Voices, Black Sounds, but Who Reaps the Fruits?," *Africa Events* (May 1987): 77–78, situates Dade Krama and African Dawn against white curators and DJs in the United Kingdom in terms of an anticolonial politics of mediation. Another take, from the same moment, is Maggie Jonas, "Is African Music Being Colonized?," *New African* (May 1987): 45–46.

6. Misty In Roots developed their powerful roots reggae approach in the mid- and late 1970s, releasing what has become one of the most successful of all live reggae LPs, *Live at the Counter Eurovision* (People Unite, 1979). They are largely acknowledged for being the most steady and long-running onstage presence in rock against racism concerts. Their 1982 trip to Zimbabwe and Zambia was followed by the very popular LP *Earth*, on which Nii Noi perfoms (People Unite, 1983) and then *Musi O Tunya* (People Unite, 1985). More recently, Nii Noi also plays on some tracks of Misty In Roots's *The John Peel Sessions* (People Unite, 1995) and *Roots Controller* (People Unite/Real World, 2002). The group is still active and maintains a website at www.mistyinroots.ws. On Misty In Roots's later trip to Ghana, with quotations on their reception from Nii Noi, see Klevor Abo, "Music and Struggle," *West Africa*, February 1, 1988, 174.

7. A VU (volume unit) meter is an analog device for representing volume level, ubiquitous on radio and audio equipment from the early 1940s.

8. I'm grateful to Efua and Nii Noi for a copy of the revealing book about

Bernie that Efua's father, Eric Grant, so passionately worked to finish just before his own death: *Dawn to Dusk: A Biography of Bernie Grant* MP (London: Ituni Books, 2006). The Bernie Grant Archive's website is www.berniegrantarchive .org.uk; the Bernie Grant Arts Centre's is www.berniegrantcentre.co.uk.

9. The late Coltrane sound of 1965–67 is represented by the LPs *A Love Supreme, Ascension, New Thing at Newport, Kulu Sé Mama, Meditations, Live at the Village Vanguard Again,* and *Expression,* all on Impulse.

10. Nii Noi's references were Klaus Wachsmann, ed., *Essays on Music and History in Africa* (Evanston: Northwestern University Press, 1971); J. H. K. Nketia, *The Music of Africa* (New York: W. W. Norton, 1974); Paul Berliner, *The Soul of Mbira: Music and Traditions of the Shona People of Zimbabwe* (Los Angeles: University of California Press, 1979); Charles Keil, *Tiv Song: The Sociology of Art in a Classless Society* (Chicago: University of Chicago Press, 1979).

11. *The World According to John Coltrane,* DVD, BMG Special Products, 2002; we also watched the full version of the Coltrane quartet's "Alabama" performance on *Ralph Gleason's Jazz Casual: John Coltrane,* DVD, Rhino/WEA, 2003.

12. Coltrane's song "Alabama" is on his LP *Live at Birdland,* Impulse, 1963; see the discussion of the song in Porter's *John Coltrane,* 331.

13. The work of Mau Mau Muziki and African Sound Project was documented on two cassettes, now out of print, produced and published by Nii Noi's Anyaa Arts Library. A sampler of both groups drawn from those cassettes is *Made in Ghana: Mau Mau Muziki (1990–1997) and African Sound Project (1999–2004),* CD, Anyaa Arts Library, 2008. Accra Trane Station (2005–8) is heard on the CDs *Tribute to A Love Supreme* (2005), *Meditations for John Coltrane* (2006), *Another Blue Train* (2007), *Topographies of the Dark,* with Alex Coke and Jefferson Voorhees (2008), all on VoxLox.

14. Charles Keil explores this theme, powerfully linking the mysteries of double-reed legacies from Africa, Asia, the Middle East, and Europe, in "The Most Important Instruments in the World," his introductory chapter to Dick Blau, Charles Keil, Angeliki Keil, and Steven Feld, *Bright Balkan Morning: Romani Lives and the Power of Music in Greek Macedonia* (Middletown: Wesleyan University Press, 2002), 23–86. On the role of the alghaita in African Islamic music, also see Eric Charry, "Music and Islam in Sub-Saharan Africa," in *The History of Islam in Africa,* ed. Nehemia Levtzion and Randall Pouwels (Athens: Ohio University Press, 2000), 545–73.

15. Nii Noi's columns were published in the Chicago-based journal *The Rising Firefly: Kemetic Magazine of Culture, Philosophy and Spirituality,* edited and largely written by his friend Naba Lamoussa Morodenibig, whose teachings are introduced at www.theearthcenter.com.

16. Norman Weinstein, *A Night in Tunisia: Imaginings of Africa in Jazz* (London: Scarecrow Press, 1992); the Coltrane chapter is "Sounding the African Cry for Paradise" (60–72).

17. I've not gone into my conversations with Nii Noi about Kwame Nkrumah here, but want to signpost both how deeply Nii Noi has read Nkrumah's writings and how significant they remain for his narration of the connections between musical and political action in the work of Ghana's nationalism and Pan-Africanism. Some of this is revealed in Nii Noi's comments in the *Accra Trane Station* film. Another key location for the Nkrumah story here comes through the way Nii Noi's sculptures are surrounded by books; sometimes the books even become part of the sculptures. Nii Noi often pointed out to me the importance of education and libraries in Nkrumah's vision of nation building. As presented in the film, Nii Noi's A–Z wall charts (A–Z of Ghanaba, A–Z of Coltrane, etc.) developed one way to bring education, nation, and pedagogy together with creative artistry. Of course, education was a place where Nkrumah's emphasis on the intertwining of nationalism and Pan-Africanism always triangulated to embrace international cosmopolitanism ideals. For example, in his speech at his installation as first chancellor of the Kwame Nkrumah University of Science and Technology (November 29, 1961), Nkrumah put it this way: "Knowledge is international, and scientific knowledge especially cannot be restricted to any one particular nation, in other words, science knows no frontiers." The speech, titled "Flower of Learning," is in Samuel Obeng, comp., *Selected Speeches of Kwame Nkrumah*, vol. 2 (1979; Accra: Afram, 1997), 153–60; quotation at 155.

18. Joel Augustus Rogers's books were largely self-financed and self-published. After his death in 1966, many of the books continued to be published with the name of his wife, Helga M. Rogers, as publisher. Those still in circulation include *World's Great Men of Color* (New York: Macmillan, 1972); *Selected Writings of Joel August Rogers* (New York: Pyramid Publishers, 1988); *One Hundred Amazing Facts about the Negro with Complete Proof: A Shortcut to the World History of the Negro*, illustrated ed. (1934; St. Petersburg, Florida: Helga M. Rogers, 1980); *Sex and Race: Negro-Caucasian Mixing in All Ages and All Lands*, vol. 1, *The Old World*, and vol. 2, *A History of White, Negro, and Indian Miscegenation in the Two Americas* (1943–46; St. Petersburg, Florida: Helga M. Rogers, 1989).

19. Rogers, *One Hundred Amazing Facts about the Negro*, 12.

20. Deborah D. Moseley's "Beethoven, the Black Spaniard," is posted at several places including the website of *ChickenBones: A Journal*, at www.nathaniel turner.com. Two of the other widely posted and reposted Internet articles are by Cecil Adams, "Was Ludwig van Beethoven of African Ancestry?" (see, e.g., www .straightdope.com), and Kwaku Person-Lynn, "Beethoven: Revealing His True Identity" (e.g., www.ghanaweb.com).

21. Anton Felix Schindler, *Beethoven as I Knew Him*, ed. and annotated by Donald W. MacArdle (trans. of 1860 German ed., 1966; New York: Dover, 1996); Donald W. MacArdle, "The Family Van Beethoven," *Musical Quarterly* 35 (1949): 528–50; Dominique-René de Lerma, "Beethoven as a Black Composer," *Black Music Research Journal* 10, no. 1 (1990): 118–22, originally in *Black Music Research*

Newsletter 8, no. 1 (1985): 3–5; also at the Myrtle Hart Society website, myr tlehart.org.

22. Nadine Gordimer, *Beethoven Was 1/16th Black and Other Stories* (New York: Farrar, Straus and Giroux, 2007).

23. Nicholas Mathew, "Beethoven and His Others," *Beethoven Forum* 13, no. 2 (2006): 148–87.

24. Jürgen Habermas, *The Divided West* (London: Polity Press, 2006); Kwame Anthony Appiah, *Cosmopolitanism: Ethics in a World of Strangers* (New York: W. W. Norton, 2007).

25. When she heard this part of the story, the jazz producer and historian Maxine Gordon reminded me that the former secretary general is also a drummer, and provided this link to the 2008 Tällberg Forum, where he sits in on congas: youtube.com/watch?v=g2nMekOx1KU.

26. Hon. Charles B. Rangel of New York in the House of Representatives, "Tribute to the 50th Anniversary of the Republic of Ghana," *United States Congressional Record—Extensions of Remarks, E899-E900, May 1, 2007.* The text incorporates the April 25, 2007, report by the BBC correspondent David Willey, "La Scala Brings Beethoven to Ghana," originally published at news.bbc.co.uk.

Third Chorus, Back Inside

1. The RWAFF (Royal West Africa Fontier Force) effort in Burma represented one of the largest colonial army campaigns in the history of the British Empire; see A. Haywood and F. A. S. Clarke, *The History of the Royal West African Frontier Force* (Aldershot: Gale and Polden, 1964); also see Adrienne M. Israel, "Measuring the War Experience: Ghanaian Soldiers in World War II," *Journal of Modern African Studies* 25, no. 1 (1987): 159–68. Burma Camp is today the name of the main army base in Accra; the camp was renamed at the time of independence to commemorate the role of Ghanaians in the Second World War Burma Campaign.

2. The Bosavi research by me and my colleagues is reported in Steven Feld, *Sound and Sentiment: Birds, Weeping, Poetics and Song in Kaluli Expression,* 2nd ed. (1982; Philadelphia: University of Pennsylvania Press, 1990); Bambi B. Schieffelin, *The Give and Take of Everyday Life: Language Socialization of Kaluli Children* (Cambridge: Cambridge University Press, 1990; 2nd ed., Tucson: Fenestra, 2005); Edward L. Schieffelin, *The Sorrow of the Lonely and the Burning of the Dancers* (London: St. Martin's Press, 1976; 2nd ed., New York: Macmillan Palgrave, 2004).

3. Claude Lévi-Strauss, *Tristes Tropiques* (1955), trans. John Weightman and Doreen Weightman (New York: Atheneum, 1973).

4. Donna J. Haraway, *A Companion Species Manifesto: Dogs, People, and Significant Otherness* (Chicago: Prickly Paradigm, 2003); *When Species Meet* (Minneapolis: University of Minnesota Press, 2007).

5. On relational ontologies, see Sylvie Poirer, "Reflections on Indigenous Cosmopolitics-Poetics," *Anthropologica* 50 (2008): 75–85; Philippe Descola, *Par-Delà nature et culture* (Paris: Gallimard, 2005); Eduardo Viveiros de Castro, "Exchanging Perspectives: The Transformation of Objects into Subjects in Amerindian Ontologies," *Common Knowledge* 10, no. 3 (2004): 463–84; John Clammer, Sylvie Poirer, and Eric Schwimmer, eds., *Figured Worlds: Ontological Obstacles in Intercultural Relations* (Toronto: University of Toronto Press, 2004); Tim Ingold, *The Perception of the Environment* (London: Routledge, 2000); Nurit Bird-David, with comments by Eduardo Viveiros de Castro, Alf Hornborg, Tim Ingold, Brian Morris, Gisli Palsson, Laura M. Rival, and Alan R. Sandstrom, "'Animism' Revisited: Personhood, Environment, and Relational Epistemology," in "Culture: A Second Chance?," special issue, *Current Anthropology* 40 (1999): S67–S91; Philippe Descola and Gisli Palsson, eds., *Nature and Society: Anthropological Perspectives* (London: Routledge, 1996); Roy Ellen and Katsuyoshi Fukui, eds., *Redefining Nature: Ecology, Culture and Domestication* (Oxford: Berg, 1996); Arturo Escobar, "After Nature: Steps to an Anti-essentialist Political Ecology," *Current Anthropology* 40, no. 1 (1999): 1–30.

On acoustemology as relational ontology, and nature as a cultural construction in Bosavi, Papua New Guinea, hear Steven Feld, *Voices of the Rainforest*, CD, Rykodisc, 1991; *Rainforest Soundwalks*, CD, EarthEar, 2001; also see Steven Feld, "Waterfalls of Song: An Acoustemology of Place Resounding in Bosavi, Papua New Guinea," in *Senses of Place*, ed. Steven Feld and Keith Basso (Santa Fe: SAR Press, 1996), 91–135, and "Poetics of Place: Ecological and Aesthetic Co-evolution in a Papua New Guinea Rainforest Community," in Ellen and Fukui, eds., *Redefining Nature*, 61–88. Also see "Multispecies Ethnography," special issue, *Cultural Anthropology* 25, no. 4 (2010).

6. Yubi (Jubi) played a major role in my Bosavi research in the 1970s and early 1980s; see especially chap. 2, "To You They Are Birds, to Me They Are Voices in the Forest," in Feld, *Sound and Sentiment*.

7. Ulahi played a major role in my Bosavi research in the 1970s, 1980s, and 1990s. She is a featured composer and performer on my *Voices of the Rainforest* CD and on disc 2, *Sounds and Songs of Everyday Life*, in *Bosavi: Rainforest Music from Papua New Guinea*, three-CD collection and book (Washington, D.C.: Smithsonian Folkways Recordings, 2001). On Ulahi's poetics see Steven Feld, "Waterfalls of Song: An Acoustemology of Place Resounding in Bosavi, Papua New Guinea," in Feld and Basso, eds., *Senses of Place*, 91–135.

Ulahi was also one of the Bosavi singers most central to the dialogic editing and auditing experiments I made with my Bosavi sound recordings. When I recorded *Voices of the Rainforest* in 1990, presenting twenty-four hours in the life of the Bosavi community in one hour, Ulahi listened to playback of each of her songs, helping me to hear the height-depth parameters of voice and ambience. For example, on the songs recorded at the Wolu creek, where she sings while sitting on a rock in the water, the mix involved four different sets of stereo tracks. The initial recordings were of Ulahi singing. Then more close-up recordings were made of the water surrounding her. Then recordings were made of both the height and depth of forest sounds behind her. The four constituent tracks were then transferred to cassette and played back simultaneously on four cassette recorders, with Ulahi adjusting their volume levels to indicate figure and ground shifts in the forest's space-time surround. From this we arrived at a dialogic representation of the life of forest ambiences and the way her voice was woven into them. That experimental process of dialogic auditing and editing underlied the studio mixing for the final CD recording.

8. Steven Feld, "Aesthetics as Iconicity of Style, or 'Lift-up-over Sounding': Getting into the Kaluli Groove," *Yearbook for Traditional Music* 20 (1988): 74–113, reprinted, expanded, in Charles Keil and Steven Feld, *Music Grooves: Essays and Dialogues* (Chicago: University of Chicago Press, 1994), 109–50.

9. On the lexical items, see Bambi B. Schieffelin and Steven Feld, *Bosavi-English-Tok Pisin Dictionary* (Canberra: Pacific Linguistics, Australian National University, 1999); Francis Mihalic, *The Jacaranda Dictionary and Grammar of Melanesian Pidgin* (Milton, Australia: Jacaranda Press, 1981). On the image of the shotgun at a pig's head, and remembrances of such early contact scenes by Papua New Guinea highlanders, see Bob Connelly and Robin Anderson's film *First Contact*, 1983, and their subsequent book by the same name (New York: Penguin, 1988). Contact in the Southern Highlands and Papuan Plateau areas around Bosavi is treated in Edward L. Schieffelin and Rob Crittenden, eds., *Like People You See in a Dream: First Contact in Six Papuan Societies* (Stanford: Stanford University Press, 1991). On the acoustics of power, see Jacques Attali, *Noise: The Political Economy of Music* (Minneapolis: University of Minnesota Press, 1985).

10. Odo Gaso's guitar songs and instrumental innovations with the instrument are presented on disc 1, *Guitar Bands of the 1990s*, and discussed in the booklet accompanying *Bosavi: Rainforest Music from Papua New Guinea*.

11. Dick Blau, Charles Keil, Angeliki Keil, and Steven Feld, *Bright Balkan Morning: Romani Lives and the Power of Music in Greek Macedonia* (Middletown: Wesleyan University Press, 2002).

12. Steven Feld, Dick Blau, Charles Keil, and Angeliki Keil, *Bells and Winter Festivals of Greek Macedonia*, CD, Smithsonian Folkways, 2002.

13. Following the model of *Bells and Winter Festivals of Greek Macedonia*, some of my other bell sound research presented as soundscape composition can be heard on the CD series *The Time of Bells*, vols. 1–4, VoxLox, 2004–7. These sound essays theorize relations between animal, church, musical, and carnival bells in Greece, Italy, France, Finland, Norway, Denmark, Ghana, and Japan. For an Italian comparison to the *Bells and Winter Festivals* recording, listen to bells and double-reed instruments in winter festivals in Basilicata on my CD for *Santi, Animali, e Suoni*, ed. Nicola Scaldaferri, CD/book, Nota, 2005.

14. Alain Corbin, *Village Bells: Sound and Meaning in the 19th Century French Countryside*, trans. Martin Thom (New York: Columbia University Press, 1998).

15. Jean-François Millet's painting *L'Angélus*, 1857–59, at Musée d'Orsay, Paris, remains, together with his 1850 painting *The Sowers* and 1857 *The Gleaners*, a major work of naturalist realism responding to peasant country life in nineteenth-century France. I am grateful to Catherine Mazière for explaining the significance of these paintings in representations of French village life, and for pointing out their influence on later works by Vincent van Gogh and Claude Monet. For a more contemporary resonance, see Agnès Varda's film *The Gleaners and I*, 2000.

16. M. M. Bakhtin, *Rabelais and His World*, trans. Hélène Iswolsky (Bloomington: Indiana University Press, 1993), exposes the power of suppressed linguistic, literary, and social registers in the Renaissance works *Gargantua* and *Pantagruel*, by the French writer François Rabelais, particularly around the centrality of bodily control, denial, and transformation in the carnivalesque and the grotesque. Lars Van Trier's film *Dogville*, 2003, is a strong contemporary drama illustrating how a bell shackle can mark and punish the bodily threat of female sexuality.

17. The classic references for Michel Foucault's work on authority, power, heterotopias, and social institutions include *The Order of Things: An Archaeology of the Human Sciences*, 2nd ed. (London: Routledge, 2001); *The Archaeology of Knowledge and The Discourse on Language* (New York: Vintage, 1982); *The History of Sexuality*, 3 vols. (New York: Vintage, 1990); *Discipline and Punish: The Birth of the Prison* (New York: Vintage, 1995); *Essential Works*, vol. 1, *Ethics: Subjectivity and Truth* (New York: New Press, 2006); *Essential Works*, vol. 2, *Aesthetics, Method, Epistemology* (New York: New Press, 1999); *Essential Works*, vol. 3, *Power* (New York: New Press, 2001). For critical contextualizations, early, and more recent, see Herbert L. Dreyfus and Paul Rabinow, *Michel Foucault: Beyond Structuralism and Hermeneutics*, 2nd ed. (Chicago: University of Chicago Press, 1983); François Cusset, *French Theory: How Foucault, Derrida, Deleuze, and Company Transformed the Intellectual Life of the United States*, trans. Jeff Fort (Minneapolis: University of Minnesota Press, 2008). Likewise, the classic references for M. M. Bakhtin's work on carnival, disruption, polyphony, heteroglossia, and dialogism and "nonfinalizability" include *The Dialogic Imagination: Four Essays*, ed. Michael Holquist, trans. Caryl Emerson and Michael Holquist (Austin: University of Texas Press, 1981); *Problems of Dostoevsky's Poetics*, ed. and trans. Caryl Emerson (Minneapolis: University of Minnesota Press, 1984); *Speech Genres and Other Late Essays*, trans. Vern W. McGee (Austin: University of Texas Press, 1986); *Art and Answerability*, ed. Michael Holquist and Vadim Liapunov, trans. Vadim Liapunov and Kenneth Brostrom (Austin: University of Texas Press, 1990). Jane H. Hill's "The Refiguration of the Anthropology of Language," *Cultural Anthropology* 1, no. 1 (1986): 89–102, played a major role in

bringing Bakhtin's work into new conversations between cultural and linguistic anthropologists. It was a critical point of introduction for me. Other key reference works are Michael Holquist, *Dialogism: Bakhtin and His World*, 2nd ed. (London: Routledge, 2002); Gary Saul Morson and Caryl Emerson, *Mikhail Bakhtin: Creation of a Prosaics* (Stanford: Stanford University Press, 1990); Tzvetan Todorov, *Mikhail Bakhtin: The Dialogical Principle*, trans. Wlad Godzich (Minneapolis: University of Minnesota Press, 1984).

18. J. H. Kwabena Nketia, *African Music in Ghana* (Evanston: Northwestern University Press, 1963), 78; John Miller Chernoff, *African Rhythm and African Sensibility* (Chicago: University of Chicago Press, 1979), 43.

Over the years of my Ghana visits, Nketia has always been a generous host and most gracious conversationalist. Early on, in 2006, I went to his office to present a copy of my CD *The Time of Bells*, vol. 3, *Musical Bells of Accra*. In response he completely blew my mind by quietly removing a pamphlet from his desk drawer and passing it over to me to inspect. It turned out to be the program from Kwame Nkrumah's 1957 inauguration. Imagine my surprise and his smile; "Prof" was in fact the bell ringer at the ceremony! I also want to acknowledge here a long friendship with John Chernoff, and to thank him for his reflexive and musically nuanced take on how a simplification of "timeline" principles is part of the way Ghanaian teachers in the United States have communicated about the structure of drum-dance ensemble music in the pedagogic encounter with American undergraduate music students.

19. Mark-Oliver Rödel, *Herpetofauna of West Africa*, vol. 1, *Amphibians of the West African Savanna* (Geneva: Edition Chimaira, 2000).

20. Alex Coke, Tina Marsh, and Steve Feld, *It's Possible*, CD, VoxLox, 2008.

21. Nii Otoo Annan and Steven Feld, *Bufo Variations*, CD, VoxLox, 2008.

22. Kakraba Lobi was a master of gyil, the most important instrument of the Dagara and Lobi people spread through Ghana, Côte d'Ivoire, and Burkina Faso. He became internationally famous as a soloist and teacher, was regularly heard on radio in Ghana, and was, for some twenty years, associated with the Music Department and the Institute of African Studies at the University of Ghana, where he worked with Professor J. H. K. Nketia. Among his recordings is a widely admired collaboration with the American musicians Valerie Dee Naranjo and Barry Olsen, the CD *Song of Legaa*, Lyricord, 2000. Brian Hogan's film about his funeral, *A Great Man Has Gone Out*, can be seen at lobimusic.org. Kakraba Lobi's work as a performer and teacher is carried on in Ghana and elsewhere today by his son, S. K. Kakraba Lobi, whose first CD as a leader is *Gandayina: Xylophone Music of Ghana*, Pentatonic Press, 2004.

23. Phonetic open o (ɔ) signifies the initial sound in American English "awful," the medial sound in "bought," and the final sound in "saw." Phonetic epsilon (ɛ) signifies the initial sound in English "Edward" or the medial sound in American English "bet" or "when." These sounds and phonetic symbols are common in

Ghanaian languages. Both can be duplicated; an example critical here is "por por," the "or" of each word signifying a double open o, hence the pronunciation transliteration "paaw paaw."

24. On indigenous mathematics as embodied cognition, see Jadran Mimica, *Intimations of Infinity: The Cultural Meanings of the Iqwaye Counting and Number Systems* (London: Berg, 1988). Named for Johann Gottlieb Goldberg, presumed the work's first performer, the *Goldberg Variations* by Johann Sebastian Bach (1741, BWV 988) consists of an aria and thirty variations for harpsichord. It is one of the most historically valorized exemplars of the concept of variation in Western European art music.

25. For example, see the frequency of hand-crossings indicated in Bach's notations for Variations 1, 5, 8, 11, 14, 17, 20, 23, 26, and 28. The two harpsichord performance recordings that Nii Otoo and I listened to, played on very different sounding instruments, were by Keith Jarrett (ECM, 2000) and Trevor Pinnock (Deutsche Gramophone Arkiv, 1985).

26. Peter Williams, *Bach: The Goldberg Variations* (Cambridge: Cambridge University Press, 2001).

27. Dimensions of those genealogies are explored recently in Allen S. Weiss, *Varieties of Audio Mimesis: Musical Evocations of Landscape* (New York: Errant Bodies Press, 2007), and Theodore Levin with Valentina Süzükei, *Where Rivers and Mountains Sing: Sound, Music, and Nomadism in Tuva and Beyond* (Bloomington: Indiana University Press, 2006).

28. John Coltrane, *Live at the Half Note: One Up, One Down*, CD, Impulse, 2005 (recorded in 1965).

29. An iconic photographic image of Jones sweating while in play, often reproduced, is the one famously part of the four-plex inside-cover of the John Coltrane Quartet LP *Live at Birdland*, Impulse, 1963.

30. Jones's three against two could play out in the feel of an underlying six-pulse cycle where one hand-foot combination emphasized one, three, and five against another that emphasized one and four. His four against three could play out in the feel of an underlying twelve-pulse cycle where one hand-foot combination emphasized one, four, seven, and ten against another that emphasized one, five, and nine.

31. The composition "Shiny Stockings" is by tenor saxophonist Frank Foster and is performed as a trio with Elvin Jones (drums) and Richard Davis (bass) on *Heavy Sounds*, LP, Impulse, 1967. Nii Otoo's "He will mess you up" response to the complexity of Elvin Jones's drumming reminds me of a story I heard from the jazz producer and historian Maxine Gordon long before I first went to Ghana. On a trip to Accra in 1973 Gordon had occasion to listen with some local musicians to a recording of Elvin Jones. All of them insisted that they were hearing two or more drummers, that it was impossible for one drummer to simultaneously sustain and interlock so many rhythmic layers. This is indeed

what Nii Otoo loved and emulated in his own listening in and APK feedback response to Jones's style. It was a pleasure, years after first hearing Maxine's story, to tell her that drummers in Ghana almost uniformly say the same thing about Nii Otoo, and that this is also the response of so many listeners to his *Bufo Variations*.

Nii Otoo's later CD, *Ghana Sea Blues* (VoxLox, 2011) demonstrates the stratigraphy of groove as sustained interlock in a related but different way. In Accra, in January and June 2010, we recorded fifteen of his compositions for solo electric guitar. Then in October 2010 he came to New Mexico and overdubbed those original guitar solos from seven to ten times on each song, sequentially adding different bells first, then shakers, then apentema and conga drums, then gome bass drum, then electric bass, and vocals. This is deeply unlike the typical practice of first putting down a percussion or guide-pulse "click" track and then adding melody instruments and vocals. It indicated the extent to which as a percussionist who also plays melody instruments like guitar, bass, and xylophone, Nii Otoo hears the entire gestalt of a piece as he plays, no matter which instrument he uses as the reference or which one he records first.

32. John Coltrane and Rashied Ali, *Interstellar Space*, LP, Impulse, 1974 (recorded in 1967).

33. M. J. Field, *Religion and Medicine of the Ga People* (1937; 2nd ed., London: Oxford University Press, 1961); also six articles and a book by Marion Kilson: "Libation in Ga Ritual," *Journal of Religion in Africa* 2, no. 3 (1969): 161–78, quotation at 166; "Ambivalence and Power: Mediums in Ga Traditional Religion," *Journal of Religion in Africa* 4, no. 3 (1971–72): 171–77; "Women in African Traditional Religions," *Journal of Religion in Africa* 8, no. 2 (1976): 133–43; "Taxonomy and Form in Ga Ritual," *Journal of Religion in Africa* 3, no. 1 (1970): 45–66; "The Structure of Ga Prayer," *Journal of Religion in Africa* 9, no. 3 (1978): 173–88; "Prayer and Song in Ga Ritual," *Journal of Religion in Africa* 12, no. 1 (1981): 16–19; and *Kpele Lala: Ga Religious Songs and Symbols* (Cambridge: Harvard University Press, 1971).

34. On the story of water and twins, see Marion Kilson, "Twin Beliefs and Ceremony in Ga Culture," *Journal of Religion in Africa* 5, no. 3 (1973): 171–97. The act of an elder pouring libation while reciting invocations is a critical ritual to pay homage to ancestors, to invoke their presence, and to invite their participation in ceremonies both public and private. Bishop Peter Sarpong's classic work of indigenous anthropology, *Libation* (Accra: Anansesem Publications, 1966), is a key text for understanding how the practice of libation in Ghana involves an intersection of newly invented traditions and locally taken-for-granted practices, as well as their rewrapping in contemporary Christian beliefs. Dmitri van den Bersselaar, *The King of Drinks: Schnapps Gin from Modernity to Tradition* (Leiden: Brill, 2007), tells how schnapps gin, a Dutch import from the late nineteenth century, became the recognized medium for libation in twentieth-century Ghana.

35. John Coltrane, *Live at the Village Vanguard Again*, LP, Impulse, 1966.

36. These issues are taken up in the exhibit catalogue by Henry John Drewel et al., *Mami Wata: Arts for Water Spirits in Africa and Its Diasporas* (Seattle: University of Washington Press, 2008); for deeper elaboration see the extensive volume edited by Henry John Drewal, *Sacred Waters: Arts for Mami Wata and Other Water Divinities in Africa and the Diaspora* (Bloomington: Indiana University Press, 2008).

37. Historical books on the castle-forts include William St. Clair, *The Door of No Return: The History of Cape Coast Castle and the Atlantic Slave Trade* (New York: BlueBridge, 2007); Christopher R. DeCorse, *An Archaeology of Elmina: Africans and Europeans on the Gold Coast, 1400–1900* (Washington: Smithsonian Institution Press, 2001); Kwesi J. Anquandah, *Castles and Forts of Ghana* (Paris: Atalante, for the Ghana Museums and Monuments Board, 1999); A. Van Dantzig, *Forts and Castles of Ghana* (Accra: Sedco, 1980); I. S. Ephson, *Ancient Forts and Castles of the Gold Coast* (Accra: Ilen Publications, 1970); A. W. Lawrence, *Trade Castles and Forts of West Africa* (London: Jonathan Cape, 1963). Also see UNESCO World Heritage documents for historical summaries and contemporary activities concerned with preservation of West African forts and castles and the memory of slavery, at whc.unesco.org/en/list/34.

On the representation of history at Cape Coast, see Christine Mullen Kreamer, "Shared Heritage, Contested Terrain: Cultural Negotiation and Ghana's Cape Coast Castle Museum Exhibition 'Crossroads of People, Crossroads of Trade,'" in *Museum Frictions: Public Culture/Global Transformations*, ed. Ivan Karp, Corinne Kratz, Lynn Szwaja, and Tomás Ybarra-Frausto (Durham: Duke University Press, 2006), 435–68. Bayo Holsey's *Routes of Remembrance: Refashioning the Slave Trade in Ghana* (Chicago: University of Chicago Press, 2007), powerfully contrasts the levels of embarrassment and national silence in Ghana about the slave trade with the upsurge of African American tourist visitation of the castles as the work of remembrance and commemoration. The book's appearance at the same moment as Saidiya Hartman's chilling exploration of loss, *Lose Your Mother: A Journey along the Atlantic Slave Route* (New York: Farrar, 2007), opens the possibilities for an important juxtaposition, bringing out how a locally sensitive anthropological exploration of place and disjuncture can be read alongside a deeply personal literary evocation of slavery's harrowing history at exactly the same sites. The interactive impact of the two is a strong reminder of the overlapping emotional, personal, biographical, historical, literary, and social issues intertwined in diasporic discourse about the memory of slavery and the relational positionality of its representation.

Kevin Gaines's deeply informed book of the same moment, *American Africans in Ghana: Black Expatriates and the Civil Rights Era* (Chapel Hill: University of North Carolina Press, 2007), provides an excellent contextualization of how and why African Americans responded to Nkrumah's political and cultural vision, and what this signals for a nuanced understanding of diaspora, nationalist and non, in the intertwined histories of Ghana and African America. The legacy of Du Bois plays an equally central and ongoing role in diasporan affairs in Ghana, and is carefully unpacked in Jesse Weaver Shipley and Jemima Pierre, "The Intellectual and Pragmatic Legacy of Du Bois's Pan-Africanism in Contemporary Ghana," in *Re-Cognizing W. E. B. Du Bois in the 21st Century*, ed. Mary Keller and Chester J. Fontenot (Macon: Mercer University Press, 2007), 61–87. The place of Du Bois in anticolonial history is told in Penny Von Eschen, *Race against Empire: Black Americans and Anti-Colonialism, 1937–1957* (Ithaca: Cornell University Press, 1997).

The passing, on July 5, 2010, at age ninety, of Dr. Robert (Bobby or Uncle Bobby) Lee—someone interviewed by Gaines and just about everyone else who has done any serious research on diasporan history in Ghana—opens up another occasion for exploring Nkrumah's appeal to African Americans and the question of how to remember and preserve the castles. Lee's story, end-chronicled in a touching forty-seven-page booklet distributed at his burial service at the W. E. B. Du Bois Centre for Pan-African Culture on July 24, 2010, recounts how he went to Lincoln University with Nkrumah, then to dental school, and after a 1953 trip moved with his family to Ghana in 1956, becoming the first African American to be naturalized as a citizen in 1961. He was close to Nkrumah, Du Bois, and numerous politicians, diplomats, internationals, and dignitaries, Ghanaian and non. He was also a people's professional, operating a local dental practice for fifty years, many of them with his wife, Sara, also a dentist. He was also a leader in efforts to restore Fort Amsterdam (Abanze). This is where I first heard his name, mentioned in fact, by Ghanaba, who told me that he very much respected Lee's insistence that the term "slave fort" always take precedence over (the more standard) "castle." The dark side of the story of this distinguished diasporan concerns his son, Flight Lieutenant (Robert Lowry) Kojo Lee, a longtime friend and Air Force Academy contemporary of the Provisional National Defense Council chairman, J. J. Rawlings. By all accounts Kojo Lee was a troubled man, menacing, trigger-happy, notorious for intimidation by fire and acting above and outside the law. When, after years of harassing altercations, he openly murdered a military man in La, he was tried by the Public Revolutionary Justice Tribunal, and Rawlings was forced, most unhappily, to sign the warrant for his execution, locally reported in "They're Executed by Firing Squad," *Daily Graphic*, September 29, 1984. Also see Roger Gocking, "Ghana's Public Tribunals: An Experiment in Revolutionary Justice," *African Affairs* 95 (1966): 197–223; Joseph R. A. Ayee, "A Decade of Accountability under Ghana's PNDC Government," *Research Review* 10, nos. 1–2 (1994): 61–76; George Tagoe, *Genesis Four* (Victoria, B.C.: Trafford Publishing, 2006), 249–55. An account of how the Kojo Lee story speaks to the complexities of African American experiences of in-and-outsider-ness in Ghana is James T. Campbell, *Middle Passages: African American Journeys to Africa, 1878–2005* (New York: Penguin, 2007).

There's also a water spirit part of this story. To this day just about anyone in La will tell you that the drowning accident at the Lee family swimming pool that took the life of one of Kojo's young daughters was retribution from the god of La, Kpa, for the number of lives that Lee took during indiscriminate shooting sprees into the Kpeshie Lagoon.

38. Virginia Ryan and Steven Feld, *The Castaways Project*, CD/DVD/catalogue, VoxLox, 2007; also see Steven Feld, in conversation with Virginia Ryan, "Collaborative Migrations: Contemporary Art In/As Anthropology," in *Between Art and Anthropology*, ed. Arnd Schneider and Chris Wright (London: Berg, 2010), 109–25.

39. Nii Otoo's "chiefs," "bosses," and "small boys" phraseology points to the pervasive local significance of male power hierarchies, their taken-for-granted character in everyday affairs, and their operations at all levels in social institutions and political culture in Ghana. For an earlier perspective, see Robert Prince, "Politics and Culture in Contemporary Ghana: The Big-Man Small-Boy Syndrome," *Journal of African Studies* 1, no. 2 (1974): 173–204, and for a more recent summary, Paul Nugent, *Big Men, Small Boys, and Politics in Ghana: Power, Ideology, and the Burden of History* (London: Pinter, 1995). The placement of women in this picture is detailed by Claire Robertson in *Sharing the Same Bowl: A Socioeconomic History of Women and Class in Accra, Ghana* (Bloomington: Indiana University Press, 1984); the larger class hierarchy perspective is laid out in Ansa K. Asamoa, *Classes and Tribalism in Ghana* (Accra: Woeli Publishing Services, 2007). The theme of gendered and classed hierarchies of power, so fundamental to *habitus* in Accra and so frequently embedded in Nii Otoo's words, brings me back to the complexities of describing how they underlie so much about the workings of the jazz cosmopolitanism I encountered. Sherry Ortner's theoretical sensitivity to the intertwining of gender, class, and agency has long helped shape my understanding of the centrality of these issues to social theory; see her collection of essays, *Anthropology and Social Theory: Culture, Power, and the Acting Subject* (Durham: Duke University Press, 2007). Stephan Miescher's *Making Men in Ghana* (Bloomington: Indiana University Press, 2005) is also quite helpful for understanding productions of authority in Ghanaian masculinity. This work, which concentrates on the life stories of eight elder men, takes us to the crossroads of layered local and imported masculine standards of authority and obligation, and with them, to contradictions in desires and burdens of being (and being perceived as) leaders. The point is that life is no more simple or easy for leaders of all sorts (chiefs, bosses, etc.) than for the small boys beneath them; power can work in remarkably contradictory and disempowering and/or reempowering ways. These themes are taken up by several writers considering intricacies of postcolonial subjectivity in Richard Werbner, ed., *Postcolonial Subjectivities in Africa* (London: Zed Books, 2002). Professional musicians are placed in these issues in sometimes quite distinctive ways; for a deep reading

of masculinity in the history of highlife music, see Nate Plageman, "Everybody Likes Saturday Night: A Social History of Popular Music and Masculinities in Urban Gold Coast / Ghana, c. 1900–1970," Ph.D. dissertation, Indiana University, 2008.

Fourth Chorus, Shout to the Groove

1. On Ga funerary musical practices see Barbara L. Hampton, "Music and Ritual Symbolism in the Ga Funeral," *Yearbook for Traditional Music* 14 (1982): 75–105. Her deep ethnographic and musical scholarship is reported in "Adowa Lala: A Synchronic Analysis of Ga Funeral Music," M.A. thesis, University of California at Los Angeles, 1972; "The Impact of Labor Migration on Music in Urban Ghana: The Case of Kphehe Gome," Ph.D. dissertation, Columbia University, 1977. Also see her classic LP and liner notes, *Music of the Ga People of Ghana*, vol. 1, *Adowa*, Ethnic Folkways Recordings, 1978.

Other contextualizing pieces on Ga religious music include Hampton's "The Contiguity Factor in Ga Music," *The Black Perspective in Music* 6, no. 2 (1978): 33–48, and the classic piece on historical methodology by J. H. Kwabena Nketia, "Historical Evidence in Ga Religious Music," in *The Historian in Tropical Africa*, ed. J. Vansina, R. Mauny, and L. V. Thomas (London: Oxford University Press, 1964), 265–83. Also see Marion Kilson, *Kpele Lala: Ga Religious Songs and Symbols* (Cambridge: Harvard University Press, 1971), and M. J. Field, *Religion and Medicine of the Ga People* (London: Oxford University Press, 1937; rev. ed., 1961).

2. Annette Weiner, *Women of Value, Men of Renown: New Perspectives in Trobriand Exchange* (Austin: University of Texas Press, 1983), and *Inalienable Possessions: The Paradox of Keeping-While-Giving* (Los Angeles: University of California Press, 1992).

3. Steven Feld, "Wept Thoughts: The Voicing of Kaluli Memories," *Oral Tradition* 5, nos. 2–3 (1990): 241–66, reprinted in *South Pacific Oral Traditions*, ed. Ruth Finnegan and Margaret Orbell (Bloomington: Indiana University Press, 1995), 85–108. Also see Steven Feld, "Weeping That Moves Women to Song," chap. 3 of *Sound and Sentiment: Birds Weeping, Poetics, and Song in Kaluli Expression* (Philadelphia: University of Pennyslvania Press, 1982; 2nd ed., 1990).

4. Fred Myers and Barbara Kirschenblatt-Gimblett, "Art and Material Culture: A Conversation with Annette Weiner," in *The Empire of Things: Regimes of Value and Material Culture*, ed. Fred Myers (Santa Fe: SAR Press, 2002), 269–314, quotation at 277.

5. While por por horn honking is unique to Accra's La Drivers Union in Ghana, the practice of pumping a tire while rhythmically beating wrenches on its rim has a larger West African legacy. This can be seen in a tire-pumping scene in Jean Rouch's 1968 film *Un lion nommé "L'Americain,"* a sequel to his better-known

1957–64 documentary feature, *The Lion Hunters*, filmed in the Niger/Mali hinterlands. In the sequel the hunters track the lion that eluded them in the first film, a lion so tenacious that they named him "the American." Rouch's description of the film is in his *Ciné-Ethnography* (Minneapolis: University of Minnesota Press, 2003), 364. I thank Antonello Ricci for reminding me of this scene.

6. H. B. Goodall, *Beloved Imperialist: Sir Gordon Guggisberg, Governor of the Gold Coast* (Bishop Auckland, U.K.: Pentland Press, 1998). The background to unionized public transport in Ghana, and particularly in Accra, receives deep historical contextualization in Jennifer Hart, " 'Suffer to Gain': Citizenship, Accumulation, and Motor Transportation in Late-Colonial Ghana," Ph.D. dissertation, Indiana University, 2011. A basic document on the background to trade unions in Ghana, which lays some groundwork for understanding drivers unions, is Blay Peter Arthiabah and Harry Tham Mbiah, *Half a Century of Toil, Trouble and Progress: A History of the Trades Union Congress of Ghana* (Accra: Gold-Type Publications, 1995).

7. An incisive review of the La-Labadi name debate can be found in Mary Esther Kropp Dakubu, *Korle Meets the Sea: A Sociolinguistic History of Accra* (New York: Oxford University Press, 1997), 5–7.

8. Some images of the contemporary coffin carving scene in Nungua, Teshie, and La can be found in Thierry Secretan, *Going into Darkness: Fantastic Coffins from Africa* (London: Thames and Hudson, 1995), and Kyoichi Tsuzuki, *Buried Spirit: Incredible Coffins of Ghana* (Tokyo: Aspect, 2000).

9. The ocean liner M.V. *Aureol* was built in 1951 for Elder Dempster Lines of Liverpool (originally the African Steamship Company, from 1852). Named for a mountain in Sierra Leone, the ship operated on its popular Liverpool–Nigeria–Ghana route until 1974.

10. The La Drivers Union Por Por Group, *Por Por: Honk Horn Music of Ghana*, Smithsonian Folkways, 2007.

11. The song "M.V. Labadi" is track 10 on the CD; the text here was transcribed by Kwame Assenyoh with revisions from Nii Yemo Nunu. A forthcoming short film, featuring commentary by Nii Yemo Nunu to his family photographic album, is *M.V. Labadi: The Story of Ataa Anangbi Anangfio*, part of our collaborative photographic and oral history of por por music and the drivers of La; Nii Yemo Nunu and Steven Feld, *Por Por He Sane/The Story of Por Por*, DVD and book, Santa Fe: VoxLox, 2012.

12. *No Time to Die*, poems by Kojo Gyinaye Kyei with drawings and photographs by Hannah Schreckenbach (Accra: Kyei, 1975). An image of Al Haji Okantey's vehicle from the rear graces the book's front and back covers, with the inscription "No Time To Die" on the tailgate, and on the top signboard above, "Still It Makes Me Laugh."

A listing of popular trotro names and signs observed in the late 1970s can be found in Eugenia Date-Bah, "The Inscriptions on the Vehicles of Ghanaian

Commercial Drivers: A Sociological Analysis," *Journal of Modern African Studies* 18, no. 3 (1980): 525–31. For a comparative Nigerian perspective, see Olatunde Bayo Lawuyi, "The World of the Yoruba Taxi Driver: An Interpretive Approach to Vehicle Slogans," *Africa* 58, no. 1 (1988): 1–12; and Wole Soyinka, "Hot Wheels: The Art of Mammy-Lorry Paintings Offers Keen Insights into the Politics of Ordinary Africans," *New Statesman*, November 1, 2007.

13. The 1960s highlife compilation by E. T. Mensah and the Tempos, *Day by Day*, CD, Retroafric, 1994, ends with a song whose Ga language title is "Mee Be Obada," "When Will You Come?" The words "Sea Never Dry" are called out in English well into the song. According to Nii Yemo Nunu and Nii Noi Nortey, most people in Accra know the song more by that English shout-out than by the actual Ga title.

14. M. M. Bakhtin, *The Dialogic Imagination: Four Essays,* ed. Michael Holquist, trans. Caryl Emerson and Michael Holquist (Austin: University of Texas Press, 1981).

15. The anthropological linguist C. F. Voegelin told me the "TAke the CAke" story during my graduate student years at Indiana University, 1971–75. I remain grateful to Carl for many quirky and entertaining conversations, and especially for his insights into the Sapir and Jakobson legacies on poetics and sound symbolism. See Roman Jakobson and Linda Waugh, *The Sound Shape of Language* (1979; 3rd ed., Paris: Mouton de Gruyter, 2002); *Roman Jakobson, Selected Writings*, ed. Stephen Rudy, vol. 3, *The Poetry of Grammar and the Grammar of Poetry* (The Hague: Mouton, 1980); Roman Jakobson, *Verbal Art, Verbal Sign, Verbal Time*, ed. Krystyna Pomorska and Stephen Rudy (Minneapolis: University of Minnesota Press, 1985). Many of Jakobson's critical insights are thoughtfully detailed in a deep essay by Steve Caton that I've returned to quite often: "Contributions of Roman Jakobson," *Annual Review of Anthropology* 16 (1987): 223–60.

16. Populist skepticism about the presidential visit was also recorded in local newspapers, including one with the large-font front-page headline "Bush Bullshits," *Daily Guide*, February 21, 2008.

17. "Respect," was written and originally recorded by Otis Redding on Stax in 1965, but was a much bigger (and Grammy award–winning) hit for Aretha Franklin, with backing vocals by her sisters Carolyn and Erma, in 1967 on Atlantic Records. It became her signature anthem. Luther Ingram and Mack Rice's song "Respect Yourself" was recorded by the Staple Singers (Roebuck "Pops" Staples, and his children Cleotha, Yvonne, Pervis, and Mavis) in 1971 for Stax. Both songs are among the best-known and most covered and rerecorded hits of the late 1960s and early 1970s soul music era. The songs' themes of respect and self-respect encompass a rich history of messages—Christian, secular, political, civil rights, independence, women's rights, familial—resonant in Ghana and among Ghanaians in America and Europe. For America Man these songs remain deep placeholders for the America he knew.

18. "The Lord works in mysterious ways" has become a formulaic phrase in the English register of many working-class Christian Ghanaians. It announces the ubiquitous idea of unseen but aware presence.

19. The on-the-bandstand composition story for "Goodbye Porkpie Hat," long part of Mingus-lore, is told in Gene Santoro, *Myself When I Am Real: The Life and Music of Charles Mingus* (New York: Oxford University Press, 2001), and, earlier, in Brian Priestley, *Mingus: A Critical Biography* (New York: Da Capo Press, 1984). The story was also retold more recently, in January 2008, by the saxophonist John Handy, an eye/ear witness who was playing in Mingus's group on that night. Hear his radio interview on WFIU with David Brent Johnson, at the website indianapublicmedia.org. Mingus's recording of "Goodbye Pork Pie Hat," made just a few months following Lester Young's passing, appears on his LP *Mingus Ah Um*, Columbia, 1959. Joni Mitchell's version of "Goodbye Pork Pie Hat," on her *Mingus* (Elektra, 1979), adds lyrics not just to Mingus's melody but also to the melody of that recording's saxophone solo, as improvised by John Handy. Mitchell's lyric for "Goodbye Pork Pie Hat" can also be newly heard in resonance with the por por story. Evoking midnight in New York, her last stanza sings of emerging from the subway, the sounds of Mingus's bass and Young's tenor saxophone "in taxi horns and brakes." (I've actually heard some singers change that phrase-final line to "in taxi horns' embrace" but am unsure if this is a mishearing of the original or a deliberate rephrasing.)

20. Leo Touchet, *Rejoice When You Die: The New Orleans Jazz Funerals* (Baton Rouge: Louisiana State University Press, 1998). Some other photographic sources for New Orleans brass bands and jazz funerals include William J. Schafer, *Brass Bands and New Orleans Jazz* (Baton Rouge: Louisiana State University Press, 1977); Al Rose and Edmond Souchon, *New Orleans Jazz: A Family Album* (Baton Rouge: Louisiana State University Press, 1984); Luke Fontana, *New Orleans and Her Jazz Funeral Marching Bands: A 10-Year Collection of Photography, 1970–1980* (New Orleans: Luke Fontana, 1980); Tom Morgan, *Historic Photos of New Orleans Jazz* (New York: Turner Publishing, 2009); Michael P. Smith, *In the Spirit: The Photography of Michael P. Smith from the Historic New Orleans Collection* (New Orleans: Historic New Orleans Collection, 2009); William Claxton, *New Orleans 1960* (New York: Taschen, 2006); Richard Knowles, *Fallen Heroes: A History of the New Orleans Brass Bands* (New Orleans: Jazzology, 1996). Film sources for New Orleans brass bands and jazz funerals include Barry Martin, *Sing On: A Film of New Orleans Brass Bands* (a historical overview with footage from as early as 1914), VHS, 2000; David M. Jones and Milton Batiste, *New Orleans Jazz Funerals from the Inside*, DVD, 1995.

21. This is not a matter of taking sides in debates about "retentions" or the meaning of diaspora. No stretch of call-and-response imagination is necessary to connect the long Black Atlantic histories of parades, community participation, mobile drum and horn ensembles, social welfare societies, dancing in the streets,

and the need to celebrate life while mourning death. At the same time, there is no need to indulge in simple or unilinear origin stories; there is plenty of distinctive long and recent history in the emergence and circulation of both por por and New Orleans jazz funerals, no matter what commonalities they share at the surface.

Listening to Nii Yemo and Vice's riffs reminded me to reread Richard Price and Sidney W. Mintz's cautionary reminder, written in 1972, in the emergent moments of black studies, about the problems of replacing grounded historical research with "shared culture" ideology; see their *The Birth of African American Culture: An Anthropological Perspective* (Boston: Beacon Press, 1992). All the same, newer openings to pursue the meanings of "live dialogue" in the Black Atlantic are particularly resonant to me as I watch and listen to por por today, and read, on the other side, the work of recent chroniclers of the history of music in New Orleans. Overall theoretical perspectives particularly helpful on the "live dialogue" approach include the masterful essays by J. Lorand Matory, "Afro-Atlantic Culture: On the Live Dialogue between Africa and the Americas," in *Africana: The Encyclopedia of the African and African American Experience*, ed. Henry Louis Gates and Kwame Anthony Appiah (New York: Basic Civitas Books, 1999), 36–44, and "The 'New World' Surrounds the Ocean: Theorizing the Live Dialogue between African and African American Cultures," in *Afro-Atlantic Dialogues: Anthropology in the Diaspora*, ed. Kevin A. Yelvington (Santa Fe: School of American Research Press, 2006), 151–92. On anti-essentialist wheres and whys of race's centrality to national music history in the United States, see Ronald Radano, *Lying Up a Nation: Race and Black Music* (Chicago: University of Chicago Press, 2003). On the persistence of hearing African echoes with New Orleans ears, see Jason Berry, "African Cultural Memory in New Orleans Music," *Black Music Research Journal* 8, no. 1 (1988): 3–12.

I've recently been guided into a contemporary synthesis of New Orleans brass band nuances through the current work of Matt Sakakeeny, "Instruments of Power: New Orleans Brass Bands and the Politics of Performance," Ph.D. dissertation, Columbia University, 2008; "'Under the Bridge': An Orientation to Soundscapes in New Orleans," *Ethnomusicology* 54, no. 1 (2010): 1–27; and "New Orleans Music as a Circulatory System," *Black Music Research Journal* 31, no. 2 (2011): 291–325. Sakakeeny takes to the road with the concept of circulation to investigate the distributional routing of effects and practices over the long history of musical movements; his theoretical inspiration for this is an important recent essay by Benjamin Lee and Edward LiPuma, "Cultures of Circulation: The Imaginations of Modernity," *Public Culture* 14, no. 1 (2002): 191–213. Further to the contemporary historiography of New Orleans music, some recent detailed studies are Bruce Raeburn, *New Orleans Style and the Writing of American Jazz History* (Ann Arbor: University of Michigan Press, 2009); Ned Sublette, *The World That Made New Orleans: From Spanish Silver to Congo Square* (Chicago:

Lawrence Hill Books, 2008); Charles Hersch, *Subversive Sounds: Race and the Birth of Jazz in New Orleans* (Chicago: University of Chicago Press, 2007). On New Orleans brass bands in particular, some additional musicological and anthropological perspectives are found in Michael White, "The New Orleans Brass Band: A Cultural Tradition," in *The Triumph of the Soul: Cultural and Psychological Aspects of African American Music*, ed. Ferdinand Jones and Arthur C. Jones (Westport: Praeger, 2001), 69–96; Helen A. Regis, "Blackness and the Politics of Memory in the New Orleans Second Line," *American Ethnologist* 28, no. 4 (2001): 752–77, and "Second Lines, Minstrelsy, and the Contested Landscapes of New Orleans Afro-Creole Festivals," *Cultural Anthropology* 14, no. 4 (1999): 472–504.

As I've worked my way through the New Orleans literature of this endnote I've also had a long read of Paul Gilroy's recent *Darker Than Blue: On the Moral Economies of Black Atlantic Culture* (Cambridge: Harvard University Press, 2010). Wow! Talk about race politics being all over style and aesthetics and vice versa! Gilroy is at his strongest when he worries out loud about the effects of corporatism selling blackness as American style, about the general selling seductions that shift "culture" and particularly black culture into consumerist positions that have lost the authority of the outside. But there is no simple authenticity versus resistance narrative here, only a deep analysis of how subjugated race/class configurations are diminished in moral authority through the Catch-22 of imagining that power comes principally through exemplary consumerist participation. Gilroy's "whither the black community" questioning then is not anticontemporary, not the familiar anxieties over the misogynist gangster bravado regressions of some hip-hop artists. Rather, it deeply deconstructs corporatism, sees through the cynicism of capital strategies to manage and market blackness, and burrows far into the question of how moral and cultural corruption is the entry price for a stake in the big-time global culture money-pie. In the context of this por por chapter I'm totally taken by Gilroy's focus on the central place of cars and music in the contemporary politics of struggle for a black culture that is not completely overwhelmed by corporatist marketing and consumerist complicity. In the story of class struggles and aspirations he sees the centrality of black vehicle worship and consumption, the iconizing of vehicles as status objects that put individual ownership and buying power ahead of any social consciousness. Gilroy's riff on vehicles and music as alpha and omega contemporary black status commodities, and particularly on style competition as creation of voracious desire for consumption in new regimes of value, honks a wonderfully ironic embrace on the streets of La, where the truly powerful vehicles are the ones that have already been rebuilt two or three times, and where some of the highest status community funerals use the town's oldest horns to reveal what can only be called the noise of reputation.

22. Miles Davis's *Birth of the Cool*, nonet recordings from 1949 to 1950 with classically tinged arrangements in "third-stream" postbebop voicings by Gil

Evans, John Lewis, and Gerry Mulligan, was originally released on LP in 1957 by Capitol. While the phrase "birth of the cool" circulated in the pool of Ghana independence-era formulas and tags, I cannot find any evidence that the music from this LP had radio play in Ghana or was in any way known there in the 1960s.

23. *Rebel without a Cause*, Nicholas Ray's famous 1955 film about a rebellious teenage bad-boy, starred James Dean and opened in Hollywood just weeks after Dean was killed in a car crash. On the Kool brand, and their extensive marketing of menthol cigarettes to African Americans, see S. Lochlann Jain, " 'Come Up to the Kool Taste': African American Upward Mobility and the Semiotics of Smoking Menthols," *Public Culture* 15, no. 2 (2003): 295–322. Another K for Kool America reference here was likely the funk/soul band Kool and the Gang, whose 1974 album *Light of Worlds* included the songs "Jungle Boogie," and "Summer Madness," both of which were radio hits in Ghana.

24. Shirley Temple Black served as U.S. ambassador to Ghana from December 6, 1974, to July 13, 1976. The text of her conversation on November 12, 1974, with President Gerald Ford about her posting was declassified in 2004 and is available at the Ford Presidential Library, fordlibrarymuseum.gov. Her husband, Charles Alden Black, is widely remembered for his informality and friendliness. In Nii Yemo's words, "Yeah, we could always see him around there in his shorts, walking the dog."

25. Lori Black, also known as Lorax, was the bassist in Clown Alley, a 1980s Bay Area thrash punk band that recorded *Circus of Chaos* in 1985 on the Alchemy label. In the late eighties and early nineties she played with the slush metal band the Melvins and recorded with them on *Gluey Porch Treatments*, Alchemy, 1987, and *Bullhead*, Boner, 1991.

26. The Ghana government's expulsion of Robert Lee Kile was reported in "Ghana Expels Four U.S. Officials; State Dept. Threatens Aid Halt," *Los Angeles Times*, November 29, 1985. Wikipedia has a page on Sharon Scranage; see at en.wikipedia.org. The Scranage-Soussoudis U.S.-Ghana CIA affair was revealed in a sequence of short articles over six months in the *New York Times*: "C.I.A. Clerk and Ghanaian Charged in Espionage," July 12, 1985; "Officials Think Spying Led to Death of C.I.A. Informant in Ghana," July 13, 1985; "U.S. Grand Jury Indicts an Ex-C.I.A. Employee," August 7, 1985; "Espionage Trial of Ghanaian in U.S. Put Off until November 12," October 15, 1985; "Swap in Spy Cases Made with Ghana," November 26, 1985.

Valerie Plame's identity as a CIA operative was exposed in a July 2003 column by the *Washington Post* journalist Robert Novak. Plame and her husband, Ambassador Joseph Wilson, contended that the identity leak was an act of retaliation for him exposing the manufactured lie in President Bush's claim (during his 2003 State of the Union address) that Iraq was attempting to purchase uranium from Niger. Plame and Wilson brought a civil lawsuit, later dismissed, against Vice President Dick Cheney, and in the course of it many fingers pointed to the possible role of Karl Rove, a presidential advisor, in outing Plame's identity. Plame and Wilson tell their tales in a pair of revealing memoirs: Valerie Plame Wilson, *Fair Game: My Life as a Spy, My Betrayal by the White House* (New York: Simon and Shuster, 2007); Joseph Wilson, *The Politics of Truth; A Diplomat's Memoir: Inside the Lies That Led to War and Betrayed My Wife's* CIA *Identity* (New York: Carroll and Graf, 2004). The 2010 feature film *Fair Game*, starring Naomi Watts as Plame and Sean Penn as her husband, is based on Plame's book. Both the film and book title refer to Karl Rove's claim that Plame was "fair game."

27. Susan Stewart, *On Longing: Narratives of the Miniature, the Gigantic, the Souvenir, the Collection* (Durham: Duke University Press, 1993).

28. *Wulomei Returns*, CD, Creative Storm Records, 2007, features a cover image of the band in an old wooden tsolorley; the CD title is written across the flank and the headboard is signed "Brand New Sounds." Wulomei was formed and led in the early 1970s by the multi-instrumentalist and composer Nii Tei Ashitey, and quickly became popular in Ghana as what was called a "traditional" or "folklore" group, terms signifying that they played pop-infused music of very local origins. The group toured internationally and despite changes of personnel and repertory remained well known in Ghana over many years. The CD *Wulomei Returns* joins nostalgic repertory to contemporary production styles and slick marketing, reworking some of the group's best-known 1970s and 1980s hit songs, including "Aklowa," "Kaagba," "Jalelele," "Meridian," "Takoradi," and "Menye Menye Menye." The new versions, produced in a state-of-the-art studio by the director of Creative Storm, Kwesi Owusu, employ the skills also of Ghanaian popular music standouts including Kari Bannerman on guitar, Ray Allen on saxophone, and Osei Tutu and John Bilson on trumpets. On Wulomei's history see John Collins, "Wulomei and the Ghanaian Folk Revival," in his *Musicmakers of West Africa* (Washington: Three Continents Press, 1985), 101–4.

29. A few final horn-to-horn outtakes from the jazz age treasure chest: the arrival of *America: An Epic Rhapsody* in 1927 . . . echoing across the water in 1928 with *An American in Paris* . . . marching in 1929 to the klaxophone . . . and taking to the screen in 1930 with boop boop be doo. . . . *America: An Epic Rhapsody* was composed by the Swiss-born émigré Ernest Bloch, the composer whose name endows the lecture series in which these essays were originally read. His three-part work is dedicated to the memory of Abraham Lincoln and Walt Whitman. Its final movement, "1926 . . . The Present—The Future," uses car horns along with blaring brass and jazz syncopations to bring the piece to its apex of cacophonous noise. The following year, the acoustic and musical turbulence of Bloch's jazz age America was more fully announced in George Gershwin's wind symphony *An American in Paris*, whose instrumentation score formally includes four taxi horns, pitched A, B, C, and D; original instruments were brought from Paris for the American premiere. The year after that, Henry Fillmore composed "The Klaxon March" for the Cincinnati Automobile Show and for the occasion fea-

tured a new musical instrument of unique invention, the klaxophone, twelve battery-powered automobile horns mounted on a table stand. No recordings of the piece with Fillmore's invention survive, but an image of the klaxophone can be seen on page 88 of *Hallelujah Trombone! The Story of Henry Fillmore* by Paul E. Bierley (New York: Carl Fischer, 2003). One year later, in 1930, Max Fleischer created the animated cartoon character Betty Boop, whose vocal signature "boop boop be doo" is introduced in her cartoons with an AABA song sung by a male crooner. He begins with the words "a hot cornet can" followed by the sound of the hot cornet in play, and then returns with the words "but a hot cornet can't boop boop be doo like Betty Boop can do." On the second iteration the "hot cornet" is replaced by "a saxophone" and then its sound, and after the bridge the third restatement substitutes "an auto horn," again with the instrumental sound rendered in juxtaposition to the crooner's voice and Betty's girlishly ultra-[u]-gendered high pinched nasality. For a sono-geneology of "boop boop be doo," see Robert O'Meally, "Checking Our Balances: Louis Armstrong, Ralph Ellison, and Betty Boop," in *Uptown Conversation: The New Jazz Studies*, ed. Robert O'Meally, Brent Hayes Edwards, and Farah Jasmine Griffin (New York: Columbia University Press, 2004), 278–96.

But it's the high-art guys who keep coming back for the big honks. Gyorgy Ligeti's fondness for African polyphonies and polyrhythms, encouraged by the work of the ethnomusicologist Simha Arom in Central Africa, takes Banda-Linda multipart animal horn music into the "Car Horn Prelude" for *Le Grand Macabre*, his mid-1970s opera (or antiopera, given its high irony about the genre itself). Both the pitches and rhythms of the car horns are notated and involve intricate interactions. See Ligeti's foreword to Arom's *African Polyphony and Polyrhythm: Music Structure and Methodology*, trans. Martin Thom, Barbara Tuckett, and Raymond Boyd (New York: Cambridge University Press, 1991), xvii–xviii, and the musicological contextualization of it by Stephen Andrew Taylor, "Ligeti, Africa and Polyrhythm," *World of Music* 45, no. 2 (2003): 83–94. A couple of other examples literally take to the road. "Car Life: A Traffic Jam Session for Automobile Orchestra" by the University of Maine music professor Philip Carlsen features forty-five vehicles honking, while "Cartet," by Bill Damur, professor of music at Alberta College Conservatory of Music, was performed in a parking lot at the University of Alberta to introduce and announce the lecture I was about to give on por por during the university's centennial celebrations in September 2008. All of these modernist musical honk-outs again serve to foreground the difference of por por cosmopolitanism as acoustemological bricolage. Beginning with recycled and reworked car horns, the La Por Por Group makes instruments ready for the road, ready for street life, and undertaking the afterlife, creating musical parades that sound out funerary passage, and through it, the deep sociality of memory.

1. Two deeply illuminating works on this theme by Saskia Sassen are *Guests and Aliens* (New York: New Press, 1999), and *Territory, Authority, Rights: From Medieval to Global Assemblages* (Princeton: Princeton University Press, 2008). Also see Arjun Appadurai, *Modernity at Large: Cultural Dimensions of Globalization* (Minneapolis: University of Minnesota Press, 1996); Aihwa Ong, *Flexible Citizenship: The Cultural Logics of Transnationality* (Durham: Duke University Press, 1999); Tiffany Ruby Patterson and Robin D. G. Kelley, "Unfinished Migrations: Reflections on the African Diaspora and the Making of the Modern World," *African Studies Review* 43, no. 1 (2000): 11–45; Stephen Castles and Alastair Davidson, eds., *Citizenship and Migration: Globalization and the Politics of Belonging* (New York: Routledge, 2000).

2. Steven Feld, " 'They Repeatedly Lick Their Own Things,' " *Critical Inquiry* 24, no. 2 (1998): 445–72; Svetlana Boym, "On Diasporic Intimacy: Ilya Kabakov's Installations and Immigrant Homes," *Critical Inquiry* 24, no. 2 (1998): 498–524, quotations from 499–500.

3. Architectural phenomenology, grounded in experiential psychology, informs Gaston Bachelard's view of home and the intimacies of dwelling in *The Poetics of Space* (Boston: Beacon, 1994), a translation of *La poétique de l'espace* (1958). One of his chapters is titled "Intimate Immensity" and there he explores the "delicate dwelling in the forest of ourselves." Bachelard's work prefigures Boym by explicitly citing the role of dreams in mediating the memory gaps between the place where one was born and the places where one later lives/d. A deep contextualization of Bachelard's ideas of place, space, and home in phenomenological psychology is found in Edward S. Casey's *The Fate of Place: A Philosophical History* (Berkeley: University of California Press, 1998); also see the new edition of his earlier *Getting Back into Place: Toward a Renewed Understanding of the Place-World*, 2nd ed. (Bloomington: Indiana University Press, 2009).

4. While our projects invoke the notion of "intimacy" to address somewhat different issues, I want to acknowledge with deep thanks a series of critical conversations with Jocelyne Guilbault about how musical intimacies intertwine what she calls their "emancipatory and repressive potentials." See her "Music, Politics, and Pleasure: Live Soca in Trinidad," *Small Axe* 31 (2010): 16–29.

5. Also referred to as *Barcelona Sphinx*, Salvador Dalí's 1939 thirty-by-forty-inch original is in the collection of the Museum Boijmans Van Beuningen in Rotterdam, Netherlands; for a digital copy, see the museum website, collectie .boijmans.nl.

6. Bill "Bojangles" Robinson and Shirley Temple were paired in four films, *The Little Colonel* (1935), *The Littlest Rebel* (1935), *Just Around the Corner* (1938), and *Rebecca of Sunnybrook Farm* (1938). Some of the stories I heard in Accra about them are mirrored in a very short article, "Shirley Temple Recalls That

Bias Experienced by 'Bojangles' Robinson Taught Her about Racism," *Jet*, December 21, 1998. For much more on racism and Robinson's career, see James Haskins and N. R. Mitgang Haskins, *Mr. Bojangles: The Biography of Bill Robinson* (New York: William Morrow, 1988).

7. Because he was employed by the United States Embassy and the United States Information Services, Kweku Asiedu neither holds copyright nor has copies or control over most of the images he made from 1970 to 2000. He told me that on a visit to his daughter in the States he was looking through some library books about Ambassador Temple Black and saw many of his photographs, but they were only mass-credited to the USIS.

8. The dancing-up-and-down-the-stairs sequence from *The Little Colonel* can be seen at youtube.com.

9. Paul Gilroy, *The Black Atlantic: Modernity and Double Consciousness* (Cambridge: Harvard University Press, 1993), quotation at 58.

10. Paul Gilroy, *Against Race: Imagining Political Culture beyond the Color Line* (Cambridge: Harvard University Press, 2000); *Between Camps: Nations, Cultures and the Allure of Race* (London: Routledge, 2004); and *Postcolonial Melancholia* (New York: Columbia University Press, 2006). Kwame Anthony Appiah, *Cosmopolitanism: Ethics in a World of Strangers* (New York: W. W. Norton, 2006).

11. Quite resonant with the chronotopia of Gilroy via Bakhtin is the centrality of the freedom float trotro and train/Trane in Nii Noi Nortey's material worlds of sound into sculpture and sculpture into sound. The centrality not just of motion but of the vehicle to slavery and all of its aftermath in the water, underground, on the railroad, in the car, moves into a virtuosic level of historical analysis in Marcus Rediker, *The Slave Ship: A Human History* (New York: Viking, 2007). The story of the crews and boatmen, oppressors and oppressed, abusers and abused, is beautifully interwoven here with a terrifically detailed account of how the ships were constructed, and how understanding their materiality helps understand the experience of the passage.

12. E. T. Mensah and the Tempos Dance Band, "Ghana Freedom," 1956, anthologized on *Day by Day*, CD, RetroAfric, 1994.

13. Lord Kitchener, "Birth of Ghana," 1956, anthologized on *London Is the Place for Me: Trinidadian Calypso in London, 1950–1956*, CD, HonestJons, 2002. Some additional information can be found in Markus Coester, "Ghana Is the Name We Wish to Proclaim: Two Popular Caribbean Voices and the Independence of Ghana," *Ntama Journal of African Music and Popular Culture*, April 26, 2004, at the journal's website uni-hildesheim.de/ntama.

14. John Collins, *E. T. Mensah: King of Highlife* (London: Off the Record Press, 1996), 23–26; Robert Raymond, *Black Star in the Wind* (London: MacGiddon and Kee, 1960), 215–47.

15. With trumpet, Benjamin Odoi can be seen just right of Louis Armstrong in a 1956 picture in Gary Giddens, *Satchmo* (New York: Doubleday, 1988), 161.

16. *Satchmo the Great*, LP, Columbia, 1957; CD reissue 2000, where the Murrow narration and the song "All for You, Louis" appear together as track 8.

17. Penny von Eschen, *Satchmo Blows up the World: Jazz Ambassadors Play the Cold War* (Cambridge: Harvard University Press, 2006), quotation at 58.

18. On his second trip to Ghana, in 1960, when he met Ghanaba, Louis Armstrong the musical ambassador was also very much Satchmo the capitalist ambassador. *Time Magazine*, October 31, 1960, in a short piece titled "Promotion: Akwaaba, Satchmo," reports that "Pepsi shelled out some $300,000 to send Satchmo and the All-Stars on the tour to promote five new West African bottling plants worth $6,000,000, and help Pepsi in its war with Coca-Cola. The plants, owned and operated by Africans under license from Pepsi-Cola, will have a capacity of eight million cases of Pepsi a year. In changing West Africa, where the people love sweet, fizzing drinks and where foreign businessmen are finding that they must hard-sell for the first time, Satchmo's long-holding C note was an advertising message understood by even the many illiterate citizens. Pepsi-Cola's C notes were also holding well. Sales in Ghana have gone up by 53 percent since Satchmo arrived."

The only eyewitness print source I know for the Nixon story that Armstrong told to Ghanaba in 1960 is found in the epigraph to David E. Apter, "Ghana's Independence: Triumph and Paradox," *Transition* 98 (2008): 6–23. It reads: "At the Independence Day banquet, the representative from the United States, then Vice President Richard M. Nixon, was seated between K. A. Gbedemah, Ghana's Minister of Finance and someone with whom he was not acquainted. Turning to the latter, Nixon asked, 'Well, how does it feel to be free?' The reply was immediate: 'Who's free? I'm from Alabama.'" Apter, a political scientist, was present on both sides of the Gold Coast–Ghana transition and wrote compellingly about the complexities then of transforming colonial institutions into plural democratic ones, particularly in the context of a one-party state. See his *The Gold Coast in Transition* (Princeton: Princeton University Press, 1955), updated as *Ghana in Transition*, 2nd rev. ed. (Princeton: Princeton University Press, 1972). Variations on the Nixon story, situating it among a group of revelers, and questioning its veracity, have circulated for years and can be found, recently for example, in the previously cited books by Kevin Gaines and James Campbell. When I told Ghanaba that some contemporary scholars consider the tale an item of folklore he smiled and shook his head, "No."

19. The most detailed account of the early history of "Sly Mongoose" is John Cowley, "West Indies Blues: An Historic Overview, 1920s–1950s—Blues and Music from the English Speaking West Indies," in *Nobody Knows Where the Blues Come From*, ed. Robert Springer (Jackson: University of Mississippi Press, 2007), 187–263. Also see Donald R. Hill, *Calypso Calaloo: Early Carnival Music in Trinidad* (Gainesville: University of Florida Press, 1993), 122–23, 272–75. I'm grateful to Jocelyne Guilbault for sharing her deep knowledge of Caribbean

music historiography and the harmonic history of early calypsos like "Sly Mongoose."

20. Ghanaba, "Setting the Records Straight," editorial, *Ghanaian Times*, September 23, 1996.

21. In his "Jack Sneed: Making 'Sly Mongoose' a Hit," an as-yet-unpublished manuscript generously shared by the virtuosic calypso discographer Ray Funk, we learn how an obscure singer named Jack Sneed made a hit of the song in the late thirties and was thus the most likely source of the piece for the jazz versions that followed by Ella Fitzgerald, Benny Goodman, and Charlie Parker. Sneed's recording also could have been a source for Armstrong, although I have not been able to verify that it is held in Armstrong's collection, as is the Goodman version. While Sneed's "Sly Mongoose" is not presently in commercial circulation, listen to his recording of "Jamaica Mama," which uses the same harmonic bridge; Jack Sneed and His Sneezers, "Jamaica Mama," on the anthology *Jazzin' the Blues 4: 1929–43*, CD, Document, 2000. Currently available sources for these versions of "Sly Mongoose" are Lionel Belasco, *Goodnight Ladies and Gents*, CD, Rounder, 1999; Sam Manning, *Sam Manning*, vol. 1, *Recorded in New York 1924–1927*, CD, Jazz Oracle, 2002; Ella Fitzgerald, *Live at the Savoy 1939–40*, CD, Hep, 2007; Benny Goodman, *All of Me*, CD, Jazz Colours, 2009; Lord Invader, *Calypso in New York*, CD, Smithsonian Folkways, 2000; Charlie Parker, *Be-Bop, The Best of the Bird*, CD, Mastersong, 2000; *Autumn in New York*, CD, Charly UK, 1999.

22. Cole Porter, "High Society Calypso," performed by Louis Armstrong and the All-Stars, *High Society*, MGM, 1956 (a musical version of *The Philadelphia Story*).

23. Currently available sources for these versions of "Sly Mongoose / All for You" are "Almer Bou" and "Tin Ka Tin Ka" on *West African Instrumental Quintet 1929*, CD, Heritage Music, 1994; Euphenia Cooper, "All for You, Baby," *The Arthur S. Alberts Collection: More Tribal, Folk, and Café Music of West Africa*, Library of Congress Endangered Music Project, CD, Rykodisc, 1998.

Although Belasco's claim of copyright on "Sly Mongoose" in Venezuela dates to 1924, the U.S. Library of Congress registration for the song is not until April 17, 1939, as words and music by Lionel Belasco and Clarence Williams, Clarence Williams Music Publishing Company, Inc., New York. Clarence Williams's name appears as co-composer only because he bought outright all rights to many songs he published, a common practice in the music business at that time. In 1943 Williams sold his back-catalogue to Decca Records; he died in 1965. It is unclear if a Decca claim (through the current owner of their catalogue, Universal Music Group, part of Vivendi) has ever been asserted or remains valid today. All research indicates that E. T. Mensah did not register or copyright "All For You" when he recorded it in 1952. I am grateful to Mensah's biographer, John Collins, and the highlife historian Markus Coester for confirming that detail, and for the following additional confirmations. Collins agrees with what Ghanaba told me, that Mensah was aware of the song's Caribbean origins, and that his source was Liberian and Sierra Leonian seamen in central Accra in the 1940s. Coester adds that following common practice it was not the musician but a Decca producer who registered the recordings. Unfortunately it has not been possible to find any documentation of that registration with the British copyright society. Collins and Coester also confirm another of Ghanaba's assertions: that Mensah was never paid composer royalties for the song.

24. The Mensah, Warren, Krupa, and Armstrong wall paintings at the Hotel Demina were made circa 1962 by Y. K. Anang. Born in 1940 in La, Accra, Anang was already painting professionally as a teenager, and the faded remains of some of his large 1950s and 1960s Accra hotel exterior and courtyard mural paintings can still be seen today. Among documented works in Accra he painted large Louis Armstrong images in 1958 for Super Service Adabraka and Miami Hotel, and another for the Broadway Hotel in 1960. His photo memory album also shows that he painted Armstrong images for Cape Coast Hotel in 1960, and in 1959 painted a full-wall image of Armstrong, Trummy Young, Edmund Hall, and Lionel Hampton for the Hotel de Tarso in Ho. In 1960 he painted a similarly larger-than-life-size wall image of E. T. Mensah and the Tempos, featuring Guy Warren at the conga drums, for the Christmas in Egypt Hotel, Mamprobi, Accra. The paintings are testimony to the power of Armstrong's presence in Accra between and around his 1956 and 1960 visits, and the Cape Coast and Ho paintings are further testimony to the reach of his story outside of Accra. They are also testimony to the importance of hotels in creating a space for emergent African urban modernities and cosmopolitan musical interchange.

The official Obama speech, "Remarks by The President to the Ghanaian Parliament, Accra International Conference Center, Accra, Ghana, July 11, 2009," is available at whitehouse.gov/the_press_office, the website of the White House, Office of the Press Secretary.

I want to recall here an insightful comment by the late Joe Nkrumah, when I spoke to him about the Accra memory of Armstrong's visit. Joe said that one of the things Ghanaians most loved and remembered about Armstrong was his ubiquitous white handkerchiefs, draped over his trumpet and alternately waved as he took the instrument from his lips or signaled the band or acknowledged the crowds. That waving was taken as a sign of a local knowing, and particularly an embrace of white cloth as a victorious symbol of pride. That this emplaced memory signs and gestures the diasporic intimacy of jazz cosmopolitanism loops back to Ghanaba's *Hallelujah!* film. There, in the final sequence, you see members of the Winneba Youth Choir pull previously hidden white handkerchiefs from their outfits and begin to wave them during the performance of "Eyi Wala Dong"/"That Happy Feeling," marking off the concluding dance-and-get-down African section of the *Hallelujah!* performance from the initial rigid-bodied European Handel portion.

25. John Miller Chernoff, *Hustling Is Not Stealing: Stories of an African Bar Girl* (Chicago: University of Chicago Press, 2003). Also see the sequel, John Miller Chernoff, *Exchange Is Not Robbery: More Stories of an African Bar Girl* (Chicago: University of Chicago Press, 2005). On self-success and other registers of contemporary hustling in Accra, see Jesse Weaver Shipley, "Aesthetic of the Entrepreneur: Afro-Cosmopolitan Rap and Moral Circulation in Accra, Ghana," *Anthropological Quarterly* 82, no. 3 (2009): 631–68; also see his larger perspective on assertion as performance and performance as assertion: Jesse Weaver Shipley, "National Audiences and Consuming Subjects: A Political Genealogy of Performance in Neoliberal Ghana," Ph.D. dissertation, University of Chicago, 2003.

26. See, for example, Aihwa Ong, *Neoliberalism as Exception: Mutations in Citizenship and Sovereignty* (Durham: Duke University Press, 2006). Pnina Werbner's ethnographies include *Imagined Diasporas among Manchester Muslims: The Public Performance of Pakistani Transnational Identity Politics* (London: James Curry, 2002) and *Pilgrims of Love: The Anthropology of a Global Sufi Cult* (Bloomington: Indiana University Press, 2004). On the early invocation of the term "vernacular cosmopolitanism," see Homi K. Bhabha, "Unsatisfied: Notes on Vernacular Cosmopolitanism," in *Text and Nation: Cross-Disciplinary Essays on Cultural and National Identities*, ed. Laura Garcia-Moreno and Peter C. Pfeiffer (Columbia, S.C.: Camden House, 1996), 191–207. For a deeply thoughtful take, one considerably more critical of simple celebration, see Charles L. Briggs, "Genealogies of Race and Culture and the Failure of Vernacular Cosmopolitanisms: Rereading Franz Boas and W. E. B. Du Bois," *Public Culture* 17, no. 1 (2005): 75–100.

27. Pnina Werbner, "Vernacular Cosmopolitanism," *Theory, Culture, and Society* 23, nos. 2–3 (2006): 496–98, quotations at 496, 497. Also see her introduction, "Towards a New Cosmopolitan Anthropology," to her edited volume *Anthropology and the New Cosmopolitanism: Rooted, Feminist and Vernacular Perspectives* (London: Berg, 2009), 1–29. For related perspectives on cosmopolitanism from below, and sideways, see the essays in the "Cosmopolitanism" issue of the journal *Public Culture*'s Millennial Quartet, reissued as Carol A. Breckenridge, Sheldon Pollock, Homi K. Bhabha, and Dipesh Chakrabarty, eds., *Cosmopolitanism* (Durham: Duke University Press, 2002); Jason D. Hill, *Becoming a Cosmopolitan* (New York: Rowman and Littlefield, 2000); Ifeona Kiddoe Nwankwo, *Black Cosmopolitanism* (Philadelphia: University of Pennsylvania Press, 2005); Manthia Diawara, "Homeboy Cosmopolitanism," in his *In Search of Africa* (Cambridge: Harvard University Press, 1998), 237–76; also see "After Post-Colonialism?," Cynthia Foo's interview with Benedict Anderson, *Invisible Culture* 13 (2009): 4–21.

On the call for more attention to "lived cosmopolitanism" amidst diverse theoretical agendas, see Ulrich Beck and Natan Sznaider, "Unpacking Cosmopolitanism for the Social Sciences: A Research Agenda," *British Journal of Sociology* 57, no. 1 (2006): 1–23; Ulf Hannerz, "Cosmopolitanism," in *A Companion to* the *Anthropology of Politics,* ed. David Nugent and Joan Vincent (Oxford: Blackwell, 2004), 69–85. While less directly about cosmopolitanism, the depictions in Charles Piot's insightful book on village modernity in Togo resonate deeply with my concern to engage complexly expansive agency in seemingly contracting or contradictory settings: *Remotely Global: Village Modernity in West Africa* (Chicago: University of Chicago Press, 1999). For a wonderfully nuanced excavation of the utopic dimension of cosmopolitan desire in contemporary West Africa, see his *Nostalgia for the Future* (Chicago: University of Chicago Press, 2010).

28. James Clifford, *Routes: Travel and Translation in the Late Twentieth Century* (Cambridge: Harvard University Press, 1997).

29. Caryl Phillips, *A Distant Shore* (New York: Knopf, 2003); *Dancing in the Dark* (New York: Vintage, 2006); *Cambridge* (New York: Vintage, 1993); *The Nature of Blood* (New York: Vintage, 1998); *The European Tribe* (New York: Vintage, 1987); *The Atlantic Sound* (New York: Knopf, 2000), quotation at 197. A resonant recent narrative by a British Ghanaian, about going "home" not to find one, and then of return to the United Kingdom with a better understanding of what he imagined escaping in the first place, is Ekow Eshun, *Black Gold in the Sun: Searching for Home in Africa and Beyond* (New York: Pantheon, 2007).

30. David Price, *Threatening Anthropology: McCarthyism and the FBI's Surveillance of Activist Anthropologists* (Durham: Duke University Press, 2004), and *Anthropological Intelligence: The Deployment and Neglect of American Anthropology in the Second World War* (Durham: Duke University Press, 2008).

31. Franz Boas, "Scientists as Spies," *The Nation*, December 20, 1919, 797. The piece that was most memorably discussed in Vietnam War teach-ins when I was an anthropology undergraduate was Eric Wolf and Joseph Jorgenson, "Anthropology on the Warpath in Thailand," *New York Review of Books*, November 19, 1970, 26–35.

32. The picture I mentioned to Ghanaba comes from the early 1950s and shows William Bascom with clarinet, together with the ethnomusicologists Alan Merriam, also with clarinet, and Richard Waterman, at the bass, playing with a Northwestern University faculty jazz band, the Academic Cats. It appears, courtesy of Patricia and Chris Waterman, in Charles Keil and Steven Feld, *Music Grooves: Essays and Dialogues* (Chicago: University of Chicago Press, 1994), 13. The "general treatise" by Bascom that Ghanaba cited would likely have been his small 1969 book, *The Yoruba of Southwestern Nigeria* (New York: Holt, Rinehart, Winston), but I never saw a copy of it in Ghanaba's library.

Alan Merriam was an avid jazz and African music discographer and record collector and I know that he had heard some of Warren's music, if not live in Chicago, certainly later on LP. Merriam's *African Music on LP: An Annotated Discography* (Evanston: Northwestern University Press, 1970) lists Warren's three Decca LPs *African Rhythms: Guy Warren, Jungle Drums,* and *Africa Speaks, America Answers* (all on page 30) but says "no information available" and provides no annotations for them. However, a detailed annotation is provided for the 1959 RCA LP *The Guy Warren Sounds: Themes for African Drums* (97). I saw this LP in Merriam's collection and recall him telling me (a trombonist) about the significant presence on several tracks of Lawrence Brown, the famous Duke Ellington Orchestra trombonist. Merriam liked to teach his classes early in the mornings. He would always come to the room well in advance of the class with a few jazz LPs, and be playing them as we students would arrive. I still have lists of LPs and LP tracks he played or mentioned. They include selections from Olatunji's *Drums of Passion* LP. Indeed, three classic Olatunji LPs are annotated in *African Music on LP* and Merriam mentions there that Robert Farris Thompson, the Yale art historian, was responsible for some of their liner notes. Merriam also played for us "Tears for Johannesburg," the Olatunji feature with Max Roach, from the 1960 *We Insist! Max Roach's Freedom Now Suite*. So even though he was aware of Warren, it is fair to say that Merriam was, like most jazz enthusiasts and Africanist scholarly listeners at that time, far more familiar with Olatunji.

33. Nat Nuno Amarteifio, text, and Kofi Setordji, photographs, *Architectural Heritage of Accra: 1920–1940* (Accra: Nubuke Foundation, with the support of the Ghana Cultural Fund, 2009). Amarteifio is currently writing a book about the architectural history of Accra.

34. Kwame Nkrumah is known to have had several affairs but only with Auntie Vicky was he said to have had a love child; the young man died in his late teenage years.

35. Another cosmo-complex sidebar: While the Bartók Prize of one thousand euros was awarded to me personally, I made the decision to disburse it to those who worked with me in the United States on the film's editing and translation, and in Ghana with the band, the drivers union, additional musicians who played, Ashirifie's family, and my coproducer Nii Yemo Nunu. Knowing of the pride that the band would feel about international recognition for their works, I commissioned Nicholas Wayo to make a painting for the occasion, and in the presence of local and international dignitaries, we presented it at a celebration in La in mid-July. A week before the event, I prepared a press release at the request of the union secretary, and everyone was pleased to see the articles "Film on Por Por Music Wins Award," in *Graphic ShowBiz*, July 15–21, 5, and "Por Por Music Grips International Ears" in the *Daily Graphic*, July 17, 20. I also delivered the press release to the local TV stations. None came to film the event. When repeatedly questioned afterward about this by the band, I had no answers as to why. Some days later, I casually mentioned this to an acquaintance from the Accra banking community. He responded, equally casually: "So how much did you pay when you gave them the press release?"

"Nothing," I said, "I just went to their offices and gave them the release."

"Oh! C'mon man," he replied, "you've been around! You know that's not how it works here. Everything has a price. If you want your music on the radio or story in the paper or picture on the TV, you have to show your appreciation. And let's be honest, whites are expected to show more appreciation because everyone knows you can afford it more than locals."

"Well," I responded, a bit more defensively than necessary, "it didn't cost me anything to get the articles in the *Graphic*!"

"Really? You got an article and picture in the *Graphic* twice and didn't pay? Hey man, you really must know someone inside!"

Yes, I have been around, and am well aware of the gaps between Western moralistic discourses on "corruption" and locally taken-for-granted ideas about "showing appreciation," not to mention the bit about showing more of it if/when one is white and foreign. All the same, my ethnographic awareness of how gifts lubricate the actualization of desires was sometimes, as in this instance, jolted by the unstated necessity to pay an additional "dash" for things that seem like they should simply be part of somebody's job description. Of course such things are often matters of degree, and signify differently when dealing with those much more powerful or menacing (liked armed police officers) or with equals or everyday workers and functionaries. On the complexities of the press and "objective" reporting in Ghana, as well as accusations about "anything for a price" undermining journalism, see Jennifer Hasty, *The Press and Political Culture in Ghana* (Bloomington: Indiana University Press, 2005).

36. Lest this seem one-sided, here's a mirror-view beamed back to the United States in 2005 from Jake Obetsebi-Lamptey, Ghana's then minister of tourism and diasporan affairs: "We want Africans everywhere, no matter where they live or how they got there, to see Ghana as their gateway home"; quoted in Lydia Polgreen, "Ghana's Uneasy Embrace of Slavery's Diaspora," *New York Times*, December 27, 2005.

37. Svetlana Boym, *The Future of Nostalgia* (New York: Basic Books, 2002), quotations at xviii, 49, 49, and xviii.

"Dedicated to You"

1. "Dedicated to You," with music and lyrics by Sammy Cahn, Saul Chaplin, and Hy Zaret, was recorded by the John Coltrane Quartet with vocalist Johnny Hartman: *John Coltrane and Johnny Hartman*, LP, Impulse, 1963.

INDEX

Page numbers in *italics* refer to illustrations.

Asiedu, Kweku, 209, 291n7
Ataa Jata, 145–47
Atlantic Sound, The (Phillips), 231–32
Attali, Jacques, 128
Austerlitz (Sebald), 250n15
Awuley, Ataa, 165
Ayler, Albert, 17–18, 20, 99
Azangeo, Amoah, 75

Bach: The Goldberg Variations
(Williams), 140
Bach, Johann Sebastian, 139–40, 157
Bachelard, Gaston, 205
Baker, David, 252n15
Baker, Ginger, 73–74, 263n33
Bakhtin, Mikhail, 130, 177, 274nn16–17
Band on the Run (McCartney and
Wings), 74, 263n33
Barenboim, Daniel, 48, 115–16, 210
Bartók, Béla, 252n15
Bascom, William, 233–34, 296n32
Basie, Count, 43, 77, 186
Basso, Keith, 8, 250n12
Beatles, 75
Beat of My Drum, The (Olatunji), 67
bebop, 59, 62, 71–72
Bechet, Sidney, 18
Becker, Sandy, 64
Beethoven (Solomon), 112
Beethoven, Ludwig van, 40, 77, 90, 94,
103, 110–18, 157, 202, 210
Beethoven as I Knew Him (Schindler),
112
Beethoven, His Life and Times (Orga),
112
"Beethoven, the Black Spaniard"
(Mosely), 111–12
"Beethoven Was 1/16 Black" (Gor-
dimer), 112–13
Belafonte, Harry, 65, 68
Belasco, Lionel, 218, 293n23
bells, 2, 5, 23, 129–30, 132, 140, 273n13
*Bells and Winter Festivals of Greek Mac-
edonia* (Feld, Blau, Keil, and Keil),
273n13
Bellson, Louis, 58

"Ben Hur" (lorry), 190
Benjamin, Walter, 204
Berlin, Irving, 253n23
Berliner, Paul, 102
Bernstein, Leonard, 73
Bertone, Bruno, 64
Bey, James Hawthorne, 40, 65, 67–68
Bhabha, Homi, 48, 229
Birth of Ghana (Kitchener), 212, 216
Birth of the Cool (Davis), 191, 286n22
Black, Charles Alden, 287n24
Black, Shirley Temple, 192, 207–10,
287n24, 290n6
Black Atlantic, 3, 27, 150–53, 219. *See
also* Africa; Ghana
Black Atlantic, The (Gilroy), 210–11
"Black Heat" (Accra Trane Station),
93–94
"Black Man's Story, The" (lorry), 166
Black Music Research Journal, 112
Black Star in the Wind (Raymond), 214
Blakey, Art, 40, 66–67, 260n22
Blau, Dick, 128
"Blessings" (lorry), 176
Blind Faith (band), 74
Bloch, Ernest, 288n29
Bloch Lecture series, 6, 8
"Blood Brothers 69" (Warren), 74,
263n33
Blue Train (Coltrane), 29, 91
Boas, Franz, 233
Bobo, Willie, 74
Bosavi rainforest, 124–34, 140, 162–63,
204–5, 271n1
Boym, Svetlana, 49, 205–6, 242–43
brekete (drum), 124, 134, 137
Bright Balkan Morning (Blau, Keil, Keil,
and Feld), 128, 269n14
Brotherhood of Breath (group), 16
Brown, James, 13, 65
Brown, Lawrence, 40, 66
Brown, Marion, 20
Buddhism, 36, 40, 54, 77, 203
bufo toads, 132–35
Bufo Variations (Annan), 5, 24, 121,
133–40, 149, 155, 161

Pozo, Chano, 59
"Prelude to a Kiss" (Ellington), 80
Presley, Elvis, 64
Price, David, 233, 296n30
Price, Leontyne, 65–66
Price, Richard, 284n21
Prophet, The (Gibran), 54, 255n1
"Psalm" (Coltrane), 19
(Psychedelic) Aliens, 75
"Pursuance" (Coltrane), 19

Rabelais and His World (Bakhtin), 274n16
race: Accra Trane Station and, 225–26; American music industry and, 41, 55, 65–69, 75, 202–3; American politics and, 217; Beethoven and, 110–16, 157, 210; border-crossings and, 238–39; funerals and, 188–89; Ghanaba on, 53, 55, 58–62, 65, 203, 259n15, 264n37, 266n45; Gilroy and, 210–11; hybridity and, 211; jazz and, 3, 6, 41, 49, 53, 59–62, 69, 75, 78, 82, 202–3, 259n15; Nortey and, 95–100; Shirley Temple and, 210
Ramblers (band), 141
Rangel, Charles, 116, 271n26
Rastafari, 99–100, 203
Ravel, Maurice, 40
Rawlings, J. J., 81, 84, 182, 192, 278n37
Raymond, Robert, 214, 291n14
RCA (label), 40
Reagan, Ronald, 192–93
Rebel without a Cause (film), 191
Redding, Otis, 283n17
"Red Roses for the Blue Lady" (Kaempfert), 64
Red Saunders Orchestra, 60
Reeves, Jim, 141
reggae, 97–100, 157
Rejoice When You Die (Touchet), 47, 188
Religion and Medicine of the Ga People (Field), 84
"Resolution" (Coltrane), 19
"Respect" (song), 182, 283n17

"Respect Yourself" (song), 283n17
Rice, Mack, 283n17
Rich, Buddy, 59
Roach, Max, 31–35, 40, 58, 67, 70–73, 77, 82, 213, 262n29
Robinson, Bill "Bojangles," 57, 208–10, 290n6
Rödel, Mark-Oliver, 132, 275n19
Rogers, Joel Augustus, 110–11, 270n18
Rollins, Sonny, 109
Roney, Antoine, 16
Roots (Haley), 262n30
Rouch, Jean, 35, 252n16, 281n5
Rouse, Charlie, 109
Routes (Clifford), 7, 231
Rove, Karl, 193, 287–8n26
Russell, George, 252n15
Russo, Bill, 252n15
Ryan, Virginia, 3, 9, 29, 93, 152, 250n16, 267n3, 280n38

Sahlins, Marshall, 56
Said, Edward, 48
Sanders, Pharoah, 13, 15, 18, 150
sankofa, 56–57
Sankofa (Gerima), 73, 76, 262n30
sanza (instrument), 102
Sargent, Malcolm, 77
Satchmo Blows Up the World (Von Eschen), 216, 292n17
Saunders, Red, 60–61
Scaldaferri, Nicola, 118
Schindler, Anton, 112
Schulkovsky, Robyn, 82
Schuller, Gunther, 33, 252n15
Schuricht, Carl, 77
Schwartz, Jean, 28, 252n11
"Scientists as Spies" (Boas), 233
Scranage, Sharon, 192–93, 287n26
"Sea Never Dry" (lorry), 176
Sebald, W. G., 9, 250n15
See It Now (Murrow), 65
Setordji, Kofi, 234
Shane (film), 182
Shearer, Ollie, 73,
shenai (instrument), 91–92

STEVEN FELD IS AN ANTHROPOLOGIST AND MUSICIAN who teaches at the University of New Mexico and the University of Oslo. His books include *Sound and Sentiment: Birds, Weeping, Poetics, and Song in Kaluli Expression*, and, with Charles Keil, *Music Grooves: Essays and Dialogues*. He is also a recipient of the prestigious MacArthur Fellowship (1991).

Library of Congress Cataloging-in-Publication Data
Feld, Steven.
Jazz cosmopolitanism in Accra : a memoir of five musical
years in Ghana / Steven Feld.
p. cm.
Includes bibliographical references and index.
ISBN 978-0-8223-5148-1 (cloth : alk. paper)
ISBN 978-0-8223-5162-7 (pbk. : alk. paper)
1. Jazz—Ghana—Accra. 2. Jazz musicians—Ghana—Accra.
3. Jazz—2001–2010. 4. Accra (Ghana)—Music. I. Title.
ML3509.G4F45 2012
781.6509667—dc23   2011035963